Laughing Allegra

Laughing Allegra

*The Inspiring Story of a Mother's Struggle
and Triumph Raising a Daughter with
Learning Disabilities*

ANNE FORD
with
John-Richard Thompson

Newmarket Press  New York

This book is published in the United States of America.

First Edition

10 9 8 7 6 5 4 3 2 1

ISBN 1-55704-564-X

Library of Congress Cataloging-in-Publication Data

Ford, Anne
Laughing Allegra : the inspiring story of a mother's struggle and triumph
raising a daughter with learning disabilities / by Anne Ford,
with John-Richard Thompson.— 1st ed.
p. cm.
Includes index.
ISBN 1-55704-564-X
1. Ford, Allegra Charlotte 2. Learning disabled children—United States—
Biography. 3. Learning disabled children—United States—Family relationships.
4. Parent and child. I. Thompson, John-Richard. II. Title.
LC4705.F67 2003
649'.151'092—dc21
2002156094

QUANTITY PURCHASES

Companies, professional groups, clubs, and other organizations may qualify for special terms when ordering quantities of this title. For information, write Special Sales Department, Newmarket Press, 18 East 48th Street, New York, NY 10017; call (212) 832-3575; fax (212) 832-3629; or e-mail mailbox@newmarketpress.com.

www.newmarketpress.com

Designed by M. J. DiMassi

Manufactured in the United States of America.

Contents

7974

From my study I see in the lamplight,
Descending the broad hall stair,
Grave Alice and Laughing Allegra,
And Edith with golden hair.

A whisper and then a silence,
Yet I know by their merry eyes
They are plotting and planning together
To take me by surprise.

—HENRY WADSWORTH LONGFELLOW

Foreword
by Mel Levine, M.D.

Students who struggle are not soloists. They perform as part of a cast as in an opera, play, or rock concert. Much of their destiny will depend on the talent and commitment of the other players who act on their behalf in the drama of their daily lives. The real life plot of *Laughing Allegra* is vivid testimony to the significant role of the entire cast—in particular, their power to lessen the power of failure (to borrow a phrase from "The Gov," Hugh Carey). Some intriguing roles are portrayed as we encounter on these pages the unfolding plot of Allegra's childhood, and these players have made a dramatic difference. First, there is her remarkable costar, Anne Ford, an extraordinary woman, who teaches us one of the core lessons of this book when she points out (and also demonstrates) that "the most finely tuned expert about a particular child is the child's parent." I can say that, as a seasoned pediatrician, I have learned, perhaps more than anything else, to listen to parents, to respect their unique expertise and tap into the X-ray vision they possess when it comes to their child.

The supporting roles in Allegra's life and in the lives of so many students like her include family, educators, mentors, adult friends, and peers. When these people are truly onboard, when they are sufficiently resourceful and sympathetic, the frustrated life of a child with academic woes acquires resiliency; the acts of learning become hopeful and, ultimately, rewarding. That's when and how Allegra has reason to laugh. On the other hand, when one or more of these individuals is insensitive, uninformed, or biased, the Allegras of the

childhood world become vulnerable to spiraling failure and shame.
Their laughter ceases or never even begins. Making matters more
complex is the reality that the members of the cast are forever chang-
ing, year by year, grade by grade, life stage by life stage. A fourth-grade
teacher may be magical in her effectiveness only to be followed by
one who assumes that all learning problems are forms of moral
turpitude (i.e., "she can do it if she tries" or "I treat everyone exactly
the same in my class"). That instability of support over time intensi-
fies the tumultuous challenge of advocating for a struggling child or
adolescent, staying aboard the chaotic roller-coaster ride that is her
life. Thank goodness for supportive parents; they are the purveyors of
unfailing continuity and unyielding advocacy—as is so vividly seen
in the tenacity of Anne Ford's loving heroism. But Anne's role is far
more than that of a devoted mother; she must serve as well as the
producer and director of a long-running show with that ever-changing
cast. It is her job to foster communication and collaboration onstage, over time, and behind the scenes of Allegra's performance. And
she judges which of the characters is potentially helpful to her
daughter and which will need to have their influence minimized.
What a valiant and indispensable role!

In Allegra's case, as well as in so many others like hers, not all of
the players were helpful. Some were unable to discern her array of as-
sets and decipher her breakdowns in learning. Somehow they pi-
geonholed her unfairly, sought to write her off, were unwilling to
look beyond the rigid reductionism that comes with sole reliance on
test scores. They failed to unearth the glimmering promise of a developing human being. These cast members became obstacles mas-
querading as helpers. Some were my fellow clinicians. Regrettably,
such professionals stifle too many suffering students and their parents. They are not mean-spirited; they are yet to be educated and
properly sensitized. For a start, they need to read *Laughing Allegra*!

One might argue that Allegra isn't very typical because she has
grown up in a family environment that has allowed her access to the
very best professional services and custom-fitted private schools. Suf-
ficient resources have been available to meet all of her needs on a
consistent basis. Moreover, her mother has been a compassionate,
uniquely well-informed, and influential advocate for her. No one
could replicate Anne Ford! But bear in mind that even with these
tremendous advantages, life often has been painful, bruised repeatedly by humiliating rejection and stabbing pangs of disappointment.
The parable of Allegra and Anne illustrates that, even in the presence
of optimal life circumstances, meeting the learning needs of a

struggling student becomes a strenuous and frequently heart-rending campaign. But we also learn that through unwavering persistence and wise planning, a family can ensure that a child is understood and worked with. The question and answer section of this book, along with the comprehensive list of resources, should serve to help parents acquire the wisdom they will need at the same time that they identify and utilize programs that can function as their allies. In the Hippocratic Oath we physicians must take, there is the phrase *"primum non nocere"* ("first, do no harm"). More than anything else, parents must protect a promising mind from being harmed by those who lack understanding and sympathy. And that's what's most challenging and vital under any environmental conditions!

Allegra herself, much like every child, provides us with some cogent lessons. First, she represents the fact that traditional notions of learning difficulties are far too narrow in their scope. The wounds are far deeper and wider than delays in reading, spelling, or mathematics. In Allegra's case, the dysfunctions extend to confused relationships with peers, overdependency on certain adults, trouble acquiring organizational and life skills, problems recognizing and responding to matters that keep recurring in a curriculum, and perhaps most importantly, incomplete formation of concepts. The latter breakdown has made it hard for her to master the true nature of numbers and deal with much of the abstract and technical thinking that permeates educational subject matter. Allegra needed to be taught the concept of a concept and carefully guided through concept formation in her mind. Allegra has also endured some problems with her attention. However, too often, we are too glib about such difficulties. Because a child is distractible or can't seem to focus, we simply invoke the magic (and ultimately unhelpful) label "ADD" (Attention Deficit Disorder). In Allegra's case, as with quite a few others, it is likely that weak concentration is largely the result of her problems processing information. Her inconsistent attention constitutes a desperate distress signal rather than a straightforward disorder. After all, why keep listening when you do not understand?

In *Laughing Allegra*, we are taught about the critical importance of diagnosing and activating a child's innate strengths and affinities. I believe that the salvation of most children with academic difficulties rests in the discovery of their minds' specialties, their areas of unique ability and interest. They all have these. Call it niche-finding. In Allegra's case, figure skating and working with young children were passions awaiting a stage upon which to act. Happily, those who knew her were able to provide the stages on which she could perform, so that Allegra could savor and display her authentic forms of mastery. We can find the right rink for any child!

For Allegra, the show must go on. I believe she will continue to enjoy the happy life her name symbolizes. No doubt, as an adult, this woman will keep tripping over pesky developmental obstacles, but don't we all? Along her chosen pathways, she will find delight in the unique rewards of jobs well done. Anne Ford and her very special daughter forever will have the satisfaction of knowing they have offered shrewd guidance to countless readers of this book whose children are deprived of the chance to sample the tasty flavors of mastery. They will absorb from these pages not only usable advice for helping their kids but they will gain unforgettable insights into the miracles of mothering and fathering fortified with the empowering knowledge of how a parent and a child can enrich and validate each other's lives.

—January 2003

Introduction
A Guide to the Heart

Hear are my thoughts about my mom writing this book...I think mom has done well...
And telling those people out there that you CAN get help...
I didn't want my life in a book at first so I told mom that and we talk it over and after I talked with mom I thought about it. If it helps other kids then we should do it and so I told my mom ok.

—E-mail from Allegra Ford

In 1972, I was living in Manhattan with my six-year-old son Alessandro and my newborn daughter Allegra. We had a very happy life, with no sign of trouble on the horizon. Alessandro was in kindergarten and was doing fine and Allegra was a happy, healthy baby. This continued for four years, but then our lives took a turn that forever altered the course of our future. My daughter began to exhibit what I thought at first was a small behavior problem. This problem soon escalated into something I had never seen or imagined before. When I tried to find help, I was confronted by a medical establishment that offered me conflicting opinions and seemed to know as little about her condition as I did. This uncertainty was the beginning of a terrifying and bewildering ordeal, filled with dire predictions from all sides telling me that my child's education and future prospects and even her happiness were in question.

I had no signposts to follow back then. I had no idea what to do or who to turn to. Worst of all was the crushing sense of isolation, the feeling that I was the only one going through it and that no one—*no one*—could possibly understand. I even had difficulty talking to my own family about this. My father was extremely busy as the head of the Ford Motor Company and was always traveling. My mother, although she was nearby, had instilled the concepts of discretion and stoicism in us at an early age—problems were something to be handled quietly, preferably without imposing them on anyone else. Nothing in my background or upbringing prepared me to handle this new, unexpected challenge.

What was the cause of all this confusion and pain? It is something that sounds very simple, but it is not. It is complex and devastating, not only for the child but also for the entire family.

It is called a learning disability. Most people equate a learning disability with dyslexia—reversing letters and words—and that is, indeed, a form of LD. But there are varying levels of severity, some mild and some so severe that every aspect of a child's life is affected: reading a book, playing a game, interacting with other children. Such ordinary daily occurrences as these have the potential to become a confusing, often paralyzing, ordeal and can turn what should be a happy childhood into a life of endless frustration and isolation.

LD is a neurological disorder. Information isn't processed as straightforward information but as a chaotic jumble of words, numbers, and thoughts tumbling over each other in the brain. Social cues are often misunderstood and can lead to tension in relationships. Often attention deficit disorder will accompany LD, adding more confusion and disorder to the mix. This is not mental retardation, autism, or Down's syndrome, and often there is no outward sign of the turmoil within.

When Allegra was diagnosed with multiple severe learning disabilities in 1976, there was little or no literature on LD and I was going through this on my own. I needed information to explain my daughter's condition and what I could do to help her, but I also needed a guide to the heart. I needed to connect with someone who had been through it already and could offer words of comfort and the most simple reassuring statement a parent can hear: "Your child will be fine."

I didn't have that, and that is my reason for writing this book, to enlighten parents and give them hope and help guide them on their oftentimes-treacherous journey. *Laughing Allegra* is the book I could not find when I needed help. It is not an academic work. I have access to many of the leading experts in the field of learning disabilities, but I have chosen to stay close to my own experience and opinions—not because I discount those of the experts but because my intention is to be the friend across the table, the one who listens and shares lessons learned through similar experiences. It is critical for parents to seek out the advice of teachers, pediatricians, and other experts. At the same time, there is great value in simply knowing that someone else understands exactly what you are going through, feels the same emotions, and has suffered the same doubts and fears.

There are four sections to the book. The first and longest is a memoir of my journey from denial to acceptance, which mirrored Allegra's own from a confused, often lonely child into a young woman of remarkable courage and dedication.

After writing the memoir, I realized there was still more to the story, especially for those whose child has been newly diagnosed. For them, I have included a section called "Questions Parents Ask," which addresses many issues common to parents of children with learning disabilities. These issues range from the most basic question of all, "What is a learning disability?," to questions on a parent's legal rights and how best to navigate the system when problems arise in school.

In the third section, "A Mother's Perspective," I offer advice on everyday matters such as homework, driving, relationships, and how to help your child as they begin life as an independent young adult.

The final section is an in-depth resource guide that directs parents to various organizations that will help in their quest to help their child.

Coping with learning disabilities is an ongoing process. It does not come to an end when the child leaves school or joins the workplace or becomes involved in a relationship. Allegra is thirty and still confronts many of the same issues she faced as a child. Our role as parents also does not end, no matter how old our children are. There are new challenges every day.

Laughing Allegra is a story of pain and frustration, but far more important, it is also a story of achievement and success. It can be the same for every child, for success comes in many forms.

I am well aware that many parents do not have the same resources that were available to me. These resources have been important, yes; but they are not the full story. Lifestyle, income level, social circles— all the externals that too often separate us—diminish when a mother is sitting alone somewhere, wondering if there is anyone out there who can help her child. With *Laughing Allegra*, I have tried to reach beyond external differences, deep into the core of what makes every parent of a child with LD the same, no matter who we are or where we live or how many resources are available for our use.

This book is intended to inspire parents, to show them they are not alone and that we all—as parents of children with learning disabilities—share the same language of hope.

PART I

♥

Laughing Allegra

Prologue

It is May, but in this small town in the Adirondacks, there is still a hint of winter in the air. The tops of the surrounding mountains are white with snow and everyone is wearing a sweater or jacket. Back home in New York City, the tulips have come and gone, but here the daffodils are in bloom.

I have come to watch my daughter Allegra compete in her final competition for the U.S. Figure Skating Association's Adult Nationals. My sister Charlotte is with me. So are my best friend Melinda and my son Alessandro. This is usually a quiet, peaceful town, but on this day, hundreds of skaters from across the country have descended for the competition. Every hotel is booked, the shops are crowded, and the sidewalks are as busy as those in New York City. In the afternoon, the town's enormous skating arena is crammed to capacity with skaters and coaches, friends and strangers who love the sport.

It's much colder inside the arena than outside. I can feel the chill of the smooth ice as we pass the rink on our way to the bleachers. Elegant men and women move beside us—sparkling with sequins, stretching, warming up, fitting in one last practice of their routine. They glide by like a flock of brilliantly colored birds, each one deep in solitary concentration. I study the swirling skaters, hoping to catch a glimpse of my daughter, but I cannot find her anywhere.

Charlotte knows I am anxious. "Will you *please* calm down?" she asks in her bemused, mock-impatient way. "You're going to make the rest of us nervous."

"She already has," Alessandro observes. We each carry a small bouquet of spring flowers to hand to Allegra when it's all over. The stems of mine have been twisted and broken by my restless hands.

"How can she do this?" I wonder. "How can she stand the pressure?" By now I should know the futility of such questions. Allegra has always surprised me. She has always surpassed my expectations. We take our seats in the bleachers, and still I cannot see her. "Where is she?" I ask again. I know she's in the arena—but where? Her coach, Tammy, approaches.

"Is everything all right?" I ask.

"Everything's fine," she says with a reassuring smile. "Allegra's raring to go. I wanted to tell you the line-up. She'll be competing against seventeen skaters in her level. She'll be number sixteen."

Not great news. I always hope she'll be first or second, anything to decrease the worry time.

Five, ten, fifteen skaters step onto the ice and perform for two minutes. They are all wonderful athletes—no falls, no breaks in their routines. I search the darkness at the edge of the rink. I still cannot see her but I know she is there, standing in the shadows, waiting for the applause for the fifteenth skater to die down.

A loud voice echoes through the cavernous arena: "Please welcome skater number sixteen, Miss Allegra Ford!"

The spotlight swings to the side and there she is, perfectly lovely as she steps onto the ice. She stands at 5"8," taller now because of the skates. Her hair is dark auburn with blond streaks, medium length, and pulled up into a braid. She is nearly thirty years old, but appears to be much younger. Her strenuous workouts and natural poise combine to give her an elegant, statuesque quality. When the spotlight hits her, I see the feature that defines her most: a great big Allegra smile.

This is her hometown and she has a cheering section. We applaud and her friends shout and call her name as she takes her place in the center of the rink, standing alone in a pool of light, wearing a turquoise dress studded with diamond rhinestones, her arms lifted in a graceful ballerina pose.

The music begins. It is the theme to *The Proposition*, a film produced by her brother, Alessandro. She steps forward, her arms sweep out to the side, and she is off, moving effortlessly over the ice.

There is an ancient saying that a journey of a thousands miles begins with a single step. Profound and true, but as I watch Allegra take that first graceful step in her routine, I cannot help but think of it as a first step at the *end* of a long painful journey measured not in miles, but in years.

This was the girl who did not fit in, the one who had few friends, and who was "different." This was the girl who could not run with the others or understand their games. This was the girl who struggled every single day with something called a learning disability—a term not in common use when we began our journey together. Hers was not a mild disability. It was far more severe than most, and nothing in our lives has had such a devastating and long-lasting impact.

As I look back over the years before that final skating competition, I search for the moment when her story begins. Was it her first day of school when she held me by the hand and we walked together down the sidewalk to a school none of my friends had ever heard of? Or was it earlier, when the nursery school teacher first mentioned that something might be wrong?

Or was it even earlier, at the age when all stories truly begin? Yes, I think I'll start there—on a day in early January, the day she was born.

Chapter 1
Baby Girl Uzielli

hellow momie its me :) well i know we talk alot on the
phone. but i just wanted to seend you a email. i hope you are
doing well with things. like work, and your book. i know its
hard but im with you all the way throught. god brought 2
big miracles to your life a son who loves you more then you
know. and daughter who just thinks the world of you. and
knows that things are to fine.
                                    —E-mail from Allegra Ford

I was in New York Hospital. The drugs were not working. An epidural
was a fairly new procedure back then and may have needed a few re-
finements. I was injected again and again, but it didn't help. I felt
everything and sensed everything around me—doctor, nurses, hospital room, and mostly, intense pain. My husband Gianni Uzielli was
there also, pacing in the room or standing beside me, but his mind
was elsewhere. If he had a choice he would rather have stayed home.
Husbands rarely came into the delivery room in those days, and for
Gianni, it was an ordeal. He was unnerved by the experience and left
every few minutes for a cigarette. He was joined several times by my
obstetrician, and when they returned and stood over me, trying to
comfort me, a stale odor of cigarettes cut through the pain. I was
grateful for it: the smell gave me something to focus on until 8:15
p.m. when my daughter came into the world.

That was January 3, 1972, one of the two favorite days of my life
(the other being a day six years earlier when my son Alessandro was
born). I never imagined I could love another person as intensely as I
loved Alessandro, and I was amazed by how quickly my heart ad-
justed to include this new little stranger. It was an instantaneous reaction, from stranger to adored daughter in a fraction of a second. The
first time I held her I knew I would never be able to imagine my life
without her. She was beautiful, a pale little angel with delicate features. She had no hair at all, which made her look even more angelic.
Alessandro, by contrast, had been a hearty baby, red and robust, born
with a wonderful Roman nose and a full head of thick black hair.

I had not wanted to wait six years between children, but I lost a baby shortly after Alessandro was born, and it was five years before I was able to have another child. Six years was a long time for my boy to be an only child and the center of his family's love and attention. How would he react to a new person dropped into the middle of this? Would he adjust? Would he share the spotlight?

Gianni brought him into the room to see me. Alessandro was never shy, but on this day he held back a bit before his curiosity got the better of him and he approached the hospital bed.

"This is your new sister," I said, moving away the folds of her blanket to give him a better look. He stared with his big brown eyes and then he smiled, and I knew he was smitten. Allegra took her own unique and equal place beside him and has never left it since.

"What's her name?" he asked.

I looked at Gianni—he looked at me—we had discussed a few names but never made a final choice. Officially, she was "Baby Girl Uzielli."

"We don't know that yet," I told him, but within a day I was able to announce her name to the world: Allegra Charlotte Uzielli. Years later, long after Gianni and I were divorced, Allegra decided to take on my name and became Allegra Charlotte Ford.

I called her Allegra for two reasons. First, because it means *happy* in Italian. I had been toying with the idea for a while, and it was finalized after a chance meeting with a stranger. We were in the nursery, standing in our bathrobes, hair a mess, happily watching our newborns through a window. She told me all her children had names beginning with the letter *A* and for some reason I thought: "That's very cool!"

Then I thought, "Well, that settles that." I already had Alessandro, my first *A*, my "Big A" as I sometimes called him. Now I had my second, my little A.

Happy Allegra, laughing Allegra.

I met my husband at a party given by my mother in New York City. He was a charming rogue, an Italian with a flair for witty banter. We were married soon after and a year later, in 1966, our son was born. My sister Charlotte's daughter Elena was born six months earlier and my friend Melinda's daughter Ashley was born around the same time, so all three of us had the happy experience of being new young mothers together.

My happiness as a mother was offset by growing difficulties in my marriage. Some people are simply not equipped to be parents. That was the case with Gianni. He was a boisterous carefree man, and when children came and the good times were threatened by early nights and crying babies and new responsibilities, our relationship began to founder. We stayed together and dealt with our separate views of our life goals as best we could. I wanted a close family, loving and peaceful. Gianni wanted a family, but for him, life outside our home was a long exciting party, and he could never quite bring himself to leave it.

When Alessandro was in nursery school, we made a move that we hoped would bring our separate views a little closer together, and for a while it did. Gianni accepted a job managing a restaurant on the island of St. Martin in the Caribbean. It was a perfect time and place to live a carefree beach-bum existence, and that's exactly what we did. We lived a fairly basic life, with no phones and very little communication with the outside world. I brought books so I could work with Alessandro to make sure he didn't fall behind, but for the most part, his classroom was the beach, with lots of time for exploring and collecting shells and sitting by my side to talk about the waves. There were tropical storms and sunburns to deal with, but all in all it was an idyllic lazy life.

After several months of this, I began to feel unwell. I thought it might be the water or the food, or even worse, some exotic illness. I didn't want to take any chances, so I took a short trip back home with Alessandro to try to figure out the problem.

Once there I discovered it wasn't the food, it wasn't the water. It wasn't a problem at all. Far from it! I came out of the doctor's office elated by the news that I was pregnant with my second child.

We decided to return to New York City as a family then, and we moved into a new apartment a few weeks before she was born. We took her home on that cold day, all wrapped up in a pink blanket. I still remember thinking how tiny she was. I could barely see her face inside all those pink folds. She was a smaller baby than Alessandro. Her birth weight was 6 pounds, 6 ounces compared to his 7 pounds, 6 ounces.

When Alessandro was born, I had the usual apprehensions of a new mother. I questioned my abilities and wondered if I would know what to do if he cried or was sick, but that is common among first-time mothers. I was not a major worrier with Alessandro, and had no reason to become one with Allegra. But soon after she was born, I did something I had never done with my son. Late one night, very late, at maybe two or three o'clock in the morning, I woke up from a deep sleep. The only sound from the monitor on my bedside table was Allegra's steady breathing, telling me she was asleep. I lay in bed for a moment, listening for—I still don't know what. For reasons I did not understand, I suddenly felt the need to be beside her. I reached into a drawer and pulled out a flashlight.

Down the dark corridor I went on tiptoe, careful not to make a sound. I reached the door to Allegra's room and touched the handle. I stopped for a moment, surprised to find that my heart was racing and I could barely breathe. I opened the door and aimed the flashlight into her crib and there she was, sleeping peacefully. Nothing wrong. Nothing out of place.

My heart calmed down at once. I stood there for a long time, watching her sleep and wondering what on earth had compelled me to check up on her like that. And why was I so alarmed? My pulse had been racing as if I was having a minor anxiety attack. But why? She had not been crying, she had not made a sound.

I dismissed it with a laugh—one of those mood swings after giving birth, I guess, and I leaned over and kissed her lightly on her silky head, then went back to my room.

The next night I did it again. Awakened in the early hours, the flashlight, the fluttering heart, the walk down the hall to check up on her…night after night I did that, all the time wondering why. I never did this with Alessandro. So what was it about my daughter? Was there a fragility there, sensed at a level deeper than the five senses? Did some form of mother's instinct, primal and subconscious, know there was something more than the usual childhood complaints in her future and that the nagging anxiety that began to grow within me would someday be justified?

There was also the baby I had lost. Perhaps that loss affected me more deeply than I realized. I had been four and a half months pregnant when I began to hemorrhage. Gianni took me to the hospital and left me there, assuring me that everything would be fine. I don't remember why he couldn't stay or where he went that night, but it doesn't really matter. By then, the responsibilities of fatherhood were beginning to close in around him and constrict his lifestyle. As far as our marriage was concerned, he was already halfway out the door. I was on my own when the doctor came into my room and told me they couldn't save the baby.

I wondered if my nighttime vigils with Allegra were proof of the lingering effects of that experience.

I did not know the answers. I did not even fully realize there were questions. All I knew was that I was compelled to leave my bedroom night after night and go to hers. Once there I knew—and I knew it to my core—that the baby I saw sleeping in the glow of my flashlight was perfect: a perfect baby, soon to be a perfect young girl, and one day, a perfectly lovely woman.

We project so much future happiness on such small helpless children. I used to sit in a chair beside her crib with the flashlight off, and my mind would wander far ahead. I imagined her as a toddler, and wondered what color her hair would be and if it would be straight and dark like Alessandro's or maybe wavy like mine was when I was a child? I saw her as a schoolgirl in one of the nearby schools, dressed in a cute little uniform and giggling over boys with her friends. And later, in college, I saw her poised to enter the world as a professional of some sort, confident and enthusiastic about her future. Oh, those were wonderful dreams, and there was no excuse for even a single one of them not to come true.

When she was less than a month old, the weather took a turn for the worse. We had one of those cold spells that hits New York City every once in a while, when the air is so cold it actually hurts to breathe it in. I had an errand to run, so I left Allegra with a babysitter. When I returned home, shivering in spite of my heavy coat and gloves, I ran into the babysitter, also on her way back to the apartment. She had the baby carriage. She had been in the park, taking Allegra out for a stroll.

I was a bit shocked, but I didn't dare criticize her. She was a very experienced woman, and I realized that she must have known it was all right. Allegra was bundled up and looked warm enough, but still, the cold was so bitter I worried that any exposure at all might be too much.

A day or so later, Allegra developed a deep bronchial cough and had some difficulty breathing. I called the pediatrician, but she assured me it was nothing. Once again, I thought, "What do I know?" and followed her recommendation without question.

I spent the night with a humidifier, aiming the steam into Allegra's blanket-covered bassinet. Her cough deepened. By the time the sun came up the next morning, I decided there was a small chance that I might know more than the babysitter and the pediatrician (at least in this instance). That soft inner voice that compelled me to check up on her night after night for reasons I did not understand now proved to be very useful. Against all expert advice, it told me to take her to the emergency room at New York Hospital, and I am very thankful that I did.

She had pneumonia. She spent two days in the hospital. I sat beside her the entire time without sleeping. We were in a dark room. In the middle of the room was an adult-sized hospital bed, and in the very center of the bed, inside a tent, was tiny, tiny Allegra. I've never seen a baby look so small before, so helpless.

Hours passed slowly. I couldn't sleep. I couldn't eat. I didn't dare leave her side.

Once in a while I was allowed to put my hand inside the tent. Allegra grasped my pinkie and held it tight, and there we sat until I was told to take my hand away. I was tense the entire time. I listened to her breathing. I focused on the sound, alert to even the smallest change, and I told the nurses immediately if I thought something was wrong. They were understanding at times, annoyed at others, but I was no longer paying attention to them. I honestly believed she was in danger of dying and I was focused entirely on her.

After she came home, the flashlight vigils intensified. I woke up every night at some point, imagining I heard her cough or wondering if she was breathing freely, and every night I crept into her room to watch her sleep in her crib. My anxiety grew in other ways, too. I didn't trust anyone with her. Babysitters came and went. My standards were high, as most parents' are, but mine may have been ridiculously high. I counted once and was amazed to discover that I had gone through seventeen babysitters in Allegra's early years.

Some left on their own, others left at my request. Most were very nice and none would have harmed her, but I could not overcome my fears. And what were those fears? I still don't know. Vague apprehension, something not quite right...something I couldn't define even if I had tried.

Many times I left my apartment and got halfway down the block only to stop in my tracks, dead still. A companion might stop with me and ask what was wrong.

"I have to go back."

"Did you forget something?"

"No, but I have to go back. I can't leave Allegra alone." I would return to the apartment as quickly as I could. This happened over and over, and did not end until—seventeen babysitters later—I finally found someone I trusted. She was my cousin, Sheila Murphy, the daughter of my mother's youngest sister. With Sheila I could relax. I could leave the children with her, confident they would be all right. But even then there were times when I had to go back—just once more—to check on things.

Not all my days and nights were filled with anxiety and fear in those early days. I was surrounded by friends and family and constant expressions of joy over our new arrival.

Six weeks after she was born, she was christened in our home. My best friend Melinda was her godmother, and she had two godfathers, my brother Edsel and Gianni's brother Philip.

The choice of godparents was an obvious one. Melinda had been a wonderful and important part of my life for many years. We met on my first day of high school. I had been enrolled in the Sacred Heart Convent in Noroton, Connecticut. It was my mother's alma mater and she decided both her girls could benefit from the character-building discipline and rigor imposed by the nuns. Charlotte went before me and spent the summer telling me so many horror stories about convent life that I was ready to go home by the time my parents drove me up the long driveway on that first day. We got out of the car and everyone stood around waiting for the arrival of the imposing nun who was the headmistress of the school. The adults chatted amongst themselves while their downcast daughters eyed each other, fearful of bursting into tears. For most of us, it was our first time away from home, and we felt like we were being sentenced to prison.

One girl caught my attention. She was about my age and was the most beautiful girl I had ever seen, with long dark hair and a huge flower in her lapel. I was a little shy, but she smiled and I found the courage to introduce myself.

"Hello," I said. "My name is Anne."

"I'm Melinda Fuller."

Those were the first words exchanged between two girls who became best friends and have remained so ever since. We started out as school friends, but by the time Allegra was christened, our friendship had developed into something more, something extraordinary. We thought alike, we talked alike, our experiences mirrored each other's in uncanny ways. When I looked at Melinda, I saw an extension of my inner soul.

Edsel and Philip were also perfect choices to share the role of Allegra's godfather. My brother Edsel didn't live in New York, but he did manage to spend many weekends with Gianni and me in the summer. On alternate weekends, Philip joined us. They were wild boys, always with a new girlfriend, but they were loving uncles to Alessandro and I knew they would be the same with Allegra. I could not imagine better godparents.

When Allegra was eighteen months old, Gianni and I decided to end our marriage. It had been coming for a while and we both knew it was the right thing to do. Allegra was so young that I wasn't concerned with her reaction, but I wondered how Alessandro would take it. I had no idea how to break the news to him.

We took him to lunch at the Rockefeller Center skating rink. I was in agony, terrified of his reaction, and was a nervous wreck by the time we sat down at the table.

"Alessandro...," I began, and he looked up at me with his big brown eyes.

"Yes, Mommy?"

I paused, glanced at Gianni and said, "Your father has something to tell you."

Gianni was as flustered as I was, so I made a second attempt. "We've decided to buy you a bunk bed."

"Why?"

"So you'll have a place to sleep—you and a friend—when you sleep over at Papa's new apartment—because Papa's getting a new apartment...."

I was still groping for words when Alessandro suddenly shrugged his shoulders and said, "Oh, I know you guys are getting a divorce. That's okay. Can we go watch the skaters now?"

They always know so much more than we think they do.

So we were on our own then, Alessandro at seven years old and Allegra approaching two. Gianni and I were no longer arguing about our separate views of life, so in some respects the end of our marriage finally allowed me to reach the place I desired: a peaceful, close, quiet family existence. It remained that way for a little while, with no dark clouds on the horizon and no overt signs to indicate what was in store for us.

There were a few hints, but to me they were simply manifestations of Allegra's unique personality and did not give me cause for concern. Now, with years behind me and far more awareness about learning disabilities, I realize that those hints may have been early warning signs.

The first one I remember came when Allegra was two years old, and my sister Charlotte and her husband Tony invited us over for a family dinner. By this time, Allegra had already answered some of my earliest questions about her future: her hair was not straight and dark like Alessandro's, but was red and curly, and her personality was shaping up to being that of an extrovert, wildly happy and vivacious and filled with laughter.

The dinner was a very casual affair—jeans and T-shirts, hamburgers and hot-dogs—an ordinary, unmemorable event until Tony pointed out that Allegra wasn't feeding herself.

"What do you mean?" I asked.

"Well, look at her. She's old enough to use a fork."

She was, but she was still eating with her fingers. She was sitting in a high chair at the table. "So?" I asked, surprised by his observation. It didn't seem that big a deal.

"So nothing," he said. He then smiled at her and said, very casually, "I just don't understand why she isn't able to feed herself at this age. There must be something wrong with her."

It was a simple statement, with no harm intended, but I was shocked. Something *wrong* with her? I don't remember how I reacted, although I'm quite sure I said nothing. I may even have consciously tried to hide my reaction. I don't remember what I said or did, but I do remember this: by the time the next family dinner came around, I made sure Allegra could feed herself.

I was determined that no one would ever again say there was something wrong with the way my children ate. "Here you go, Allegra," I said over and over again. "Hold the fork like this. No, no, honey. Like this." We practiced it until she got it down, and once she got it down, that was that. She used a fork from then on.

She learned without complaint. In my memories, she did everything easily and on time. But note those words: *in my memories*. Rummaging through old photo albums and looking at school records, I am astounded to read this in one of Allegra's earliest neurological reports from 1977: "Her developmental landmarks are recalled as being consistently slow. She was late to turn over and to sit. She did not walk until age two and she did not speak in sentences until age four."

There it is in black and white. *"Recalled as consistently slow."* Since it says "recalled," I must have been the one who was doing the recalling. But why do I remember it so differently now? In my memories, she walked on time, she talked on time, she learned to tie her shoelaces on time.

The comment at the dinner table was a minor incident, but it does hold a place of importance for I am certain it was the day on which Charlotte first suspected something was not quite right. She knew long before I did. I still didn't have a clue. The comment hurt me in the way any mother is hurt when something negative is said about her child. It was far more a matter of mother's pride than of worry or alarm.

Charlotte did not say anything to me at the time. What could she say? There was no outward sign of a disability, nothing to indicate how serious the problems were. Later, when the disability began to surface more clearly, she remembered that evening as the time she first suspected that her husband was right and that there was, indeed, something wrong with her niece.

We sat down together recently and I asked her things I had never asked before. We were at lunch and I tried to make my questions sound as casual as I could, knowing it was important for me to hear the truth unaffected by a sister's concern.

"Do you remember when you first thought something might be wrong?" I asked.

"I remember thinking it," Charlotte said, "but you never mentioned that there were any problems until much later. I thought you were avoiding it, and it's such a delicate thing to say to somebody when they haven't mentioned it first."

"That's understandable," I said. "I'd be the same way. Do you remember any specific incidents?"

"I remember when she was three or four, she didn't seem to be doing what Alessandro did at that age, or my daughter Elena did. Little things, like the alphabet or numbers. Kids test each other. They ask each other things like, 'Do you know what two and two equals?' I remember she never played those games. And if someone asked her, she didn't seem to have the answers."

Another hint came the following January, when she turned three. By this time, Allegra had fully evolved into the child I think of whenever anyone asks what she was like back then—curly red hair, freckles, an unstoppable vitality and joy for life. She was so much fun!

That year I invited some of my friends' children to our house to celebrate her third birthday. I hired a puppeteer to provide the entertainment. The puppeteer set up a small theater in the living room and the children sat on the floor to watch the show. Allegra was always so energetic and gregarious at home and with her family, and I remember being surprised to see her leave the group of children and sit off to the side by herself. She didn't interact as I thought she would. She even appeared to be a bit withdrawn, which was very unusual. I was about to go sit beside her and bring her closer to the group when she suddenly stood and went right up to the stage.

She reached out for the puppets, but I stopped her and brought her back to her place. "You have to watch them from out here," I said. She sat for a few seconds and then was up again. She stared at the puppets and then up at the strings and the puppeteer behind the theater—I sensed that she couldn't connect the two: puppet and string. She couldn't see that one controlled the other or that the puppets were not real. She believed they were real people, tiny people. Several times I brought her back to her place and each time she stayed for a moment but then she was up again, staring at the stage, fascinated by the strange little creatures and oblivious to the other children around her. I didn't think her behavior was alarming or even particularly odd, but I was bothered by it. I'm certain all the other children's imaginations translated the puppets into real people, but Allegra was the only one who felt compelled to investigate. She was only three, but so were most of the others, and I couldn't understand why she was so restless when they sat quietly, mesmerized by what they were watching. There was a strange contradiction in her behavior: she was withdrawn from the group, yet she was also outgoing, almost as though she was in her own little world where she was happily alone, with no other children in there with her.

"Well, that's fine," I thought. "She is easily distracted." That's all it was, that's what I believed. I wasn't even all that surprised by it for I had already seen how difficult it sometimes was for her to concentrate.

At bedtime, I used to get into bed with her to read a story. I loved the closeness and the warmth, but Allegra could not sit still. She fidgeted and fussed and got up and down and crawled out of bed and back into it, and I soon realized that bedtime stories were not going to be a part of our nightly routine. I was saddened as I looked back at those times with Alessandro as being some of our closest. I wanted the same for Allegra. I was about to give up when I hit upon an idea that I hoped might work.

I got into bed with her one night and pulled the covers over us. This time, instead of opening a book, I lay my head against hers and said, "Once upon a time there was a little girl named Allegra...."

She stopped fidgeting.

"And Allegra had a brother named Alessandro who was older than she was. And one night they were at the dinner table and Allegra dropped her fork on the floor...."

That very thing had happened that night. It was a story she already knew, but it held her interest. "And then what happened to the little girl named Allegra?" she asked, and I told her how Alessandro picked up the fork but wouldn't give it back to her, and how she started crying until the character named "Mommy" told Alessandro to give it back to his sister.

She never got out of bed during those stories. They were about her and about what had happened that day. She knew all the characters and easily followed the events.

Night after night I told a story about the little girl named Allegra and what had happened to her that day, and night after night Allegra cuddled beside me and was eventually lulled to sleep by the sound of my voice. Later we added *Goodnight Moon* to our nightly bedtime stories. The repetition and simplicity of Margaret Wise Brown's story was enormously appealing to Allegra, and I could count on her settling in without distraction when I opened the book and read, "In the great green room there was a telephone and a red balloon...."

I did not realize that my storytelling adventures were another example of one of the most powerful tools there is when trying to help a child, and that is good old-fashioned mother's intuition. When I closed the story books and told Allegra about her own day or returned over and over again to *Goodnight Moon*, I did not realize I was helping her compensate for an inability to focus or understand simple words and concepts. All I knew was that we were connecting as mother and daughter and that she was interested in the story and was comforted by the simple repetition of what had happened to her that day. We also devised a routine around the ending of *Goodnight Moon* that was a comfort to us both. I came to the last page and together we said, "Goodnight stars. Goodnight air. Goodnight noises everywhere."

I closed the book then, and we both said goodnight to the objects in her room. "Goodnight table," I said, and Allegra repeated it after me.

"Goodnight table," she said in her small, sleepy voice.

I got out of her bed. "Goodnight chair."

"Goodnight chair," she repeated.

"Goodnight teddy bear." I said, and I kissed her and crossed to her door.

"Goodnight teddy bear."

And I turned off the light. "Goodnight Allegra."

"Goodnight Mommy."

Chapter 2
Why Are You
Wandering Off Again?

*When I was five years old I was diagnosed with a learing
disabilitie my mom heard it through the doc. And my moms
face didn't look too happy.*
                                    —E-mail from Allegra Ford

I told stories to Allegra every night and by the age of three and a half,
she left *Goodnight Moon* behind in favor of other stories...but not
completely. We often returned to our old favorite just to hear ourselves say goodnight to the table, the stars, and the teddy bear.

I was long over the "What's wrong with her?" remark made by my
sister's husband and we carried on as if things were perfectly fine,
which they were. She had an older brother who doted on her and
aunts and cousins and grandparents who couldn't get enough of her.
My mother never quite knew what to make of her: She had rather
firm ideas about discipline and proper behavior, but all these ideas
fell by the wayside when she was in my daughter's presence. She
couldn't help it. My daughter's actions resembled a "behavior problem" insofar as she was constantly on the move and always talking,
but that's where the similarities ended. She was so funny and effer-
vescent, and her behavior was so far from being considered a "problem" that my mother gave up all attempts at discipline or even
expressions of disapproval. My father never even tried: funny and ef-
fervescent was right up his alley, and he took to Allegra at once.

Everything was clear skies and smooth sailing, and then, at age
three and a half, it was time to enroll her in nursery school.

I applied to a couple of schools near our apartment. In the interviews she didn't pay attention, didn't respond as she should, could-
n't seem to put together a fairly simple puzzle, but only because she
was distracted by the teachers and the new environment (or so I
thought). I wasn't alarmed. It was the sort of behavior I was familiar

with: clowning around, vivacious laughter, short attention span, but not undisciplined, not a "behavior problem." Allegra was never rude. She never threw a temper tantrum. She never even shouted in anger. She was spontaneous and engaging, a total extrovert.

The first two schools did not accept her, but that was not uncommon at all. It seemed that everyone I knew had children who didn't get into the first school they applied to. A third school accepted her right away. It was called the Madison Avenue Presbyterian Nursery School, and was housed on the top floor of a twelve-story building. It was close to our apartment and had a very good reputation.

I can't think of a single thing that went wrong that first year. Allegra loved school, and she seemed to get along with the other children. Her teachers never indicated there might be a problem. She was energetic, maybe a little hyperactive, but nothing out of the ordinary.

The year went by without a hitch and she returned to the same nursery school for a second year. She was now four and a half years old. A month went by, and then another, and then came the first real sign of trouble.

Miss Zimmerman, the headmistress, called me and scheduled an appointment for the two of us to meet. I went to the school, unsure of what to expect. I assumed the meeting was to discuss the coming year, which kindergarten she recommended we apply to or even the possibility of keeping her in nursery school for another year, although I couldn't imagine any reason to keep her back. She seemed to be progressing nicely, but still, anything is a possibility.

So I was calm and optimistic when I went to the school, happy to be laying plans for my daughter's future. I even had a list of kindergartens to go over with the headmistress. I knew she would have some insight into which might be the best ones for Allegra.

Miss Zimmerman was a tall, heavy-set woman. Typical of so many nursery school teachers, she was warm and loving to the children, almost motherly in her devotion. She led me into her office and asked me to take a seat. She closed her office door, muffling the children's voices outside.

A closed door…not a good sign. It made me a little uneasy, though I didn't know why. Obviously we needed a quiet place to talk, but the closed door hinted at something a little more serious than I expected. She began by praising Allegra and then, for the first time, I heard what I would come to call The Inevitable But, as in, "Allegra is very popular, *but…*" or "Allegra tries very hard to keep up with the others, *but…*"

The Inevitable But is always followed by a statement:

"She doesn't follow directions...."

"She wanders around the room when she should be sitting down...."

"She retreats into a world of her own...."

"She won't sit still in reading or in show-and-tell...."

"She can't keep up with the others...."

None of this was said unkindly. Miss Zimmerman was trying to be helpful and in this, my first introduction to The Inevitable But, I also heard these words for the first time: "You may want to have her tested."

"Tested?" I asked in alarm. "Tested for what?"

All I could imagine was a test for some physical ailment, a virus or a condition the teachers saw but which had somehow escaped my notice.

Miss Zimmerman gently touched my hand and said, "For learning problems."

"Learning problems?" I asked, a bit relieved but now confused. "You mean because she isn't paying attention?"

"That's part of it, yes."

"But she's always like that, even at home," I pointed out. "It has nothing to do with learning problems."

Miss Zimmerman was not persuaded. "I believe she may have difficulty in a regular kindergarten."

"Oh, I don't think so!" I said, and I laughed at the suggestion. It was polite laughter, somewhat nervous. "She won't have a problem, I'm sure of it. It can't be that serious. Whatever it is, she'll outgrow it."

Miss Zimmerman smiled again. She was very understanding and patient. I'm sure she had much experience with mothers of my kind before, unwilling to believe anything is wrong with their child. "This isn't easy to hear," she said, "I understand that. But I really do believe she'll have trouble in a regular kindergarten."

"But what do you mean by 'regular kindergarten'?" I asked. "What other kind is there?" I honestly didn't know. If a kindergarten wasn't "regular" what else could it be? "Is all this because she won't sit still?" I asked in amazement. Surely this was a minor problem. Irritating for the teacher perhaps, and a bit embarrassing for me, but surely it was nothing serious.

This was not the way things were supposed to be. I had my list of kindergartens in my hand. Allegra was supposed to be enrolled in one of those, a school like the one Alessandro had gone to. She would attend school with all my friends' children and with all the other little girls in her nursery school class. That was the plan. I envisioned her wearing a gray wool uniform with a white cotton blouse, its Peter Pan collar trimmed in red, and little brown loafers with white socks and a knapsack on her back—a uniform similar to the one I wore when I was in school. And like every other little girl, she would have lots of friends and play-dates. That was the plan, that was the reality I expected, and I couldn't imagine any reason it should be altered—*especially* over a behavior problem, real or otherwise.

"She'll be fine," I said, confident in my prediction.

"Why don't you try this," Miss Zimmerman said, "why don't you come to Parents Day? I think you may understand the situation a little better."

"I've been to Parents Day," I reminded her. "Several of them. There was never a problem."

"That was last year. Things have changed. I think you ought to see for yourself."

I thought about all this as I walked the few blocks to my apartment. How could things have changed so much in a year? It wasn't possible. A small child does change between ages three and four, but the changes are not all that drastic—certainly not enough to alter my plans. I felt threatened, though I now realize that it wasn't me personally who was being assaulted, but all my beliefs and assumptions about my child's education. Some of these assumptions may have been a little frivolous (like my insistence that Allegra would wear a gray uniform with a Peter Pan collar), but such small details added up to form an image of my child in a school of my choosing, receiving the very best education available. Some of this was my way of rebelling against my own school years.

I went to high school in the Sacred Heart Convent in Noroton, Connecticut. Before that, I attended school at another convent, also called Sacred Heart, in a suburb of Detroit. I never really fit in at either of them, never related to the nuns as teachers. In my mind, I see only a procession of strict, unsmiling women dressed in black.

This was how Charlotte described the convent in Noroton to me before I went for the first time: "You live in a big room with iron beds and only one straight-backed chair, and you have to wear a uniform all day long, and you have to kneel when you're wearing a skirt to make sure the hem touches the floor so you won't show your knees...." Her description was accurate but she did not go far enough. We were not allowed to speak unless we were spoken to first, even in our rooms. We were allowed one phone call a week, and that was only to our parents. Our mail was censored before it was sent.

Classes were held six days a week, with mass every morning at 6:30. On Sunday we spent most of the day in prayer.

I met Melinda there, but that was the only bright spot in an otherwise dreary experience and I vowed I would not send my children to a place like that. Allegra's school years would be much happier than mine, and more fulfilling—that's what I believed.

But now things had taken an unexpected turn. Miss Zimmerman's words stayed with me until I reached my apartment, but by then I had already decided that she was wrong. There couldn't be a problem. I knew Allegra, I knew her behavior, I knew what she could do and couldn't do. I knew she had no difficulty learning—it was the same as the fork at the dinner table back when she was two. Once the situation was pointed out to me, I worked with her and she overcame it quickly and easily. It would be the same this time. I would work with her and together we would fix whatever "learning problem" they thought she might have.

I did not realize it, but the first bricks in my wall of denial were being laid.

I almost called to cancel my attendance at Parents Day, but then I thought, "No, I'll go. It can't hurt. And besides, that will give me the chance to see for myself that Miss Zimmerman is wrong."

I arrived at Parents Day and took my place with the other parents, and there it was in full view, staring me in the face. But did I see it? No. I saw *something*, but not the reality of the situation.

The children were in a small tight circle around the teacher, all faces upturned to hers, all eyes glued to her as they listened to a story she was reading.

One child wasn't there. She was off in a corner on her own, pretending to be cooking lunch for the class, completely oblivious to the story, the teacher, the other children.

She was in her own world. When someone brought her back to the circle she stayed for a moment, but then she was off again, over into the kitchen to play in that other world.

"Now we're going to make the brownies," she said, talking to herself. "You put the mix in the pan and put the pan in the oven." She was teaching class, using the words she had heard another teacher use and imitating the teacher's voice.

I wanted to go to her, to take her back to the group, but I forced myself to watch. Other parents glanced at her from time to time, and then at me...and they smiled. What was in those smiles? Sympathy? Or was it the simple joy of watching a little girl playing on her own? I couldn't tell.

During playtime, Allegra was in another area of the room engaged in solitary games with only her imagination as her companion. The other children avoided her—not because they didn't like her, but because they couldn't understand her. She was on her own, but it didn't seem to bother her at all. Her isolation was a result of imaginary games she created in her mind, with rules only she could understand.

I now saw what Miss Zimmerman was talking about. I still wasn't alarmed, or even overly concerned, but I was a little embarrassed. Embarrassment is not an easy emotion to feel about your own child and that was the first time I ever felt it. There was nothing wrong with her (as far as I could tell), so why was she acting this way? I was convinced that it was exactly what my mother had already dismissed—a behavior problem. And again, I knew she could overcome it with my help and perhaps a little more discipline.

We began on our walk home from school that very afternoon. "Allegra, do you know what the teacher is doing when she gathers you all into a circle?"

"She has a book."

"Yes, and she's reading to you, the same way I do at night. But she wants you to listen. You need to sit with all the other children while she's reading."

I remembered my own problems keeping her still in the bed and wondered if I had contributed to her restlessness by not forcing her to listen to stories that were not about her or *Goodnight Moon*. Was I too lenient? Did I unwittingly encourage this apparently willful distraction?

Even then, on the walk home, that distraction was on display. I spoke to her but her attention wandered. The yellow bus, the blue car, a pigeon, another little girl: all were enough to pull her attention away from my words and my voice. I stopped on the sidewalk and crouched down in front of her. "Allegra," I said, firmly. "You need to listen to me when I'm talking. You need to listen to the teacher when she's talking."

She looked at me intently with her sweet brown eyes and then she glanced over my shoulder at...something, I don't know what—and I knew I had lost her again. Still, I had faith in my ability to change her behavior. It was a simple matter of paying attention, that's all. There was nothing wrong with her.

I do not know how much of this early denial was formed by my innate character and how much by attitudes learned when I was growing up, but the combination of the two formed a barrier of defenses around me that was so impenetrable that I did not realize there was any barrier at all. My "reality," the reality I was trying to will into existence, was that Allegra had no problems at all and that there was nothing to upset the perfect world I imagined for my children and myself.

This denial would grow stronger in the coming months, but in some ways it served a useful purpose. Denial is not a completely negative reaction, at least not in the beginning and in small doses. Theoretically it may be preferable to be clear-eyed and realistic right from the start but this rarely happens. Unless you have a child with a disability it is difficult to imagine the crushing pain and sense of panic that can come with this awful realization. So many things come upon you at the same time. "It can't be," you tell yourself over and over again, "it *can't* be!" The implications are so vast that it is difficult to take them in all at once. Denial may be nature's way of easing us into a process of acceptance.

Sometimes a parent's denial can be so strong it impacts the child in negative ways. The parent may seriously delay getting help for the child, for example, or refuse to seek help at all. This parent may repeatedly force the child into situations where he or she fails, all in a long, futile effort to prove there is nothing wrong. I never went quite that far with Allegra (though I came close). For me, denial was manifested in an inability to accept reality even as I made an honest attempt to deal with it. It was sort of like, "All right, I'll face the problem and deal with it, even though I know there is no problem at all."

My war between denial and acceptance began on Parents Day. It was waged within me from that moment onward, with each getting the upper hand at various times in the coming months.

Not long after Parents Day, I happened to pass Allegra's bedroom and saw that her door was closed. That was rather unusual and I wondered if she was all right. I reached for the door handle but stopped at the sound of her voice. "Goodnight moon," I heard. "Goodnight stars..."

I opened her door. She was sitting on a stool in the middle of the bedroom. Her dolls and teddy bears were arranged in a semi-circle in front of her. "Hi Sweetheart," I said as I entered the room. "What are you doing?"

"Playing school," she returned, and I realized that she was the teacher and the dolls were the students.

"Are you reading to them?" I asked.

"Yes. I'm reading *Goodnight Moon*." She held the book in her hand,

but it was upside down. I smiled at her; she had obviously memo-
rized the story, and I thought it was so cute that she was holding the
book upside down.

"Are they listening to you?" I asked.

"Oh, yes, Mommy. They're being very good."

"That's wonderful, Allegra," I said, and I smiled again as I left her
to her students. I closed the door, but not all the way. I stood in the
hall and listened as my daughter, the child who could not sit still, became the teacher and read to the class. And then I heard this: "Come
back now. You need to pay attention."

As she had when cooking lunch for the class during Parents Day,
she repeated the words she knew best, focusing on one doll in the
circle. "Come back now," she said. "Pay attention. You have to sit
down and listen while I read the story. Why are you wandering off
again...?"

I now knew that she was aware of what was happening in her
school. She knew the rules, how to sit down, how to pay attention.
She knew enough to ask it of her dolls. So why couldn't she do it herself?

Day after day I heard her talking to her dolls and one day I asked if
I could join her. I sat on the floor as if I was one of her students.
When she pretended that one of the dolls walked away from the
reading circle I asked if she had ever done that.

"Sometimes," she told me.

"Do you know why?"

She didn't answer.

"Allegra? Do you know why you walk away from the reading circle?"

"Do you think my doll's dress is pretty?"

"Yes, Allegra, it's beautiful. Why do you walk away from the circle,
sweetheart?"

"I think her red dress is pretty, too."

Miss Zimmerman called me with the name of a diagnostician. "It's
only an evaluation," she said. "Nothing to be worried about."

I wasn't worried. Allegra would pass. I knew she would.

The evaluation was simple enough. They asked me questions
about her background and family life: "Does she have brothers and
sister? Older or younger? Is there any indication that her brother or
any other family member has had difficulty in school?" They reviewed a report submitted by the nursery school. They administered
intelligence and ability tests, asking her to identify basic shapes and

colors, simple number sequences and rhymes. They asked her to say the alphabet and put together simple puzzles. There were gross motor skill tests such as running around obstacles and balancing on one foot for five to ten seconds. Fine motor skill tests included building a tower of small blocks and copying circles. This was followed with communication skill tests such as understanding sentences involving time concepts like "tomorrow" or size comparisons like "big or bigger." They asked her if she understood what it meant when she was told, "Let's pretend...."

Allegra did fine on colors and some shapes, the same with rhyming. She had difficulty with number sequences and with both the gross and fine motor skills, and she was completely unable to understand time and size concepts, or even understand "let's pretend." She didn't know what "let's pretend" meant. For Allegra, everything was based in the reality of the moment, and that included imaginary situations. If another child said, "Let's pretend a bear is behind that tree," there was no "pretend" at all for her. She was convinced a real bear was there and about to chase her. I always considered that to be a positive trait, the result of a very active and healthy imagination.

Then they asked me about her medical history. "Were there any problems at birth?"

"No," I said. "Not for her anyway."

"Were there problems for you?"

"No. Well, maybe a little problem, but nothing important. I had an epidural, but for some reason it didn't work. My doctor injected me again and again, but it still didn't work." I hesitated. "You don't think that caused any trouble do you?"

"No, I doubt it," the diagnostician said. "Anything else?"

"Not that I remember," I said. "She was smaller than her brother. Her birth weight was a pound less than his. Oh, and she had pneumonia when she was about a month old."

"I see. Was she deprived of oxygen?"

"No," I said in surprise. "No, they put her in a tent. I'm sure she wasn't deprived of oxygen."

"Did they give her the heel test?"

"What's that?"

"It is standard procedure to prick a child's heel to check for slow or nonexistent reflexes, a sign of oxygen deprivation."

I told them I didn't know if the test had been administered, but that I would look into it. I had never heard of it before. I later learned that no one gave her the test. No one asked if I wanted it done. I never asked for it because I never heard of it. There was no way to know if she was deprived of oxygen.

The evaluation was concluded and the official results came back. She was found to have a "variable level of functioning, being below her age expectation."

A horrible-sounding phrase. "What does that mean?" I asked the doctor.

"It may not mean a lot now, but I do agree with Miss Zimmerman. I believe she needs some special help before going on to first grade. A special kindergarten."

"Special...what does that mean?" I asked. "There's nothing really wrong with her, is there?"

"No, not yet, but—"

"So there's nothing to worry about, right? She's going to be fine. There's nothing wrong." My questions were not questions at all: they were statements designed to cover the diagnosis with solid reassurance. I refused to believe what I was told. I was her mother. If there was a serious problem, surely I would recognize it. I knew I would. I had already convinced myself that she had only a small behavior problem, a minor matter of distraction, an overactive imagination. I heard her with her dolls. I knew she could sit down and stay still. I knew it was possible for her to pay attention. I could help her. I could work with her, and show her how to put the puzzles together over and over again. The pieces would fall into place. Everything would fall into place. I knew it would.

This belief changed and my first defensive wall of denial was forcibly shattered on a late December afternoon when all the parents and siblings of the forty or so children in the nursery school gathered together in the auditorium at the Madison Avenue Presbyterian Church.

It was the annual Christmas Pageant.

There aren't too many things more funny or heartwarming than the sound of small children belting out loud off-key renditions of "Jingle Bells" or "Here Comes Santa Claus." I knew that my sister and mother would have enjoyed the pageant, but I did not ask them to come. I was still upset and a little hurt by the doctor's suggestions—I didn't believe Allegra had a serious problem but her inattentive behavior (which I couldn't ignore) was enough to instill some doubt. Could she stand in a structured line and sing a song? Yes, I knew she could, but *would* she? She could perform, but would she follow all the directions? I did not know the answers, and so I decided to go to the performance alone.

I can still picture the auditorium, but I have no memory of what songs were sung or what Allegra was wearing. I was sitting in the darkness in the middle of the audience. The curtains opened and the lights came up on the stage.

I couldn't see her at first. It took a moment to sort out the children.

They began to sing the first song and that's when it happened. In one instant, all the illusions I had about my daughter, the fears, even my own ignorance about her true nature, careened together in one single, heart-stopping moment.

The children were grouped together with the music director conducting, her back to the audience. All of a sudden, out of nowhere, Allegra appeared at the front of the stage and began to dance and sing a song. I couldn't hear what she was singing, but I knew it had nothing to do with what the others were singing. For me the entire world collapsed into a single moment frozen in time—my daughter standing out in front, lost and bewildered, singing something known only to her. And there I am, watching her from deep within the dark auditorium, separated from her by chairs and people, unable to reach her and hold her and take away those feelings of confusion. It was a moment frozen in time, but the feelings and impact of this moment were almost entirely internal. They were my feelings, and my perceptions. No one pointed at Allegra and laughed. Stunned silence did not fall in the auditorium. Very little happened at all. The music teacher simply reached for her arm and gently pulled her back to the group. A few of the parents did chuckle a bit, thinking it was cute and funny to see a child so expressive and extroverted she couldn't help but take center stage. I might have joined them had I not heard the recent reports from the doctor and headmistress. I, too, might have found it cute and funny. But I didn't. I saw for the first time how right they were. And I knew that what was cute and funny today would not be cute and funny tomorrow.

She had no clue she was doing something out of the ordinary. She did not know how inappropriate her behavior was. She had no idea that she had just shown me, for the first time, that the dreams I had of my daughter as a perfect little school girl were unlikely to come true.

Chapter 3
A Beautiful Squiggle

i know in life we all go through somthing thats not right or
we just donr know what to do. because we went the rong way
—E-mail from Allegra Ford

Now I knew that something was not quite right with Allegra, but I still had no idea what it was. It was an enormous, frustrating mystery. By all outward appearances, she was perfectly fine. It was impossible for me or anyone else to detect anything out of the ordinary. The same with her ability to converse. Oh yes, she mispronounced some words and sometimes got mixed up in her efforts to communicate, but so what? She was five years old. Still, all the behaviors I viewed as normal or perhaps a little out of control were viewed by the experts as symptoms of a larger problem. But what? The terms they used were so vague: "learning problems." What does that mean? Does it mean she isn't concentrating? Or that she isn't trying? Or does it mean that she *is* trying, but is incapable of doing it?

The diagnostician who conducted the first evaluation told me she had a "variable level of functioning, below her age expectation."

Oh. I see. And when I asked what a variable level of functioning meant, the answer was, "It may not mean anything." If that's the case then why not say so up front? Why not start the conversation with "This may not mean anything," instead of waiting until I asked, with my heart in my throat and a pit in my stomach, terrified to hear the answer?

It was all so unclear and so frightening. I could not gauge how serious our situation was.

Many of my friends had children when I did. We all began together, pushing our baby carriages in Central Park, comparing what our children could or couldn't do, how many teeth they had, who could walk first, who could talk first. When Allegra was an infant, there happened to be more baby girls within this circle and when we spoke of our children's future, much of the discussion revolved around which school they would attend.

Those Central Park conversations, as informal and casual as they were, instilled a sense of expectation among my friends and me. I can't imagine there is a group of happy young mothers anywhere who do not go through the same process: the light-hearted competition among them shapes their expectations and the entire group comes to an unspoken, maybe unconscious consensus about what is and what is not appropriate for the children. *All* the children. For us, one of the major expectations involved school. We all wanted a school that would provide our children with the very best education possible.

And now, here I was in Miss Zimmerman's office to discuss my options. The enthusiasm and certainties of those conversations in the park seemed to slip from my grasp as I listened to the headmistress. "We have some suggestions for kindergarten," she told me, "and I must say you are very lucky. There happens to be a very good special school on the fifth floor of this building that is appropriate for Allegra's needs. It's called the Gateway School."

It was not a school that had been on my list. I had never heard of it before. But the Christmas pageant had shown me that my highest expectations for Allegra were probably not realistic and so, with some reluctance, I agreed to take a look at this "special" school.

"But I still don't understand what you mean by 'special,'" I said.

"It's for children like Allegra."

"I understand that, but are you recommending this school because she has a learning problem? That's what you called it originally. Is it because of that or is it something more serious?"

"It's the learning problem," she said. "And it can be serious. We don't know if that's the case with Allegra. But this school is a place for children who cannot fit into a regular classroom."

I didn't respond as I wanted. I wanted to say, "What do you mean she cannot fit in? She can fit in—of course, she can fit in!" But this flash of anger was quickly overwhelmed by fear and led to the most basic question of all, still unspoken: "What's *wrong* with Allegra?" Something in Miss Zimmerman's gentle confidence made me believe that she had already given me the answer she thought was best. I thanked her and made my way from the twelfth floor nursery school to the unknown kindergarten on the fifth floor.

That elevator ride seemed to be the longest ride of my life. I tried

desperately to convince myself that Miss Zimmerman was wrong—
*she can fit into a regular classroom. And what did she mean by that any-
way? "Cannot fit in." Maybe she is a bit hyper but I can work with her on
this....*The elevator descended, rickety, clanking on its cables....*I can
work with her the same way I did after Tony said there was something
wrong with her because she couldn't use a fork. She learned quickly enough
back then, I know she can do it again...*The elevator floor lights
changed, flashing down from ten to nine to eight...*How did this happen? How did she get like this?* And then a new disturbing thought intruded: *Is it my fault?*

This new thought and the questions that followed rushed in so
quickly that it seemed they had been there for quite some time, hiding below the surface of my mind, waiting for the right moment to
strike—and that's exactly what they did. The elevator descended and
I fell into the first of many waves of guilt that would periodically
wash over me. My rational mind told me that Allegra's difficulties
were not caused by something I had done, but my heart said another
thing, and so did my memories. When you are grasping at straws, it
sometimes seems that *every* memory contains a potential clue to the
reason for the child's disability. Did I eat too much? Did I not eat
enough? Did I fall? Did I breathe in toxic fumes? Was it the epidural?
Was it the pneumonia? And why wasn't she given the heel test? And
then there were things I didn't know about. Did Allegra suffer some
sort of trauma when I wasn't around? Did something happen when I
left her with a babysitter while I was away one afternoon? Was she
dropped? Is there something genetic going on here? Was something
passed down through my family? And what about Gianni—could
this have been passed on through him?

Blame and guilt had me firmly in their clutches by the time the elevator opened.

When it did, I stepped out and looked around. The school was a
single enormous room with the hardwood floor of a gymnasium. A
narrow staircase led up to a second level of tiny classrooms, which
were accessed by a single long balcony that surrounded three quar-
ters of the main room. Kindergarten paraphernalia was in evidence
everywhere—blocks, drawings, collages made of colored paper,
schoolbags on the windowsills, little coats on hooks. Nothing all
that unusual. But then I took one step to the right and froze, devastated by the sight before me.

In the center of this cavernous room were about thirty children
gathered around a teacher for show-and-tell. To my eyes, they were
all disabled, some physically, some mentally, but all very obviously

disabled. I realized then what everyone meant by the word "special." They meant handicapped. They meant retarded or maybe "slow" as it was sometimes called. "Oh, no," I thought. "No, no, this is not going to work out at all."

My eyes filled with tears. I reached behind, hoping to stop the elevator door from closing, but it was too late. It closed with a bang. I stood there with my back to the room, staring at the gray elevator door, trying as hard as I could to keep my tears in check, but I couldn't.

I was approached by a small, stately woman with gray hair. She introduced herself as Elizabeth Freidus, the director of the Gateway School. She didn't say a word about my tears. She did not embarrass me or make me feel that my reaction was insensitive or even unusual. She simply smiled and led me toward her office.

"I understand you have come here about your daughter. What's her name?"

"Allegra."

"Oh, how lovely."

"It's Italian," I said as we passed the children playing on the floor. "It means happy."

Mrs. Freidus had started the school in a room so small it was often described as a closet. There were no special schools at the time, and when she was told of a young boy who was rejected from every school in the area, she said, "I'll take him." He was her only student for a time, but others soon joined him, and within a few years Gateway became a model school for children with disabilities. Back then, most of the children had been sent there from the Committee for the Handicapped (now called the Committee for Special Education). Every school district is required to have such a committee, which evaluates and places children with all disabilities into an appropriate school. As I first suspected, some of the children at Gateway that day were physically disabled, others were mentally disabled. To me, not a single child appeared to be *normal*. As I had passed them on the way to the office my tears had been replaced by panic: "How could I possibly send Allegra here? She isn't like these children at all! She doesn't belong here!"

Appearances—it was all appearances. The word "normal" is so subjective. Everyone has a personal idea of what it means. My concept of normal has shifted over the years, expanded, become much more inclusive. I can see a child in Gateway today and think he looks perfectly "normal." If that same child had been there on that first day so long ago, I would not have thought so. Everything is relative and sooner or later we learn to accept what we are given...but it doesn't come easy.

My tears were gone by the time we reached her office. Mrs. Freidus' aura of kindness took the edge off my first stunned reaction to what I saw, but I was devastated and I rebelled at once.

I listened to what she had to say, but I listened like someone who is plotting an escape. I was already determined not to send Allegra to this school no matter what she said.

"Why don't you bring her in for an evaluation?" she asked.

"I had one done already," I said. "She was found to be...I don't know, varying levels of functioning or something like that. I don't really understand it, but they also said it might not matter."

"And they may be right. But it never hurts to get a second opinion, or another evaluation. If you bring her in, I can see if she and Gateway are right for each other. If that's the case, we may still have some difficulties with placement. I'm not sure if there are any slots left for next year. But we'll wait on that. Bring her in tomorrow if you'd like."

I agreed, but only because I reasoned that if Allegra was not right for the school it automatically meant she was suited to a better, more "normal" school.

I brought her back the following day for the evaluation. It was similar to the one conducted by the diagnostician, using puzzles and pictures, but this one was a bit more advanced. Mrs. Freidus and a teacher named Tonya Pulanco sat at a small table with Allegra. I was asked to sit there as well, but I didn't.

"No, that's okay," I said. "I'm fine," and I pulled my chair up to the wall beside the door. Tonya says it was the place farthest away from the table. That is her memory of me—a mother seated as far away as possible, unable to handle what was happening.

Once again communication skills were part of the test. Allegra did well on all but the most complex, such as: "Do you understand the differences between "pretty," "prettier," and "prettiest"? She didn't, but I thought that was understandable at her age. Other tests evaluated her visual abilities. They showed her a busy circus picture and asked, "Allegra, can you find the clown in this picture?" She did find the clown and I relaxed a little bit. Then she was asked to draw a squiggle on the blackboard.

Mrs. Freidus drew one first, a set of spirals that started at the top of the board and looped down to the bottom. Allegra was asked to draw the exact same shape. She tried over and over, but she was unable to re-create the squiggle's gently swirling lines.

"She couldn't organize herself," Tonya remembers. "She could not organize her body or her movements. She couldn't coordinate them in a way that gave her the ability to begin to draw the squiggle. For Allegra, there was only a blank area on the blackboard—a dark, confusing space with no signposts to show her the way. She looked at Mrs. Freidus' squiggle, then back to the empty space, back and forth from line to empty space, and still she could not figure out a way to begin. So what did she do? She compensated."

Rather than create a squiggle on her own, Allegra hit upon the ingenious solution of drawing her squiggle directly over the one that was already there. There was a breathless moment...would the teacher say, as might be expected, "That's not right"?

No. Mrs. Freidus smiled and very gently said, "Very good, Allegra. Now try it again."

Allegra beamed with pride. "You see, Mom? I can do it."

"Yes, honey, you can," I said, and I smiled from my distant vantage point as she drew another squiggle on top of the first two.

"Again," Mrs. Freidus said, guiding Allegra, encouraging her; and before long, Allegra had drawn so many squiggles on top of one another that the form and rhythm and shape were in her mind, and she was able to move off into the empty space and create one on her own.

"Very good, Allegra," said Mrs. Freidus. "That is a beautiful squiggle."

After the evaluation, the teachers and administrators met in private, and then I was informed that there was no place for her at the school because, as Mrs. Freidus expected, they were all booked up for the term.

I did not hear the last part.

I only heard, "There is no place for her," and I interpreted this to mean, "She isn't right for this place. She isn't disabled enough."

I was so relieved. I *knew* she didn't belong there! Now the evaluation proved I was correct. "Yes, well, that's fine," I thought as we walked home that day. "She won't have to go to that place! I know she won't be enrolled in the school I hoped she could go to, but I'll accept that. I'll even accept the fact that she may need some sort of special school. Now I need to find the very best special school in New York City."

Christmas came and went that year, and Charlotte and I took our children on a skiing trip to Sun Valley, Idaho, in early January 1977. It was a wonderful place for them. Alessandro had a ton of friends there and both he and Allegra loved to ski. This was a positive thing in her life. She may have had trouble paying attention at show-and-tell, but she had very little trouble skiing. She took her first lessons around this time and was able to keep up with the others.

I enjoyed the snow and the cold and the sun on the mountains; and our family get-togethers were as happy as they had always been, but part of me was removed from Sun Valley that year, distracted by a constant thought that cast its shadow over everything: "Is there something wrong with my daughter?"

I can see her now on her tiny skis, all bundled up with a big smile on her face as she joined the other children on the easy trails of Dollar Mountain. And there I was, watching her, my face clouded with worry, unable to really believe there was anything serious going on with her. "Look at her," I thought. "They said she had some difficulties with coordination in her evaluation, but look how well she does on skis. There's nothing wrong with her coordination."

Charlotte approached me. "Are you okay?"

"What?" I asked, startled out of my daydream.

"I asked if you're okay. You're not yourself. You haven't been since we arrived here."

"I'm fine."

Charlotte eyed me suspiciously. "Come on, Anne. I know you too well. What's going on?"

I looked at her and my eyes began to fill with tears. I fought them back, bit my lower lip, and then I said, "Let's go somewhere where we can talk."

I told her all about the evaluations and the recommendations for special schools. She couldn't have been sweeter about it all, and it was a huge relief for me to finally talk to someone about it. "Why don't you come over to my place on Friday," she said. "I'm having a dinner party and one of the guests is a pediatrician. He lives in New York, too. He's out here on vacation."

I agreed and met the pediatrician at Charlotte's, and took the opportunity to discuss Allegra with him. I knew he was in Idaho to escape the office and relax, but I asked if he would take the time to observe her. I told him about the special school back in New York and how the teachers didn't think she should be in a mainstream school. I tried to be calm about it all, but he must have sensed my distress because he agreed.

He took time out from his vacation to observe Allegra in a social situation and to my intense relief he said, "I don't think there is anything wrong at all. But bring her by the office when we get back to New York and we'll test her."

The shadow lifted for me that day and for the rest of our vacation.

We returned to New York, I made the appointment with the pediatrician, and I radiated confidence when I brought her in for her IQ test. This, for certain, would prove him correct in his initial observation that she was fine. More important for me, it would also prove that all the other evaluations were *wrong*.

He tested her and gave me the result: "I'm afraid she has some rather serious developmental delays."

"What does that mean?" I asked. This was *not* what I had expected. I felt like the wind had been knocked out of me. "But you just saw her in Sun Valley," I stammered. "You told me there was nothing wrong with her! That was only two weeks ago, how can she be this...whatever you said."

"Developmentally delayed." He went on to explain the bell curve, a way to measure a person's intelligence. There is a small group of extraordinarily intelligent children—the child prodigies and geniuses—that is represented by a flat line on the chart. The line begins to curve upward as the level of intelligence goes "down" and the number of children falling into that category swells. The very top of the curve is the point where the highest percentage of children is located. This is the place where the "average" child is found. Then the curve begins to descend again, as smaller and smaller groups fit into categories going lower and lower on the intelligence scale. At the bottom of the curve the line straightens out again and contains the small group of children at the very bottom of the scale.

Allegra was found to be at a point just before that final flat line.

"But how can that be?" I asked. "How can she be fine in Sun Valley and now be at the lowest end of a curve?"

The doctor had no answer.

My confusion and questions now became part of a routine as I began to search for an answer and each doctor, pediatrician, psychologist, and psychiatrist tried to diagnose Allegra's problem. Their diagnosis often *was* the problem! She didn't fit into any standardized categories. One doctor gave me hope by telling me she would outgrow her difficulties and the next sent me into despair by telling me she might be mentally retarded. Another doctor might say she was fine while the next told me she was developmentally disabled and would never outgrow it. I didn't know who to believe.

And then there were the questions about her medical history. The heel test came up again and again. "Was she ever tested for oxygen deprivation?"

"No," I told them, "or at least I don't know if she was. There's no way to tell."

My denial remained strong, but with every evaluation it began to be whittled away, bit by bit, very slowly and very painfully. After her first evaluation, I refused to believe the diagnosis of "learning problems." I had to be shown indisputable proof before I could accept it (and even then I had great difficulty with the truth). But now, after being overwhelmed with psychological test results from many different doctors, I realized that I must at least try to accept their findings. Once that happened, I did what so many mothers of disabled children do: I would be by myself, having coffee in the quiet hours of the morning, or maybe driving the car or trying to concentrate on a book or magazine. But what was I really doing? I was tearing through my memories like a detective, trying to find a reason, something that might have caused this. It was useless to *try* to stop it. Memories came unbidden—even when I was not actively trying to find them, suddenly *ah!*...something half-remembered, an incident so minor at the time but now a possible clue in the search for an answer.

I thought about the pneumonia. Could that have been the cause? Was she deprived of oxygen?

No one knows the exact cause of learning disabilities, but a variety of factors have been implicated. They often run in families. A father, a mother, a grandparent, an uncle: it is not unusual to find learning disabilities running like a thread through the generations. I have sixty-eight first cousins on my mother's side and there may be one or two instances of LD, but none as severe as Allegra's. Problems during pregnancy and birth may also lead to learning disabilities. It could be an illness or injury during or before birth, or exposure to toxins such as lead paint. It may be premature labor, or lack of oxygen, or low birth weight.

So many things to consider....

It is a bewildering and dismaying list to cover, checking off each item in a "Yes," "No," or "Possibly" column, but the thing I most wish I knew back then is that there is often no specific cause at all. Parents should not spend too much time feeling guilty or wondering how the disability could have been prevented.

This is easier said than done. I wonder how many mothers hear reasons for their child's disability that have nothing to do with them, yet take them on as additional doubts and distress. She may hear something like a recent report that said PCBs cause LD, and she may think, "Oh my God, was I exposed to PCBs?" Like me, she may not know what a PCB is or looks like or if the damage is caused by eating them or handling them or standing beside them, but suddenly they take on great importance—at least until the next thing comes along to once again lead the mother to ask: "Did I do that? Am I somehow responsible?" I wish there were concrete answers that could lift the burden of blame from *all* of us. But even if there were such answers, sometimes we cannot shake the feeling that somehow we are at fault.

When these dark moments of self-doubt come, there is one extremely important thing a mother should bear in mind, and it is this: learning disabilities are a *neurological* disorder, not a *psychological* disorder. In other words, LD is a biological condition. It cannot be caused because a mother didn't love her child enough or didn't read to her child as an infant or didn't spend enough time playing with her child. Some psychological issues such as low self-esteem may eventually arise as result of the child having learning disabilities— but the psychological issues are *not* the cause.

There is more than enough heartache involved in coming to terms with the fact that your child is disabled. To be held accountable, even if only in your own mind, is too much to bear. I was as susceptible to guilt as anyone else but have come to realize that guilt and blame have never benefited a single person, especially not the disabled child.

Chapter 4
She Doesn't Belong Here

So they told us to go see some special doctor that could
help us out so we did.
And we went saw so many doctors that
The last one said I can't help anymore :(
And that was like a stab in the heart. My mom didn't
have any friends who didn't know a lot about learning
disabilities so we were on our owen.

—E-mail from Allegra Ford

All during the evaluation process I continued to search for a school
for Allegra. I applied to many schools in the city and one by one they
rejected her. It was the same each time: a voice on the phone telling
me, "She doesn't belong here." With each rejection came a deeper
sense of despair. As the list of schools grew shorter, my despair began
to be overtaken by something close to panic.

I was frightened. I didn't know what to do. What in the world can
anyone do if a child is denied even a basic education? Her future was
falling apart before my eyes. I knew the only chance she stood of making it in this world was to find a school, *any* school, that would accept
her, yet with each one I continued to hear, "She doesn't belong here."

"But I *want* her there!" I wanted to shout each time, but I never
did. I probably said, "I see. Well, thank you," and hung up the
phone. I never got angry, I never tossed a chair around or hit the wall
or even yelled at the person on the other end of the phone. I refused
to cry in front of Alessandro and Allegra. I didn't want to upset them
or let them think I was not in control of the situation.

I felt completely alone.

There was no one to go through this with me, no one to lean on
for support. There was no father for Allegra, or at least, not one who
was present and took an active role in her upbringing. I never took
my sister or Melinda to any of the interviews or to see any of the
schools. I never told my mother or father what I was going through.
No one really knew what we were up against.

Why the self-imposed isolation? Somehow I felt that something was going to happen and that she would be all right. I saw no need to burden my family and friends with my troubles.

Now desperate and grasping at straws, I sought out one of the most well respected pediatric psychologists in the city.

Allegra came with me. We walked into his office and with barely a glance in her direction he said, "Allegra, you may go downstairs now. There's a very nice woman down there who will talk to you."

Allegra was taken downstairs for a psychological evaluation while I went to the waiting room and sat for over an hour. When the tests were finished, I went to get Allegra. There she was at the secretary's desk, pretending she was the secretary, chatting away as she had heard the secretary chat. She was once again in her own world and was making appointments for other children just as a secretary would, using the same vocabulary she had heard the secretary using. It was exactly like the cooking class in nursery school and the reading circle for her dolls. Her imagination was center stage all the time and I couldn't help but smile as I watched her.

A day later I received a call from the psychologist's office, asking me to come in and discuss the report. I went in expecting a version similar to all the other discussions, although I was hopeful he might clear things up a little for me. I hoped his diagnosis and explanations might make our situation more understandable, and even acceptable. He was a renowned expert after all. He, more than anyone, should be able to offer me some hope.

Instead, he offered me something that remains burned into my memory as the single worst thing I have ever heard about one of my children.

He sat at his polished desk with the report in front of him. "I'm afraid I have to tell you that your daughter is borderline retarded, and I think you are making the problem worse."

"Who is?" I asked, not sure that I understood.

"You are."

"Me?" I asked, still convinced I had misunderstood him. "Are you saying that I'm making her problems *worse*?!"

"In a way, yes. You're taking her from doctor to doctor, trying to find the answer that you want to hear. And that answer simply isn't there. It really would be best if she was taken away from you."

I sat back in my chair, stunned. I could not take it in, could not understand what he meant by "away." Away where? And for how long? "What do you mean?" I asked.

"I mean that it would be best for you, your family, and for Allegra if she was institutionalized."

My jaw dropped. I stared in disbelief as he elaborated. "Not an asylum," he explained, "but also not assisted living. Somewhere in between."

My heart was racing. I could not believe what I was hearing. I must have misunderstood him, he couldn't have meant what I thought I heard. It wasn't possible. "Send her away," I repeated, but the words still would not sink in. "Send her away?" I tried to control my voice. "Where would I send her to?"

"There's a very nice place on the outskirts of London."

Part of me, *every* part of me, wanted to stand up, throw something, and scream at him, "She's *five* years old!"

But no—stunned and polite, I sat there as he continued. "And I'm afraid I can't be of any further assistance to you. You'll need to find someone else to take care of her because I'm too busy."

Too busy...

Essentially it came down to this: "You need to put your five-year-old in an institution three thousand miles away and I wish I could help you get through this, but I can't. So good-bye and good luck." That hurt more than anything—casting us adrift, leaving me to handle this overwhelming bit of news on my own. It was like cutting someone's arms off, throwing her in the water, and saying, "Okay, now swim to shore. Wish I could help you. Good-bye."

If only I could have told him what I thought of his diagnosis and his callous indifference, but I couldn't. I said, "Thank you, doctor," and went home. I locked myself in the bathroom and cried and cried until I could cry no more. I don't know how long I was in there or how many tears were shed but finally, exhausted and red-eyed, I stared at myself in the mirror and said the only thing I could say to my reflection, "No."

I didn't yell it, I didn't scream it. I said it quietly. "No." That was all. But the word contained so much more. It was a simple word now filled with resolve and determination. No, I will *not* accept that diagnosis. No, I will *not* send her away, and no, I will *not* give up on Allegra, no matter how many doctors tell me I am making things worse. And if this means giving up on the doctors, so be it. I will go it alone, but not completely—my children will be with me.

I tore up that damned report and threw it away.

Ever since, I have wondered how many parents receive a similar diagnosis from a similar doctor. Not long ago I spoke to a father who had received the same advice from the same prominent psychologist. Like me twenty years before, he has chosen to ignore the advice and to pursue other more humane avenues. But how many parents do not have the resources to find a way out of such a frightening situation—and I do not mean financial resources. Inner resources: courage, perseverance, those somewhat stubborn personality traits that often are the only things that keep us from the abyss.

In less than two months, I went from thinking I had an average, possibly overactive child to being told she was retarded, that she was unacceptable at every school we applied to, and that she should be institutionalized. Worst of all was the truly frightening thought, deep in the back of my mind, that maybe the doctor's suggestion was right. He was the professional, he should know, and maybe it would be best.

Second opinions are so important, especially when something so drastic and severe is recommended. And there is something else to bear in mind: experts are invaluable, yes, but the most finely tuned expert about a particular child is the child's parent. No one should blindly follow advice they believe in their heart to be against their child's best interests. I very quickly crushed any notion of the psychologist's superior knowledge of my daughter and what was "best" for me.

It was not going to happen. Could I abandon her, at five years old, alone in another country? To send her away…she wouldn't die, that's true, but to send her so far—was that any different from death?

Everything—the endless rejections, the nightmare diagnosis—came to a head on a rainy day at a pay phone on 72nd Street and Park Avenue in Manhattan. I was waiting to hear the final verdict from the very last school I had applied to. I was nervous, and I gripped the telephone receiver as tightly as I could, as if my grip would somehow change the answer from the one I dreaded (and expected) to one of acceptance.

I was standing in the rain, on hold. There was no pleasant music in the receiver to help me pass the time. Nothing but stony silence. People passed on the sidewalk, jostling each other with umbrellas. Pink tulips drooped in the rain down the center islands of Park Avenue, buses roared by, taxis blared, and there I was, surrounded by bustling life yet completely isolated within my own fear and confusion. I felt utterly alone. Every connection, every friend, every family member was nowhere to be found—not because they were insensitive or uncaring, but because I had not reached out to them or asked them to share my pain. I was not able to. I thought I could go it alone.

Most of the admissions directors at the schools we applied to had been sympathetic but firm in their decision. With each "No, I'm sorry," I scratched the school off my list. My anxiety level had increased with each rejection. Now I had reached the very last one, and I had no confidence left at all, nothing but failing hope and this one last chance.

The phone clicked, a voice came on—this time without a trace of warmth or understanding. "I'm sorry...."

I couldn't let her finish. "But why?" I asked, my voice rising in desperation. "Why?!"

"We feel this isn't the place for her."

"But why?!" I needed an answer, something I could hold onto, a reason that made sense. "I don't know how much more you can expect from her. She's only five!"

"I realize that. But she doesn't belong here."

I don't believe the woman understood the impact of her words. Her voice was as cold as the rain that day, completely devoid of feeling; but it was *what* she said and not her tone that sent a gate crashing down before me, cutting off my last hope.

I dropped the receiver into its cradle and stared at the phone in tears, stunned by the panic that surged through my body like an electrical shock. My daughter's future was unraveling before my eyes. What could I do? Who could I turn to? I had already shut down all avenues of comfort and could not face the idea of going to them now. I was too...what? Embarrassed? Ashamed? No.

It was simply that this was not how things were meant to be. Not for Allegra, not for me. I had goals and plans for her, formed in large measure by my own upbringing. I wanted her to have things I didn't have: not material things, but a chance to make it on her own for what she was, not who she was. I was completely unequipped to deal with rejection and failure and, most of all, this new thing in my family: a disability, a flaw!

I did not know it then but that final devastating phone call in the rain was to be a dividing line in my life and the lives of my children, ending all that had gone before and setting us all on a new course which continues to this day. My children became the center of my universe in ways I never dreamed possible, with all action, all thought, and all feeling revolving around them. I grew to accept that life is filled with uncertainty and that answers to the most simple, yet profound, questions such as "What is wrong with my daughter?" can be elusive. I learned to be self-reliant in ways I never had before. I learned that every spark of optimism and hope was something to be nurtured and treasured because sometimes they were the only comfort available. And I learned that worry had entered my life—sometimes it came as a fleeting thought, other times as free-flowing anxiety—but I knew even then that I would never be worry-free again.

It was over. There were no more schools. I now had to think of something unexpected and different, perhaps teaching her myself or starting a school of my own for children like Allegra.

What about a public school? To say it plainly and simply and with a touch of embarrassment: I did not know about them.

I was ignorant. After the harsh words of that doctor, I did not seek any additional help. I was so unworldly about many things. All of my school years had been spent in the convents, first in Detroit, then in Connecticut. Public schools were foreign to me. I grew up in the 1950s, yet I knew nothing of proms or sock-hops or cheerleading or what it was like to have a teacher who was a man or a high school friend who was a boy.

My knowledge of schools came from my friends who had children and who sent them to the same private school Alessandro attended.

It is amazing that in all that time I was searching for a school for Allegra, not one single person—not a teacher, headmistress, school counselor, doctor, or pediatrician—no one ever mentioned the possibility of sending her to a public school. We hear too many terrible stories today about much of the public school system, but had I known how far advanced it was in comparison to many of these "high powered private schools," especially when it came to special education classes, I would have leaped at the opportunity. But I didn't know what to search for, who to reach out to. I didn't know what was out there for us and I sometimes wonder if Allegra didn't suffer because of it. How much easier things might have been if I had only known what was available for us in the local public school.

I also wish I had sought out someone to talk to, someone to unburden myself with: a psychiatrist, someone to help me get through it all. I talked to doctors, yes, but only about Allegra, never about what our situation was doing to me. I knew of no other mother in the same predicament, no older woman I could turn to as a mentor.

In those gray days I could find no end to the tunnel, no cause for optimism. Allegra had a favorite song as a child. It was "Tomorrow" from *Annie*. Maybe I should have listened more closely to the words she sang so often. Sometimes the simple, almost naive belief that somehow "the sun'll come out tomorrow" is enough to get us through.

The sun did come out for us. It came in the form of a phone call from the Gateway School, the little school on the fifth floor, the one I had rejected as unfit for my daughter. When I had first gone there I could not see past the children I thought were not "normal," but now with my own ideas of normal forcibly expanded and reshaped, I was overjoyed. My relief on being told that someone had dropped out and there was a place for Allegra can scarcely be described. It felt like the cavalry had come over the hill to rescue us. I had rejected the school before and now I was grateful beyond belief that they would consider taking her at all.

There were some conditions (as there would be with every school she would ever go to). They would take her on a probationary basis to see if she could do it. I didn't care. Anything was preferable to the limbo we were in.

I took Allegra back to meet with the headmistress, Mrs. Freidus.

"Are we going back to the nursery school?" Allegra asked as we walked into the building.

"No, sweetheart," I said. "You're older now and soon it will be time for you to start kindergarten."

"Will I have real friends there?" she asked, and I knew she was thinking back to the days of isolating herself in the classroom, with classmates not understanding and her only friends being her dolls in the room behind her closed door.

"Yes, Allegra. This is a new school where you'll have lots of new friends."

This time the elevator went up instead of down. No longer was I apprehensive or doubtful. From the ground upward, I rode the elevator filled with gratitude instead of despair, and when the doors opened, I saw a place no longer different and uninviting but a place of light and warmth and caring teachers, where my daughter finally stood a chance of finding a space in her life where she fit in.

I signed her up at once and we went home safe and happy in the knowledge that everything was taken care of for the coming fall.

I now hoped to be able to sit back with a cup of coffee and reflect on the tumultuous fall, winter, and spring and say, "Well, thank God, *that's* over!" It was summer at last and I knew we were in for three months of beach, swimming, and tennis in my favorite place in the world—Southampton, New York.

What I did not realize is that learning disabilities are not confined to the classroom and that the problems of the spring would follow us deep into the summer.

Learning disabilities do not take vacations.

Chapter 5
Summer

in sumer we went to southhamptno : (i dindnt like it
there. because i miss new york and my new york friend
—E-mail from Allegra Ford

Southampton is located ninety miles east of New York City at the eastern end of Long Island. It is a small community of manicured hedges and beautiful green lawns bordering the Atlantic Ocean; and I can say without hesitation that the happiest days of my life have been spent in Southampton. The same is true for Alessandro. For Allegra, they were her worst days, her loneliest years.

To explain why this was so and the impact it had on my family, I first need to give a little family history.

I was born in Detroit, the second child of Anne and Henry Ford II. My first friend was my older sister Charlotte. We fought and argued like every pair of sisters on earth, but we have been there for each other for over fifty years now. Our brother Edsel came along six years after I was born. Charlotte and I were at an age where we treated him more like a living doll than a little brother, and he received a tremendous amount of affection and attention from his two elder sisters.

Our childhood was filled with many opposites and contradictions. We were a rather close, loving family, yet our family life was guided by strict rules and rigid formalities. Etiquette and manners were important, especially to my mother. So was self-restraint. To show too much emotion, especially temper, was not allowed. Our family was prominent in Detroit and came under more scrutiny than most. Because of this, we were expected to behave and conduct ourselves in a proper manner, especially in public.

Dinner was at the same time every evening, and we had to be bathed and dressed presentably before gathering in the dining room.

Such formality was the structure within which my family operated, but within that structure we had free reign. Nothing, it seemed, could prevent us from arguing or me claiming that "Charlotte's kicking me!" or Charlotte complaining about Edsel and on and on until my exasperated mother sent one of us away from the table. The dinner inevitably ended with tears, like many family dinners do.

Much of this formal informality was due to my grandmother Eleanor, known to us as Granny Ford. She was a loving, gentle woman who commanded great respect from those around her. She never asked for it or demanded it, and would have recoiled at the thought of such a thing, yet she was so dignified and elegant she acquired respect effortlessly. She believed that the most important qualities a person could have were consideration for others and modesty. They were traits she instilled in her four children and the ones they tried to instill in us.

Once a week Charlotte and I went to Granny's for tea. She lived in a big spooky house and our routine was to play hide-and-seek on every visit. Granny Ford had an endless supply of hiding places, but for some reason she felt compelled to hide behind the same set of curtains in the same hall every single time we played. If that wasn't enough, she made things even easier by taking no trouble to hide the toes of her shoes. Charlotte and I counted to ten, then tiptoed into the hall, giggling as we approached Granny's feet behind the red curtains. We didn't want to hurt her feelings by finding her too quickly so we went through an elaborate ritual of searching behind all the other curtains before approaching hers. We pulled them open and yelled, "Gotcha!" and we all collapsed in laughter. Granny was always surprised by how clever we were. What a sweet, lovely woman.

My mother was the disciplinarian in the family, and the one who helped us with our homework and taught us right from wrong. My father was more easy-going. He had a mischievous sense of humor and loved practical jokes. I once saw him horrify his guests at an elegant party by leading them in a conga line that wove out of the house and over the lawn and wound its way directly into the swimming pool.

My mother also had a sense of humor, but it was expressed in a more quiet, gentle way. She was the backbone of the family and the one who made sure there were few separations between us by taking us all along on my father's business trips. On those rare occasions when we could not accompany them, I sprayed my pillow with her perfume so I would dream of her all night long.

Detroit was a place of rules and regulations, but things were different when summer rolled around. My father's family was from Michigan, but the McDonnells, my mother's family, were New Yorkers. Mother was raised in New York City and her summers were spent in a pair of rambling stone houses in Southampton known as the McDonnell-Murray Compound. It was called a compound because there were so many relatives who lived there. My grandparents (McDonnell) and their fourteen children, plus my grandmother's sister (Murray) and *her* fourteen children all spent their summers there.

Every June my family left Detroit on a train called The Wolverine. It left at night and headed for New York City, and I can still remember my excitement when I lifted the blinds the following morning to peep out the tiny window in the sleeping compartment and catch my first glimpse of the Hudson River at Hastings-on-Hudson. The train headed south from there and an hour or so later we pulled into Grand Central Station.

There was no Long Island Expressway back then so we drove to Southampton for three hours along the Southern State Highway. Most of the land was owned by potato farmers and the highway was bordered by field upon field of potato plants, sparse at first, then more and more abundant until the air was filled with the smell of potato plants—not a lovely aroma, I assure you—but if I smelled it today, I would be instantly transported back to Southampton in the early 1950s.

There was a building shaped like a huge white duck with a yellow beak. It was on a duck farm where they sold eggs, and for us—even more than the potato plants—this marked the border of our summer home. That's when we would get *really* excited.

Southampton was like Mayberry back then, small town America. It was never called "The Hamptons" as it is now. The RKO movie theater, now a cineplex, had an old marquee surrounded by yellow lights. Jobs Lane was lined with small shops, for the most part all gone today.

So much has changed. The hedges are still there, tall and stately, lining the streets on both sides, and the beautiful lawns are as they were fifty years ago, but the potato fields are long gone, covered over with housing developments. Shep Millers, our family's clothing store, has become the Gap and Corwith Drug Store with the soda fountain where we met our friends for hot fudge sundaes is now a Rite-Aid.

My family did not live at the McDonnell-Murray Compound but in a house nearby on the dunes. It was so close to the water you could hear the waves at all times and feel the ocean spray when you sat on the porch. This was lovely in nice weather but made for some frightening moments when a storm came. There were many times when my mother came into our room to wake us and gather us all for a full-scale evacuation. I remember looking out of the window while my mother was calling, and seeing the waves thundering right up to the house.

But apart from the storms, summer in Southampton made for an idyllic childhood.

For me it was freedom. I was finally free of the rules and restrictions of the convent and my life in Detroit. It was a safe place, surrounded by friends and family, and our days were filled with activity.

In the mornings, we rode our bikes to the beach club to swim or take swimming lessons. The beach club was a rustic building, Spanish in design, with a red-tiled roof, an open cafeteria and closed dining room, and a large swimming pool. From there, it was off to the Meadow Club for tennis lessons or to play other sports. The Meadow Club hasn't changed at all over the years. It is a huge long wooden white house with a wonderful old porch that faces about twenty grass tennis courts. These grass courts make it a favorite of many famous tennis players, and there was always a pro-tournament around Labor Day. That is how I remember the end of summer. It was always the same....sitting on the old porch sipping lemonade and watching the tennis matches.

I thought Southampton would always remain central to my life. I would get married and have children. I would have a life exactly like my parents, and Southampton would always be the special place it had been for me in childhood.

A beachfront house came up for sale the year I was pregnant with Alessandro. It was an old white clapboard house overlooking the dunes and very close to the ocean.

Alessandro was born in November and we moved in the following summer. The name of the road was Fairlea and the house we called *Firenze*—Italian for "Florence." That house was and is everything to Alessandro. It embodies his childhood in the same way our old house by the sea embodied mine. It was the place he left every morning, riding his bike to the same beach club for the same swimming lessons, and the place he came back to for lunch and dinner and where he and his friends spent the evening hours playing hide-and-seek and capture the flag, the same games I played when I was a child.

Everything was fine and as it should be, and then it was Allegra's turn to take part in the Southampton rituals.

Many people who do not have disabled children are not often inclined to think about them very deeply. I suppose that is understandable. After all, before I had a child with a disability, I had sympathy and compassion but I do not remember dwelling on the subject too long. The people of Southampton were no different.

We had all grown up together, got married, had children, saw each other every Friday and Saturday night; and it was these people's children who were the friends of Alessandro and should have been Allegra's friends.

For a while they were.

There were those first four years when nothing appeared to me to be out of the ordinary. The summer before I found out about her disability, I was told she couldn't keep up in the gymnastics class, that she couldn't do a headstand or follow instructions. But that was fine: she was only four and a half, and if she went left instead of right, it was cute and funny, the way she always was. She took swimming lessons and did just fine. People brought their children over to play and she was invited to other houses in return.

By the following summer, I had gone through the Christmas pageant, the nightmare diagnosis by the renowned psychologist, and the entire grueling ordeal of discovering her disability and trying to find a way to handle it. I now knew she would be attending Gateway instead of a school on a par with the one her brother attended or where her contemporaries would be going. And now, when the Southampton gymnastics coach called two weeks into class, it had a whole new meaning for me. As soon as I heard his voice I knew what the call was about.

"She tries very hard, *but...*"

The level of gymnastics in the class was not difficult. There were no balance beams or parallel bars. It was mostly running and tumbling, and I knew she could do those things with a little help on my part.

"Come on, sweetheart, into the backyard," I said to her. "I want to play with you."

"What are we going to play, Mommy?"

"I know you like gymnastics, Allegra. And all the other little girls, you like them, too, don't you?"

"Oh, yes. It's fun playing with them."

"When the coach tells you to run, can you do it?"

She assured me that she could and she ran across the yard. "Okay, Allegra," I called. "Now run back to me!"

She did, running and laughing, and making me laugh as I watched the irrepressible joy on her face. She could run, she could do somersaults, she could do it all, and she did it with exuberance and abandon. So why couldn't she follow the coach's instructions?

"Come after me, Mommy!" she called, and I couldn't help myself. I chased her across the yard, and she screamed with laughter when I caught her. We both fell down and lay on our backs on the grass and watched the clouds. "Remember when you were in school, Allegra? And the teacher asked you to listen when she was reading a story?"

"Yes, Mommy."

"Well, this is the same, sweetheart. When the coach asks you to run or do somersaults, you need to listen to what he says. You need to look at your friends and see what they are doing. Can you do that?"

"Yes, I can do it."

I knew she could. I thought back to the previous winter in Sun Valley and remembered how well she did in her first skiing lessons. If she could do that, then surely she could manage simple gymnastics. The reason why Allegra excelled in one activity only to be confounded by another was a mystery to me, and one that would only deepen as the years went by. Children with learning disabilities often excel in artistic activities or a particular sport—especially a noncompetitive sport. I did not know this at the time, but I must have sensed Allegra's potential because I was already searching for the key that would bring her a sense of accomplishment. In the coming months and years we would try dance class, piano lessons, and tennis lessons, and each time a couple of weeks would pass before I received the phone call from the instructor, telling me that Allegra was popular and trying hard, *but....*

She could not keep up. She could not remember the simple steps. She would not pay attention. How many times did I hear that? How many phone calls from teachers, instructors, and coaches over the years? Yet there were always small grace notes in Allegra's life. Three or four attempts at sports or artistic activities would come and go without success, only to be followed by something where she could keep up with the others in her age group and sometimes surpass them. Skiing was one of those things. It may be that the gliding motion of skiing was something she could control more readily than the running and hand-eye coordination required for a sport like tennis. I've never been able to pinpoint with any certainty which activity Allegra would excel at and which would completely elude her.

I called the gymnastics coach back. "Please give her another chance," I said. "I've been working with her in the backyard, and she does everything I ask with no trouble. I *know* she can do this."

He agreed and Allegra continued with gymnastics lessons. A week went by. No call. A good sign. And then, in the second week, the coach called. "I don't know what's wrong," he said. "She's listening to me, but she doesn't seem to understand my instructions."

"Are you asking her to move right or left?" I asked. "Because she doesn't know right or left yet."

"No, I'm not. I'm asking her to run or to do a somersault, but she doesn't seem to understand."

"Please give her a little more time," I said. "All her friends are in your class. I don't want her to be singled out. I'll work with her some more at home. I know she can do it."

Once again, he agreed to let her stay on.

I spent as much time as possible in the backyard, running with her and tumbling, trying to make it all as much fun as possible. She had a little bit of difficulty at times, but nothing too extreme. When I said, "Run, Allegra!" she ran. When I said, "Let's do a somersault," she followed my moves as best she could.

As the days passed that summer, I began to notice that something else had happened. It was subtle and I might not have noticed at all it if it hadn't been for the difficulties of the previous spring.

Allegra and I were together in the backyard, running and tumbling and laughing, but we were also alone.

There were no friends there with her.

Children had stopped coming over.

Allegra was no longer invited to play at other people's houses.

It wasn't that the others did not like her, but they seemed to sense that something was different about her. It was one thing for Allegra to run across the yard from one side to the other—that was straight-forward. But children make up their own games and Allegra could not follow their made-up rules and directions, no matter how simple they were. She made up her own rules.

Near the end of summer there is an awards ceremony at the beach club, with a gymnastics exhibition and swimming races. By then I was well aware of Allegra's difficulties with gymnastics, but it never occurred to me to keep her out of the competition. I ran with her, I tumbled with her, I knew she could manage it all, yet when the games started, I could see—everyone could see—that there was sim-ply no way Allegra could keep up with the other children.

It was the Christmas pageant all over again, but in some ways it was worse. I sat with the other parents, all my friends, all the people I knew. There we were, sitting on bleachers surrounding an arena with a large blue mat in the center. The mothers were dressed identically, thin, tan, all with long blond hair, watching their perfect children perform perfectly—many with cameras to record the moment for posterity. With every activity my child was exposed as not being as "perfect" as children are supposed to be in Southampton. And there I was, hiding under a big floppy hat, wanting to melt away.

The gymnastics coach and swimming coach had spoken to me of her difficulties. They said she had trouble following instructions. But neither one had told me she couldn't do the activities at all! In fairness to them, I doubt I would have believed them even if they had told me. After all, I was the one who pushed and cajoled and persuaded them to give her another chance. "I *know* she can do it," I said, but did I believe she could do it? I don't know. All I know is that I *wanted* to believe it.

We were part of a community, we partook of every aspect of the community, and every single one of Allegra's contemporaries was involved in gymnastics. I couldn't keep her out. I didn't think it was fair to her. I didn't want her to be singled out. How wrong I was! I was told over and over that she was having difficulties, so why on earth did I send her out there, even if there was only a slight possibility she would be laughed at? I wanted her to fit in. And I wanted to fit in as well.

There were two teams. All they were expected to do was get down on all fours and crawl down the length of the blue mat as fast as they could. Allegra couldn't do it. Instead, she ran down the length of the mat as though someone had said, "Okay, everyone, down on all fours. Except you, Allegra. You do whatever you want."

The swimming races were next.

The children lined up on one side of the huge swimming pool. The coach fired a starter pistol—it scared the living daylights out of *me*, but for Allegra it was far worse. Everyone leaped into the pool and she was left behind, startled by the gun, standing there all alone, with all eyes upon her…and then she jumped in and went in one direction while everyone was coming back in the other.

I was embarrassed, for her and for myself. The same group moved on to all the other sports that day and I went along with them, dying inside for Allegra even though she appeared to be perfectly happy. She did not seem to understand that she was going in the wrong direction and not following instructions. When the competitions were over, she changed into a dry suit, went down to play on the beach, and acted as if nothing had happened. When it was time to go home, she was the same happy child she was when we arrived that morning.

The irony is that Allegra turned out to be a terrific swimmer. She didn't learn through formal swimming lessons, but by watching her brother and his friends jump in and out of the pool and following along behind them. She was very good at joining in and copying what her brother did.

I always included Allegra in every family and social situation, and I believe it was the right thing to do. However, I do not believe I used my best judgment when it came to including her (forcing her, actually) to engage in team sports or activities when it was abundantly clear she would fail. A little failure is a good thing. Total, continual failure is long lasting. I should have pulled her out after the first activity, but I didn't—again, it was a valiant, horribly difficult attempt to prevent her from being singled out as different, as though allowing her to stand in isolated confusion in front of all those spectators didn't single her out!

Once again, the saving grace was that Allegra never realized she was doing anything different. She didn't mind running down the mat or swimming the wrong way. She had a wonderful time with it all, but for me, the future was hung out to see, clearly and starkly. There would be no more competitive sports. I knew she could not do them, and I vowed I would never put her in that situation again.

All of these difficulties and realizations were compounded by questions about school. This was the end of the summer, and everyone's first question was: "Where did your child get in?" meaning "Which school did she get into?" I thought back to the summer when Alessandro was starting first grade and how proud I was to say he was going to St. Bernard's School. Now, with Allegra, I said, "Gateway," and received a blank stare in return. No one had ever heard of Gateway. I didn't say it was a special school. I just said Gateway. Again, blank stares, vacant smiles....

I wish I had known that the very best way to handle this was to come right out and say, "She has a learning disability." The term was not in use then, but I wish I had been able to come up with something!

Allegra also put me on the spot. She heard other girls mention their schools, or overheard the mothers talking, and asked me, "Am I going to Jennifer's school?"

"Not this year, Allegra."

"Why not? Jennifer and Angela said they're going to the same school. Why can't I go with them?"

"Because your new school is going to be much better for you than theirs," I said. "And I'm anxious for you to have new friends."

"But why, Mommy? I like my friends."

"I know, sweetheart. But this is a better school for you."

"But why…?"

I had no answer.

Many of the friends she liked so much stopped playing with her that summer. I asked them to come over. They declined my invitations. These were the sons and daughters of my own friends so it was difficult for me to understand when they began to drift away one by one. Allegra was never unfriendly or rude, she never pulled their hair or had a tantrum. As in nursery school, she simply could not relate to them on a social level. They could not relate to her. There were too many barriers.

No one ever said anything to me directly. I tried to make the play times at my house more fun than anywhere else, but nothing worked. Once in a while a little girl accepted an invitation to a cookout or party, but inevitably it was the last time she played with Allegra or extended an invitation in return. The parents never stepped forward and insisted that their child play with her.

Not long ago, I asked one of my friends if there had ever been a family discussion about why her daughter didn't want to play with Allegra. I asked if the reason was because Allegra couldn't keep up or wasn't the same as the others, and if so, was that a good enough reason for my friend not to say, "Look, you've got to try, once in a while you've got to include her?"

It was more than twenty years before I dared bring up the subject, but my friend was honest with me. She told me they did discuss it as a family and decided to leave the decision of whether or not to play with Allegra up to their child.

The child chose not to.

I realize that it was not easy for them. Children sometimes have a difficult time overlooking what they perceive as defects, yet if they are not taught compassion and some understanding of other people's differences, how can they grow up to be adults who truly know how to treat others with dignity and respect?

My frustration and sense of hurt was in danger of overflowing—once again, I didn't know who to talk to or how to express these feelings. I couldn't stand in the backyard and yell to the skies, hoping that somehow the message would get through to all the parents in the neighborhood. One day Melinda came over and we decided to go for a walk on the beach. She already knew about Allegra's difficulties and about Gateway School, and had always been compassionate and supportive. Still, there were things that even Melinda and Charlotte didn't know. On this day on the beach, I finally unburdened my feelings about Allegra's isolation and abandonment.

"What is wrong with these people?" I asked her. "Are they all so perfect that they can't accept or deal with any imperfection? Wouldn't you think they would look at our situation and explain it to their child? Or even insist that their child comes over, even for a short play-date? Allegra needs a friend right now, but the play-dates never come."

Melinda brought up several names of children Allegra's age, but all of them had already fallen away. "But why?" Melinda asked, obviously as perplexed as I was. Her own daughter Ashley was Alessandro's age, and for once, I wished she were a little younger. I knew Melinda would have made sure Ashley would not abandon Allegra.

"I don't know what to do," I said. "I just don't know what to do."

Melinda had no answer. We walked along the beach, listening to the waves, each wondering how friends and neighbors can so easily give up on a five-year-old child.

The next day the doorbell rang. I opened the door, and it was Ashley. I assumed she had come over to see if Alessandro was there, but she said, "Not today. I've come over to play with Allegra."

That was the first of many times she did her best to make my daughter happy. There was never a word of complaint, never a hint that her kindness was a burden. She and her mother were proof that compassion could still be found—not in Southampton perhaps, but in the hearts of a few good people.

We returned to the city in early September, and for the first time in my life I was not saddened by the end of summer. I had also given up on the idea of Allegra making friends outside of school, and I prayed that Gateway would be a place where she might develop lasting friendships. It may be that I had given up too early on the outside world because soon after we returned to New York City, someone wonderful stepped into our lives. Her name was Ali Halpern.

Like Ashley, she was six years older than Allegra. She lived on our block. I didn't know her or her family, and didn't remember seeing her before. Allegra didn't know her either. But one day they met.

This is how Ali tells the story:

"I saw this cute little girl with curly red hair playing on the sidewalk. She saw me sitting out in front of my building and came right up to me, and right out of the blue she asked: 'Do you have a cat?' I said that I did and asked if she wanted to come in and see her. Back then it was more normal, asking a stranger into your house. It wouldn't happen now. But I was eleven and she was five, and we didn't think anything was wrong at all. She came up and met my cat Kelly, and then she asked if I had a present for her. I gave her an old Holly Hobby nightgown and we've been friends ever since."

When Ali tells this story, nearly twenty-five years later, her face still lights up. I asked if she knew there was something "different" about Allegra and she said that she did. "Sometimes she had trouble with numbers or with rhyming, and some things just didn't make sense to her. But I didn't care. All I knew was that she was my friend. We used to hang out at her place or mine. I wasn't the kind of kid who was into games or instructions, so we never had any problem with that. We did things our way, like recording ourselves singing songs we made up."

I remember those days, listening to the two girls in Allegra's room singing their hearts out and laughing hysterically. What a relief it was to hear the sound of laughter echoing down the hall. It made me love Ali as if she was my own daughter. Looking at her today, as an adult, I feel the same way. "So it was a normal friendship?" I asked.

"Oh sure," she said, a little surprised by my question. "She was a happy person and she made me happy. She still does."

Chapter 6
First Day of School

So finally we went go look at some schools that some sourt of progam with specail needs.

And we came cross one last school that did take me it was called gateway school. And it was in new york city.

I meet some very specail staff and there name Ginny and some otheres too. I went there for 3 years.

—E-mail from Allegra Ford

Every mother remembers her emotions on her child's first day at school, the blend of nervousness, excitement, a touch of sadness, and a lot of optimism. We began Allegra's first day at Gateway by doing something I had never done before—packing a lunch. Alessandro always had lunch at school, and I had never packed lunch for anyone prior to Allegra. The children were running around the apartment, getting ready for school, both hollering at the top of their lungs, arguing and horsing around, and there I was, brown-bagging a peanut butter and jelly sandwich for the first time in my life. I got the hang of it pretty quickly and hoped to go on to further challenges like tuna fish or egg salad, but Allegra would eat nothing but peanut butter and jelly—day in and day out, year after year, hundreds and hundreds of peanut butter and jelly sandwiches. I'm an expert now.

Alessandro went off to school and Allegra and I walked the three blocks to the Gateway School and her new life. She wore a short royal blue skirt and white T-shirt, with a new book bag slung over her shoulder. She held my hand as we approached the buses lined up outside the building. They were small yellow buses. I'm sure I had seen them often during the two years Allegra was in nursery school, but I had never really looked at them, never noticed that they were equipped to accommodate children with physical disabilities. Now I saw them in every detail, the lifts to help with wheelchairs, the straps on the seats.

We rode up to the fifth floor in the clanking elevator and Mrs. Freidus was once again standing there to welcome us. She was such a comforting presence, especially for me. I was still reeling from the events of the previous spring and summer, still unable to fully accept that Allegra would be going to a school like this, and it took someone of Mrs. Freidus' warmth and understanding to help ease me into the situation.

Parents were allowed to stay at Gateway the entire first week. It was a way for us to help the children adapt to their new life in school. Mrs. Freidus had the children sit in a semicircle on the floor, with the parents in chairs behind them, and she talked about what school would be like for the children and how happy she was to have them there.

Above the large primary room was a wide balcony accessible by a staircase. A series of small rooms ran along the length of the balcony. These were the classrooms, each one large enough for about six students and a homeroom teacher. Allegra was assigned to Mary Zielenbach's room.

I cannot look back on my own school years and think of one teacher I can single out as "my favorite." I had none. Allegra finds this idea difficult because she has had so many favorites. I have never known anyone as loyal to former teachers as Allegra. This is doubly remarkable for a child whose educational years were not at all easy. Even today she often meets her former teachers for lunch—and I'm talking about *nursery school teachers*! How many thirty-year-old adults still meet with their nursery school teachers? Or someone like Miss Buckley, one of Allegra's tutors when she was eleven years old? She is in contact with teachers from every school she attended and she would find the idea of singling one out as a favorite to be an impossible task.

They all are favorites, and in that first year Miss Zielenbach became Allegra's very best friend in the whole world. She came to our house for dinner. Allegra called her in the evening long after school had let out. Like every single one of the teachers Allegra latched onto, Mary had an endless supply of patience. It could not have been easy but I never heard a single word of complaint from any of them.

The morning passed quickly and soon it was time for lunch. The children sat at four long tables with a teacher at each table. The lunch began with one child telling a story, usually about something that had occurred during the morning classes.

After lunch was a rest time. The shades were drawn, blue mats were unfolded and spread over the floor and the children were encouraged to lie down for a nap during this quiet time.

Well…!

There was no way Allegra was going to lie down for five minutes.

She would have loved to run around the school, talking to Mary Zielenbach and singing songs, but I did not want her to be singled out again. She sat on my lap the entire time, whispering loudly while the other children rested. "Mom, can I go talk to Miss Zielenbach?"

"Shhh, Allegra. It's time for everybody to rest."

"I don't want to rest. Why are we resting?"

"Because it's rest time."

"Why is it rest time? How come her name is Miss Zielenbach?"

I'm sure there were other children who had trouble sitting still. This was, after all, a school for children with problems similar to Allegra's. But I have no memory of them. It is only Allegra I remember, and how hopeful I was, how determined that here in this special school, she would finally fit in.

The day ended at 2:30. All the children were lined up and were taken home by their mothers or guardians. As I walked home with Allegra I could see that she had finally found a place where she felt at ease. She loved the teachers, and it didn't really matter if she acted out because the other children acted the same. The teachers understood and expected it.

You would think I would have welcomed the opportunity to share my situation with the other parents who were there that day and who were going through the same thing I was. But I didn't. I was polite, and we spoke, but it was all small talk. I did not reach out as I should have. To find another who knows *exactly* what you're going through is like finding a gold mine, but I couldn't see the opportunity for what it was. I was too busy trying to see Allegra as being "not as bad" as the other children.

Some of the feelings I had at that time were beyond my ability to mention. I couldn't acknowledge their existence to myself, much less to others. To this day, some of what I went through makes me cringe with shame, but it is very important for other parents to understand that it is common to experience a wide range of emotions (some of them rather unpleasant) when trying to deal with a child with a learning disability. For someone who has not gone through it, it is difficult to realize how deeply the tentacles of a disability can spread throughout a family. It can affect your relationships with your other children and your friends, and it can even affect a marriage.

Many feelings can lead to an enormous amount of guilt. "How can I be feeling this about my child?" we ask, but the feelings are there, and they are perfectly normal. If I had known I was not alone in this, I would have been spared a tremendous amount of pain.

I thought I was the only one who felt this way.

First there is the pain of watching your child struggle in school and in life. This is perhaps the worst of it—watching the child try and try and fail every time. It often leads to frustration for the parent as well as the child. "*Why* can't you do it?!" runs through your mind when they fail to understand what seems to be the simplest concept, as when Allegra was unable to comprehend, no matter how many times I told her, that a friend of mine named Mrs. Brady was not the mother on the television show *The Brady Bunch*. Everything you try comes to the same sense of frustrating failure. "For heaven's sake, Allegra!" I might say, "Why can't you understand this?"

Maybe you have a sense of incompetence, that you are not equipped to handle this confusing and frightening situation or that your parenting skills are not strong enough. I was twenty-nine years old and already had a child, yet I was completely at a loss. I have since come to understand it would be possible to have ten children and *still* not be prepared to deal with the eleventh child having a learning disability.

There is also the heartache of watching a lonely child. I think of the hours Allegra spent in our kitchen in Southampton, talking to our elderly housekeeper while all the other girls her age were playing on the beach. Or the mother who told Richard Lavoie, headmaster of a school for the learning disabled in Massachusetts, that she knew she had to remove her son from public school when his classmates "threw him away"—they literally picked him up and deposited him in a garbage can, telling him that was where he belonged because he was so stupid. That is the sort of thing that tears at any parent's heart.

Larger, deeper feelings often come into play. There is sadness and a sense that somehow you have been cheated. This child whom you love was supposed to be "normal," was supposed to live the life you expected him or her to lead. You want your child to be the same as your friends' children. You want them all to go to the same school, the same church groups, to play the same sports and join the same clubs. There may even be a mourning period for the loss of that "perfect" child you thought you had.

Anger. Can't forget that one. There is often no one to be angry at—God, the universe, fate—so you take it out on pediatricians, teachers, the other parent, siblings, neighbors, friends, even the child herself. Often you take it out on yourself (which sometimes comes back as placing blame—you may believe the child's disability reflects poorly on you, that somehow it is your fault: "It must have been caused by something I did wrong.").

Often fear is part of the mix. You wonder how to help your child, or if she will be accepted. You wonder if the problems will ever go away and if she'll be all right someday.

Finally, there is shame. This is a very difficult one because it often leads to a tremendous sense of guilt, but it is common and even understandable. The truth is that there are times when you are ashamed and embarrassed when your child behaves inappropriately or can't follow the rules or doesn't fit in.

All these feelings and emotions are unpleasant realities. If parents feel any of them about their own child, *they are not alone!*

My own sense of isolation was extreme. And it didn't matter how many parents I met who also had children with learning disabilities—I still found it possible to deny the obvious. "Allegra's not as bad as the others," I thought, or, "She'll outgrow this, I know she will." Because I had trouble admitting to myself that there was anything wrong with my child, I could not share my feelings or talk about the problem to others.

The road from denial to acceptance is a long and painful one, especially when you think you are the only one traveling it. But acceptance does have a way of winning out in the end. For me, there was no other alternative. Acceptance *had* to win. Denial, comforting though it was, was slowly and painfully overwhelmed by reality.

It's a little like the classic set of feelings a terminally ill patient goes through: denial, anger, fear, and finally, acceptance. Once you get over some of the darker emotions you come to realize one never-changing fact: you love your child with her disability as much as you would if she did not have a disability at all. You do not love her more or less than your other children—you love them all, equally and deeply, and you always will.

I felt every single one of these emotions at one time or another and in various combinations. Fear was the most constant one. Even on Allegra's first day at school, I knew I was in for a long period of uncertainty. She was accepted at Gateway, but only conditionally. She would go there year to year, sometimes semester to semester, and each time it was the same—uncertain, unsettled, with a cloud of fear hovering over everything. What will happen if she doesn't make it? What will happen if they don't take her back? Where will I go? What will I do?

I have tried at various times over the years to put myself in my daughter's mind, to see the world as she sees it and experience the life of a person with learning disabilities. It is not an easy prospect. No two cases of LD are alike. No textbook definitions can ever tell us *exactly* what a child is experiencing. It wasn't until I observed Allegra in school and, more importantly, heard her teachers describe what she was going through that I began to understand how difficult it must have been for her.

For most of us, information is processed in an orderly manner. We all have moments of confusion, of course, but for the most part, our brains instantly and correctly process words, sounds, and sights. Our brains guide us through the world around us and make it comprehensible. With a learning disability, information comes in a confusing and distorted manner. A simple word can be baffling. A simple concept such as *up* versus *down* or *large* versus *small* can be incomprehensible. Allegra had no concept of "next week" for instance. She lived entirely in the present. She could not understand numerical values, such as ten is greater than five.

Allegra's disabilities are more severe than most but she was lucky in one regard. She was identified and diagnosed *early*. She was five when her learning disabilities were discovered. For many children, a diagnosis comes much later. Sometimes it doesn't come at all.

I cannot stress enough the importance of early identification. It is the key to unlocking the child's potential. Without it, year after year goes by, each filled with unnecessary frustration and suffering until the defeated child becomes the defeated teen who then becomes the defeated adult. Screening tools, such as the "Get Ready to Read" Program sponsored by The National Center for Learning Disabilities, help identify children as young as four who may be at risk for reading difficulties. These tools do not offer a definitive diagnosis of a learning disability, but they do serve as a way to warn parents of possible trouble up ahead.

This is what it is like for a child who is not diagnosed and who falls through the cracks: he looks like everyone else in his class, but for some reason he has difficulty doing certain things that others do with ease. He tries and grits his teeth in frustration and anger when his teacher or parent says, "You're lazy. I know you could do it if you tried harder." Maybe he excels in certain subjects like reading but is surprisingly confused by mathematics. He can't remember information or concepts that appear to come naturally to his classmates. Once again the teacher or parent passes judgment: "I don't believe you want to learn. You're not motivated, you simply don't care."

The statement is a self-fulfilling prophecy. Faced with failure in spite of doing everything he can to succeed, the child drops out— first in his attitude toward learning and eventually by leaving school as soon as he is of legal age. And why wouldn't he? Who among us is capable of withstanding years of defeat, all the while being told that it is our own fault? School failure can lead to juvenile delinquency and substance abuse, often as an attempt to escape the crushing burdens of a life without expectations or self-esteem.

The number of adults who start out this way is staggering. LD has only been identified as a disability in the last twenty-five years. Think of the hundreds of thousands of parents and grandparents whose school days are remembered only as a long, painful, humiliating ordeal. How many secretly believe they are stupid because that was what was drilled into them day after day when they were young? How many never realize that they are not stupid at all, but have a disability that could have been alleviated had it been understood in time?

When Allegra started school that September in 1977, the term "learning disabilities" was not in general use. Most pediatricians and teachers had never heard of it. If they had, many didn't believe there really was such a thing. One of my great frustrations continued to be the lack of a firm diagnosis. Allegra's problems fell squarely into a category that could be called "unique." The combination and severity were such that no one could accurately pinpoint what was wrong. I shudder to think what might have happened had she not been diagnosed early and put into a special school. What permanent scars would remain in my daughter's life if she had been forced to compete with children in a mainstream classroom?

If patience is a virtue, then the teachers at the Gateway School are among the most virtuous people I have ever known. They sit for hours, days, sometime years, working with a child until they get it right. Sometimes they use repetition and go over the same thing again and again. Sometimes they try new things. They use their instincts to guide them in their efforts to teach. Virginia "Ginny" Nudell, for example, spent nearly five years trying to teach Allegra the concept of abstract numbers. Often she resorted to ingenious solutions such as having Allegra count the steps leading from the main classroom up to the second level. Day after day they would go up the steps—one, two, three—and down again—one, two, three—over and over again until the numbers became clear in her mind. From there, she went to counting blocks, and on and on, experimenting and working with her until Allegra acquired a foundation of understanding that she never could have gained in any mainstream school.

Allegra did not really know her own body. She had no real sense of where her body was within space—I don't mean only her place in a room or with another person, but her *own self*. Had she been aware of the problem, she could easily have asked herself, "Where is my body? Where does my body begin and end? How do I put one foot down and then put the second foot down in front of it?"

At Gateway, they have the children navigate an obstacle course made up of boxes of varying heights. They step in the boxes, one after another. You can see the difficulties some have coordinating their footsteps to match the height of the box.

The best way to understand this seeming lack of coordination is through the example of running. In Southampton, in the backyard, I saw that Allegra could run with no difficulties at all. I called to her and said, "Run, Allegra!" and I watched her, laughing as she raced across the grass into my arms. But she had trouble when she was asked to run in a regimented environment like gymnastics class. I told the teachers at Gateway that I couldn't understand how she could be such a good runner at home and not in a class. "There is a difference," Tobi explained. "It's true that Allegra can run like the wind. But if she is asked to run in slow motion, if she has to slow down and actually *think* about running instead of running naturally, she runs into difficulties. Thinking about even the simplest physical act requires a lot of mental organization and coordination. For Allegra to stop and think about where she is and what she is doing means she also has to think: 'Where am I in this space?' and that is often something she cannot easily do."

It was the same with speech. Allegra could talk at length, laughing and rambling on about subject after subject. But if she had to slow down and think about what she was saying, or what the proper response might be, or what an appropriate question might be, she often ran into trouble. Alessandro refers to it as the "loose cannon." We often didn't (and still don't!) know what she might say in a given situation or how long she would dwell on any given subject.

Allegra ran on autopilot. She had difficulty with the manual controls, but that did not stop her from trying. Like so many other children with learning disabilities, she is a determined learner. She wants to learn. The only place that determination was allowed to flourish was in a special school. If nothing else (and never underestimate the importance of this in a child's life), Gateway proved that she *could* learn. Yes, at her own pace, and yes, maybe not at the level of other children her age. But she was spared the humiliation and pain that would assuredly have come had she been forced to compete in a mainstream school setting. Gateway taught her awareness of herself, how to use her balance and control, and most important, how to use her own determination to her best advantage.

One thing I'll never know is if she was born with this determination or if she acquired it through life's experiences. I'm inclined to believe that she acquired it because she had to. Most children with learning disabilities are like that. The common thread of determination is woven into their lives.

Chapter 7
A Great Gentleman
Comes into Our Lives

i love hugh cary. because he is daddty warbucks and we going to brodway together.

—E-mail from Allegra Ford

All that terrible spring and summer of 1977 when Allegra's problems came to light, I was alone. Much of it was self-imposed isolation as I was also right in the middle of my own denial. I had been divorced for almost five years and there was no man in my life. I had no reason to expect one to be in my life. And then I received a phone call from a friend, asking me to her home for dinner.

I was seated next to Hugh Carey, then the governor of New York. He was a vibrant, larger than life man, full of laughter and good humor. He had recently instituted a financial plan that pulled New York City back from the edge of bankruptcy and was the hero of the hour.

That evening was the beginning of a long, wonderful friendship. Hugh's wife had passed away in 1974. They had thirteen children together. Hugh was elected to his first term as governor the year she died. I don't know how he managed, but if nothing else, Hugh Carey was resourceful and strong.

He came along at a vitally important time in my children's lives. Allegra was five and had just been diagnosed with LD. Alessandro was ten. Hugh would be part of our lives for the next four years, seeing Allegra through the early years of school and Alessandro through the passage from boyhood into adolescence.

He had so many children of his own yet he became a second father to mine. He often cooked for them, he helped them with their homework, and no matter how busy his schedule was, he always found the time to be there for them.

He was also directly responsible for two of the most important experiences in Allegra's life.

The first occurred when Hugh called one day and asked to speak to Allegra. "You want to come on a date with your mother and me?" he asked, and of course, she agreed. I took the phone. "What kind of date?" I asked, and he told me that he got tickets to a new Broadway musical. It was called *Annie*.

Hugh picked us up a little after 7:00, and we went to the theater. We found our seats and sat down, the house lights dimmed, the orchestra played the overture, and the curtain opened on what was to be one of the most profoundly influential moments in my daughter's life.

I can see her now, seated between Hugh and me in that darkened theater, her eyes sparkling as she sat transfixed by the story of the little orphan called Annie, who had hair as red and curly as her own. She didn't understand that the role was played by an actress. She thought the real Annie was onstage and that the struggles and triumphs of her life were unfolding before our very eyes. Daddy Warbucks, Miss Hannigan, the dog Sandy, and all the little girls in the orphanage were to become as real to her as any living person she knew. To this day she still considers it to be the most wonderful night of her life.

After the show we were invited to go backstage to meet the star, Andrea McArdle. Andrea was still in her costume and makeup, and from that moment on, Annie became Allegra's hero, the person she wanted to be. It was never Cinderella or Snow White. It was always Annie. (A few years later, Allegra saw *The Sound of Music* for the first time and added Maria von Trapp to her short list of heroes.)

Annie was perfect for Allegra. First of all, she looked exactly like her. She could have been the original model for the character. In those days, very few adults met Allegra for the first time without commenting on how much she looked like Annie, which thrilled her to no end!

Her personality also fit the role. Songs like "The Sun'll Come Out Tomorrow" spoke to her—not because she was a sad, lonely child, but because they fit perfectly with her naturally sunny outlook on life. Allegra has *always* been optimistic. If there is a dark side to anything, Allegra rarely sees it. She cries at times, but it's usually over someone else's distress. If I punished Alessandro, Allegra cried. (She's still like that—her friend Ali was laid off from a job a couple of years ago, but Ali didn't cry. Allegra did.)

Davida Sherwood, Mrs. Freidus' successor at Gateway, recently reminded me that whenever Allegra was involved in an altercation of any kind, she would always be the first to apologize, even when she was not at fault. She was an easy child to be around and so much fun. It was not unusual to find her in the living room, entertaining my friends with her rendition of "Tomorrow." In fact, it was far from unusual. You could almost plan on Allegra's performance being a part of any evening's entertainment. Dinner parties, family get-togethers, it didn't matter: "Tomorrow! Tomorrow, I love you, tomorrow...!"

I was never bothered by her enthusiasm for *Annie*. If anything, it made me laugh more than anyone else. But it drove Alessandro crazy.

Here we are at the dinner table—Allegra, Alessandro, and I. I have mentioned that when I was growing up, dinner was a very formal affair. I never put my children through a strict routine, but I hoped to create something approaching a civilized atmosphere at the dinner table. So here we are, at our civilized, casually formal table in the kitchen. With candles sometimes, and sometimes with the children in their pajamas. The conversation flows easily: "How was school today?" the sort of thing heard at every dinner table.

Suddenly, out of nowhere, the atmosphere of refinement is broken when Allegra stands for no apparent reason and sings at the top of her lungs, "The sun'll come out, tomorrow...!" Alessandro has had it. It has happened every night for the past two weeks and he can no longer bear it. He throws his napkin down and yells, "Will you shut up?"

I am shocked...well, no—it happens too frequently to come as a shock. Still, I am not happy. Alessandro's request does not quite rise to the level of conversation I'd hoped for, and so I scold him. "Don't tell her to shut up!" I say.

"I can't help it!" he cries. "She keeps singing that song! It's the same song every night!"

Allegra ignores him. Sunny optimism pours out of her, and she cannot be stopped. She will not be stopped. She sings out loud, with gusto, "When you're stuck with a day, that's gray, and lonely...!"

Alessandro, now desperate, makes a pronouncement: "Annie's dead!" he yells, which horrifies Allegra and stops her in her tracks.

"No, she's not!"

"Yes, she is! She's dead! She fell in the river and drowned!"

Now Allegra begins to cry. I yell at Alessandro, "Stop telling her that Annie is dead!" I threaten to send him to his room, which of course makes Allegra cry even harder. "She's not dead," I tell her, comfortingly. "She's alive. At the theater."

"No, she's not," Alessandro whispers. "Someone *ate* her!"

This time I do send him to his room.

So much for civilization.

Annie filled Allegra's imagination and gave her room to dream and explore. For children with learning disabilities, the power of imagination is a godsend. It brings them to a place where they are comfortable, where they know the rules and the only limits are those they set themselves. Annie, the little orphan girl, helped guide Allegra through childhood in a way that only a best friend can. Hugh Carey was the one who introduced her to Annie and the one who helped keep the imaginative fires burning at a crucial time in my daughter's life.

Charlotte, Edsel, and I threw a birthday party for my father when he turned sixty. It was a surprise party, and part of the surprise was to be a special performance by members of the family. Charlotte, Edsel's wife Cynthia, and I sang and danced (which may have been more of a nightmare than a surprise), but by far the most moving and astonishing portion of the evening's entertainment was a duet sung by Hugh and Allegra as Daddy Warbucks and Annie. He was a very busy man, yet he found the time to learn and rehearse the number, and more, to *teach* it to a child with a learning disability. The patience it took, the hours of rehearsal and the generosity of heart and spirit—to this day I still view it as one of the kindest things anyone has ever done for one of my children.

Hugh Carey was equally as important to Alessandro. They both called him "The Gov," a name he delighted in. Not long ago, I found a letter he wrote to Allegra one Valentine's Day on stationery from the governor's desk. It captures the tone of warmth, acceptance, and understanding he brought into my daughter's life:

> *Dear Allegra,*
>
> *They say there is no St. Valentine, but there has to be because we need a Special Spirit. He steals hearts when they're sad and sends them back glad. The Spirit does it with magic—like the laugh and smile, the curtsey and kiss of Allegra. That's why you are on my "Lovely List"—along with my daughters, Helen, Nancy, Marianne in Austria, etc., etc. My son Thomas has no valentine, but he smiles when I share mine with him. Speaking of sharing—give a "gooey" kiss to your sweet mummy. The way to her heart is through her tummy. Joy!*
>
> *The Gov*
>
> *P.S. Bite the bonbons—not your brother!*

There is no question that a learning disability can cause a great deal of heartache and can be a challenge within any family, yet it is equally true that it does not overshadow every single moment of a family's life. The pain was always counterbalanced with a healthy dose of laughter and downright foolishness, both of which I highly recommend. They do not make the problems go away, but they sure do help to put them in a positive, more realistic light.

Not long after Allegra's introduction to *Annie*, my father invited his three children, along with wives and husbands and children, to spend a summer vacation in Maine. I invited Hugh to come along. It was a long, lovely week in New England. Maybe it was too long, too tranquil. Whatever the reason, Hugh decided to take Alessandro and Allegra off on an adventure, just the three of them. I don't know where they went or what they saw. All I know is that they stopped at a roadside stand on the way home and bought some live lobsters.

But there was no talk of a lobster dinner when they returned. There was no mention of lobster at all. We had something else for dinner and sat up talking late as usual, then we all retired for the night.

Allegra liked to stay with me when we were away from home, but this night she decided against it. We were in my room when she asked, "Are you going to bed now, Mommy?" This was followed with a strange little giggle that was unusual even for my laughing Allegra.

"Yes," I said, a little perplexed. "You want me to read you a story?"

She glanced at the bed and shook her head. "No. I think I want to stay in Al's room tonight."

"You do?" I asked, a little surprised. "Are you sure?"

"Yes, Mommy, I'm sure."

"All right then," I said, and kissed her goodnight. After she left, I changed into my nightgown and spent a quiet moment alone looking out at the starry sky and the surf on the rocks below.

I turned off the light and climbed into bed, pulled the covers up close, and…something…wet, cold, a clammy something against my leg. I pulled back the covers at the exact same moment that Charlotte in a nearby room discovered her own personal bed-lobster. We both screamed at the top of our lungs and were quickly joined by the cries of Edsel's wife and my father's wife Kathy. Fords were screaming all through the house, throwing sheets and blankets into the air, and vowing to get whoever was responsible!

Allegra was in on the joke, of course. "So *that's* why she didn't want to sleep with me!" I realized. Hugh told me later that she had been quite conflicted: Allegra was terrified of lobsters but was so taken by the idea of the practical joke that she tried to overcome her fear. She kept Hugh in stitches as she alternated between fear and delight as they visited each bed to hide their ghastly surprise.

I said Hugh Carey influenced Allegra in two important ways. *Annie* was one but the second was even more long-lasting. Allegra's favorite book was a picture book called *A Very Young Skater*, by Jill Krementz. She was nearing six years old and couldn't read yet, but something about the little girl in the book, the ice skater Katherine Healy, appealed to my daughter. Maybe it was the costumes, maybe the petite body so like her own, or the hair with the hint of red in it. Something captured Allegra's imagination and she looked at the book whenever she had the chance.

Hugh noticed. One day he came to me and said, "Do you think Allegra would like to try ice-skating?"

I thought back to the previous summer's gymnastics and swimming races. I was still burning with the memory of her inability to keep up with the other children. "She can't do it," I said. That was my verdict. It was said without thinking, but also with certainty. I knew in my heart it would be another "She tries hard, *but…*."

I was gradually giving up on Allegra. I did not realize this, and would have been horrified at the thought. It was not a conscious process, but a slow erosion of my belief in her abilities. Now, instead of hoping against hope, I simply understood and even accepted in a deep way that she would not be able to do it, no matter what "it" was. My faith in Allegra was being tested, and I was failing the test.

Hugh must have sensed this. He also knew the importance of a parent's belief in her child, no matter what the circumstance. "You have to let her try, Anne."

"I don't want her to be singled out anymore," I said, giving him my number one reason. It was true. Experience had shown me that being singled out meant humiliation and defeat. Hugh tried to show me that it could also be viewed as taking one's own unique place in the world.

I didn't buy it. "We've tried it all," I said. "Tennis, gymnastics, she can't do it. She has no hand-eye coordination."

"I understand, but you can't give up like that. Maybe she can't do it, but there may be a chance that she can."

"I already know she won't be able to do it."

"No, you don't," he said firmly. "And if that's how you approach everything in her life, then your predictions will always be right. She will never be able to do anything if she isn't given a chance."

I was a little taken aback by his frankness, but I listened, and in my heart I hoped he was right. I agreed to let her try.

There was a tiny skating rink near our apartment called the Ice Studio. We did a little research and found out that Katherine Healy, the star of Jill Krementz's book, lived on Long Island. For Allegra's sixth birthday, Hugh invited Katherine herself to visit the Ice Studio to show Allegra the basics of skating. I was surprised by how thrilled she was. I knew she liked Katherine and the book, but it never occurred to me that she might want to skate herself. Again, I was so shell-shocked by the events of the previous year that I couldn't imagine there was anything Allegra would want to try.

I fully expected her to fall several times, to be unable to follow directions, to ask Katherine the same question over and over again.

It didn't happen.

In the musical *My Fair Lady*, Henry Higgins sits in a chair late at night with a compress on his forehead, convinced that Eliza Doolittle will never be able to properly say "the rain in Spain stays mainly in the plain." He tells her to try it again without much hope, but Eliza suddenly—unexpectedly—says it perfectly. I can still see Rex Harrison as he lowers his hands, staring in disbelief, his face hopeful but cautious as he says, slowly, "Again." She says it again, and their situation is transformed from one of frustration and futility into one of triumph.

How I wish I had a picture of Allegra's first step onto the ice.

It was immediately apparent that she had found her element. I stood at the side of the tiny rink, staring at her face, her joyful expression, her comfort and sense of place. Like Henry Higgins, I was afraid to believe it. I was cautious, fully prepared for disappointment, but still hopeful.

I looked at Hugh and he smiled at me: he knew at once that I finally understood what he had been trying to tell me. "Never give up on her," his smile said, "never give failure too much power, never doubt that your child will somehow find her way, in ways you never expect."

Katherine Healy was wonderful that day and the owners of the Ice Studio were gracious and charming, but it was the ice itself that gave that afternoon its almost mythical dimension in my mind. It was a pivotal moment in my daughter's life. I can see her now, like a young colt, unsteady on her legs, unsure of herself, holding onto the fence bordering the rink for support, her eyes sparkling with delight. "Look at me, Mommy," she called, "I'm like Katherine! I'm a skater!"

The Ice Studio became her second home, and the instructors and all the people who worked there became her extended family. It is impossible to think of Allegra as a teenager or an adult without envisioning her first in skates and a skater's costume. When I had a special birthday cake designed for her, there was no alternative to making it in the shape of a figure skate. Even her e-mail address contains the abbreviated word "sk8."

Ice became the center of her world and her life.

Thanks to Hugh, Allegra found an activity that gave her the sense of self-worth and self-esteem so lacking in all other areas of her life. I leaped upon the idea and encouraged her in every way I knew how (though she didn't need much encouragement at all!). When other children were off playing together after school, Allegra would be on her way to the studio, her skates slung over her shoulder. For hours she skated on that rink, improving in incremental ways as the years passed. She made friends there, too. One friendship with a girl named Hilary Braverman would turn out to be as long-lasting as her friendship with Ali Halpern. Hilary and her mother Judy bonded with Allegra and also with me. These relationships were invaluable. For Allegra, it allowed her to experience a friendship based in shared interests. For me, it resulted in my first opportunity to truly open up to someone who understood.

Soon after meeting Judy, she told me that Hilary was diagnosed with a learning disability. This was a new experience for me! Here was another mother like me, but unlike others I had met, she was not telling me about her daughter while we were sitting in a doctor's waiting room or in a school setting. Judy and I did not start our relationship off focused solely on the shared pain of having a child with LD. We had been brought together through our daughters' love of skating. Their learning disabilities were secondary, and for me this came as a relief. I felt I could open up to Judy in ways I hadn't with any other. As time went on, Allegra and Hilary spent more time skating together, and Judy and I spent more time talking about them, their struggles, and more importantly, their hopes and aspirations and small triumphs on the ice. We could dream again. We could talk of their future in ways that were optimistic and hopeful. We could see them living happy, fulfilling lives.

Judy passed away not too long ago, and there isn't a day that goes by when I don't think of her and miss her and thank God for allowing me to experience her wisdom and understanding.

Everyone at the Ice Studio encouraged Allegra. They all knew about her disability, but it never became an issue. No one cared about a learning disability on the ice. No one cared what school she attended or if she could understand math. No one cared that she couldn't tell her left from her right. All that mattered was music and color and the joy and freedom of the ice.

By the end of that first year at Gateway, we seemed to have settled into a routine. She passed her "conditional" status that first year and was accepted for a second. She was making some progress, though there was still a great deal of work to do. She had found something new in her life that gave her a previously unknown sense of accomplishment. She had two new friends, Hilary and Ali, who truly loved to spend time with her. And there was Hugh, a great gentleman in her life who cared about her and believed in her.

Everything appeared to be going smoothly, and I felt it was time to face my fears by telling the rest of my family and friends what we had been through.

I began with my father.

Chapter 8
Sprinkle a Little Pixie Dust

grandady gave me a aligator that we swam together with
and we have so much fun. i miss him a lot.
                                    —E-mail from Allegra Ford

My father was a prominent American businessman, but to me he was just Daddy. He was not a humble, easy-going man by any means, but he was a loving father to me. He was also a product of his upbringing, as we all are, and his upbringing instilled in him a peculiar blend of formality and playfulness. He was a tough-minded private man, but he was also extremely funny and could make me laugh harder than anyone. I was never bored with him. In many ways we were each other's confidant. I was so much like him and resembled him much more than I did my mother, and we spent hours together late at night, talking about…things. I can't remember a single conversation in detail. We simply talked, and it was wonderful.

I do know that we never had a conversation about what was going on at his office. When he came home at night the first thing he did was take off his watch, which meant it was the end of the work day. My father worked extremely hard and traveled frequently, and time at home with his family was a treasured time. He didn't want to hear a word about business and never offered one in return.

Charlotte and I have a running joke about who was whose favorite—I insist she was mother's favorite, she insists I was Daddy's. "I was too straight-laced to be Daddy's favorite," she tells me. "While you and Daddy were talking at night, I was doing homework. And if we were told to be in at 10:00, I was always in at 10:00. You were more wild and daring and might come in at 11:00."

Wow. How daring.

My father and mother were divorced when I was eighteen. That was the end of my years in Detroit, though my bond with my father did not weaken. At eighteen, I soon would have moved out on my own anyway so the sudden split in our family wasn't as traumatic as it might have been had I been younger. My sister, brother, and I moved to New York City to live with our mother.

From that point on, I saw my father only at certain periods of the year. A summer vacation, a spring break—at least two or three weeks a year were spent with him.

Alessandro was his first grandson. Daddy was so thrilled when he was born. He heard the news, rushed off to his men's club, and bought all the members cigars and champagne to toast the new arrival. He was a good grandfather—as good as he knew how to be. Often a grandparent can be blind to the reality of a grandchild. I can think of no more obvious instance of this than my father and his perception of Allegra.

First of all, to him, a disability had to be physical, something you could see. A mental disability of any kind had to be accompanied by outward signs of mental retardation or Down's syndrome for him to believe that anything was wrong. He's not alone in this, of course. Many people look at Allegra and find it difficult to believe she has a disability.

My own perceptions were very slow in coming around to reality. Now I faced the difficulty of perceptions that were not my own.

In the summer of 1978, Allegra had already been through one year of Gateway. Soon after school let out, my father invited us all to join him on vacation in Europe.

Charlotte and her daughter Elena couldn't make it, so it was only llegra, Alessandro, my cousin Sheila Murphy, and myself. Sheila ıd been babysitting my children for about three years by then. I've eady mentioned that I had gone through a series of babysitters, ʿching for one I trusted enough to leave Allegra with. My mother's ıgest sister, Margie, called one day to ask if either my sister or I ed someone to help with the kids. Her twin daughters, Sheila ıonie, were both looking for summer jobs. It was perfect. Char- nd I leaped at the opportunity, though who was to get whom ʿicult to decide because we loved them both equally. A coin ed to make the decision for us, and I won Sheila. She moved house and into our lives, not only as a babysitter but as a e stayed with us for ten years.

ften accompanied us on family vacations. My children had ʿection for her and she was a perfect traveling companion.

That year I decided to surprise them all by booking passage to Europe on a ship. They had never been on a transatlantic cruise, and I was sure they would love it. I wanted it to be a secret so I told them we were taking a plane. When the car headed toward the west side of Manhattan instead of toward the airports, Alessandro asked, "Why are we going west?"

"We're flying out of Newark," I said, and bit my lip to keep from laughing. I couldn't wait for their reaction when they saw the huge, magnificent ocean liner waiting at the pier.

We drove up to it, and Alessandro let out a whoop of joy. And Allegra? As far as she was concerned we were going to fly to Europe. That's what I had told her. That's what she believed. She stepped out of the car and gazed up at the enormous bulk of the ship looming over us, then turned to me and asked, "When is it going to take off?"

Why was I so afraid to tell my father about Allegra's disability? I had made up my mind to do so the moment she asked when the boat would fly. I owed it to her to try to get his help.

We joined up with him in Nice, in the south of France. Opportunities to break the news about Allegra came and went. I would start to say something and stop. Over and over I told myself, "Tonight, tell him tonight," and over and over I was stopped by my own fear.

I wasn't afraid of his reaction. I knew he would be understanding. I was afraid of *my* reaction. So much pain and frustration had been bottled up inside me I was terrified of making a scene in front of him. I wanted to go back in time to when I was a child and we spent hours in quiet conversation. That's how I wanted to tell him— quietly, calmly, affectionately. I didn't want my rage at the pediatric neurologist who suggested I institutionalize her to bubble to the surface. I didn't want my humiliation at being rejected by schools to send me over the edge. I wanted to tell him in a controlled adult way and I was scared to death.

One evening I joined him and his wife at a restaurant at the top of a steep hill overlooking the Mediterranean. The children stayed at the hotel with Sheila.

It was a lovely night, warm and fragrant with flowers and a beautiful view of the lights along the Riviera. We chatted amiably during dinner and all the time I was filled with warring voices: "Tell him. No, don't. Yes, tell him. No, I can't."

A bottle of wine gone, then another started. Finally....

"Daddy, I have to tell you something."

"What is it?"

"It's about Allegra."

His face changed, his smile faded, now replaced by a look of concern. "What is it? What's the matter?"

"Not long ago she was diagnosed with a severe learning disability. The neurologist in New York thought that she should be institutionalized and...."

There was no way I could finish the sentence.

My father sat back in his chair, stunned. No one said a word. Finally he said exactly what I had expected him to say: "I don't believe it. There's nothing wrong with her."

"I know that's what it looks like. You can't see it. But trust me, it's there." I told him about the neurologist, the schools, all we had gone through. I tried to be calm, tried to stay in control and soon saw that he was fighting to maintain control himself. He couldn't hide his distress. We spent hours discussing the situation and I still don't believe he ever fully accepted it.

We closed the restaurant that night and made our way down the steep hill in the dark. At the hotel my father gave me a big hug. "Don't worry, honey," he said, calling me by the name he had used in our late night talks so long ago. "We'll find the best doctor in the world for her. We'll find a cure."

I smiled at him, a sad smile...loving him for his concern and sad in my own knowledge that what he said could never be. I had always believed my father could fix anything—a phone call, a letter, a personal visit, and it was done, no matter what it was. Now I heard him assure me he would do whatever it took to find a cure.

It was the first time I knew he would fail.

We planned to continue the discussion the next day, but early that morning he received a phone call that his brother Benson had passed away. He left immediately, and we remained behind in France.

When I returned to New York, there was a message from him. "I found the best pediatric neurologist in the country," it said. "His name is Hart Petersen and he's in New York. I'm sure this will work out for the best."

Dr. Petersen was wonderful, yet despite my father's best efforts, the cure for a learning disability remained out of reach. That was true then, and it remains true now.

The following year my father made up for his early departure from France by inviting us on a cruise. All his children and grandchildren joined him for a week, and he was in heaven. I have a photograph of him from that trip with Alessandro on one shoulder and Allegra in the other arm and Charlotte's daughter Elena leaning close to his side—a proud and happy grandfather.

He spent an inordinate amount of time with Allegra on that trip. She loved to entertain him. She adored him and the feeling was mutual. When he was a young boy he developed an inner ear disorder called mastoid disease. The problem would flare up if he put his head underwater, so he never went swimming—until Allegra came along. He couldn't resist. He bought an enormous blow-up alligator and spent hours swimming off the side of the boat, doing what grandfathers do best—chasing grandchildren with a rubber alligator. It was so much fun to watch them.

My father knew of Allegra's disability by this time, but he seemed never to see anything out of the ordinary. There was no other child her age at any of the family vacations (Elena and Alessandro were both six years older), so there was no one to compare her to. Even if there had been, I seriously doubt he would have noticed.

Allegra had breakfast, lunch, and dinner every single day with my father with no difficulties at all. She did her *Annie* routine at the table. What I knew was hyperactivity came across as high spirits to my father. I tried to get her to stop, but he wouldn't hear of it.

One evening Allegra began to repeat a phrase she'd heard somewhere. She often did this. She would latch onto something and say it over and over again, sometimes to the point of driving others to distraction. This time it was a simple phrase: "Sprinkle a little pixie dust!"

On this night she wouldn't stop. She sprinkled imaginary pixie dust on her plate, on her chair, on the table, on the silverware, all the while declaring, "Sprinkle a little pixie dust!" Alessandro rolled his eyes. I sighed, hoping she might lose interest before she began to irritate my father. "Sprinkle a little pixie dust!" she said again, and this time I stopped her. "Allegra, please," I said. "We're at dinner, sweetheart. We can sprinkle pixie dust later."

My father sat in his chair, taking all this in quietly. Then he said, "Allegra, will you please pass me some of that dust?" The next thing I know, this gruff tough-minded businessman was sprinkling pixie dust along with his granddaughter. He then insisted that we all do the same. "Come on, come on!" he said. "Start sprinkling!" With that, Charlotte, Elena, Alessandro, Sheila, and I joined the two pixies in their efforts, and the more we did it, the more we laughed. It was the most ridiculous dinner, and by the end of it, that boat was covered from bow to stern with pixie dust.

Chapter 9
Separation

: (but so as i say good by. i just want you to know that i love you. and that i think of you all the today.
—E-mail from Allegra Ford

Allegra went to Gateway for five years, from age five to ten. I look back on that time as a happy one—at least when we were in New York. In those years, she was introduced to the Ice Studio. Hugh Carey had befriended us. Allegra had settled into a positive routine at Gateway, one which allowed her to learn at her own pace and to her best abilities.

However, it seemed that whenever Allegra was away from school and the teachers who understood her so well, she fell into the old difficulties of isolation and confusion. Each year during spring break, my sister Charlotte and I took our children to a vacation resort where my father rented a house. As with everything else, for the first few years of Allegra's life we had a great time. There were children everywhere, and as always, Alessandro bonded with a group of boys who remained his friends for years.

Things turned out differently for Allegra.

In the beginning, she was accepted completely. Then one year they played a game in the pool. It was something simple, but Allegra couldn't understand the rules. She asked the same questions over and over and the other children answered patiently. She still didn't understand. Rather than be rude to her, they simply walked away and began to play by themselves. She joined them, and they moved away again. Eventually she was completely left behind.

Sometimes there was no game involved at all. All the children, Allegra included, might be in the pool and suddenly one would shout, "Let's go to the beach!" and they would all explode out of the water and run to the beach. It was a happy, enthusiastic free-for-all, but for Allegra it was all bewildering—noise, sound, directions, movement, splashing, and shouting, and she was overwhelmed. She couldn't understand what they were doing, what their intentions were, or where they would end up. Inevitably, they would all run off, leaving Allegra standing by the pool, dripping wet, lost in confusion. Each year the situation grew worse as the games became more complex and soon she was isolated completely—a lonely child, an island in a sea of children.

The other children never made fun of her. Worse, they ignored her.

Once in a while a couple of girls might pass by and call to her, "Hi Allegra, hi Allegra" and she waved at them, hopefully. I saw the eagerness in her eyes. "Hi!" she called back and her eagerness was replaced by disappointment when the girls continued on without a glance back.

She watched them go. I couldn't stand it. I alternated between sorrow for Allegra and fury toward the girls, but I didn't know what to say. I couldn't find the words to explain such callous indifference in people she considered her friends.

One afternoon I was lying on a chaise lounge, reading a book by the pool. Several girls were in the water, teasing the boys, and having a great time. Allegra joined me. She stood beside me and looked at the girls. They didn't say a word. They never looked at her. Allegra said nothing to them or to me, but pulled up a chair beside mine. She sat down and picked up a book. If they wouldn't play with her, fine. She was perfectly capable of ignoring people too. She opened her book and began to read *The Diary of Anne Frank*. I found her actions a little satisfying. She wasn't going to let them get to her. I smiled to myself, but then I glanced over at her and my heart sank.

The book was upside down.

That was it. Enough silence from me. Enough hoping the situation would change if I ignored it.

"I don't feel like swimming either," I said out of the blue. "And I don't feel like lying here reading. Because we're going to do something much more fun than that."

Her mood changed. A smile lit up her face. Sadness turned to joyous expectation.

"What are we going to do, Mom?" she asked, and I put my arms around her and told her about shopping, and riding our bikes, and any one of dozens of things we would find to do by ourselves and with Alessandro. We would have a wonderful time, and that's exactly what we did. That was also one of the last times we went on vacation in a place where we knew a lot of people. It was too painful. From then on, we would go by ourselves. We knew how to have fun, the three of us. We knew how to laugh at ourselves and each other. We even learned how to laugh at an upside-down book.

I continued my struggle to accept and understand over the course of Allegra's years at Gateway. I had some success, but not as much as I wanted or needed. I had a particularly willful sense of denial—this is an awkward admission, especially since I now advise parents to face their situation head-on without illusion. But as usual, that is easier said than done. I could not extinguish that last spark of hope that something would happen to erase the learning disability from our lives. Some of my optimism was based in reality (or at least, an illusion of reality). Throughout Allegra's life there have been people close to her or to our family who have insisted that there is nothing wrong with her at all. That is not always a helpful thing, but when the news is never good and the diagnosis from the experts is always grim, the opinion of a Doubting Thomas is sometimes a welcome one.

One of those doubting Thomases was introduced to us in an odd and unexpected way in 1982. Allegra came home from visiting a school friend one day, and she announced to me that she had been invited to dinner the following night by Chuck Scarborough, the anchorman for WNBC News in New York. This was startling news from a ten-year-old, and I was curious to discover how she had received an invitation from such a prestigious and handsome man.

Allegra's friend's mother was an acquaintance of Chuck's. One afternoon he invited his acquaintance, her daughter, and her daughter's friend—Allegra—to join him for dinner with some of his colleagues.

I said, "Well, that's nice, Allegra," and marveled at the rather exotic life my daughter seemed to be leading. I thought she was only going to a friend's apartment to watch TV. I had no idea she would be lucky enough to have dinner with an anchorman!

The next evening I was dressing to go to a black-tie event and Allegra said, "Mom, I told Chuck I'd meet him down in the lobby of the apartment building."

"Don't you think you ought to call him Mr. Scarborough?"

"He told me to call him Chuck. He said to meet him downstairs in the lobby, but I'm scared to go down alone. Will you come with me?"

"I'm getting ready to go out, Allegra. Just have Chuck come upstairs to get you."

Not long after, the doorbell rang. I opened the door and there he was: tall, fair-haired, and handsome. "Hello, Mr. Scarborough," I said, and I too was given permission to call him Chuck. He asked if I would like to join them for dinner, "if you're not busy," he added.

"Actually I am," I told him, and explained that I didn't usually eat dinner alone at home in an evening dress.

Allegra had a great time that night, and when I went into her room to kiss her goodnight, she told me what a wonderful man Chuck was.

He called the next day and asked if Allegra and I would like to go down to the studio to watch him do the 6 o'clock news. We did, and it wasn't long before we were seeing a great deal of "Mr. Scarborough." Chuck and I were married two years later. Allegra was my maid of honor.

As Allegra's stepfather, Chuck became involved in her school life. He often helped her with her homework. She loved this because she had developed quite a little crush on him. And I loved it, too. This simple scene of domestic happiness, a man sitting at a kitchen table helping a young girl with homework, was something we had not experienced before. In the beginning, Chuck did not believe that she had any learning problems. For the first time, Allegra began to hear the phrases almost every child with a learning disability has heard at some time or another: "You're not trying hard enough. You're not motivated." He wasn't being mean and he never said it in an unkind way. He was acting like many fathers do. Unable to accept the problem, he began looking past the obvious in his search for an easier logical explanation. Chuck saw Allegra as a normal, healthy ten-year-old, and simply could not comprehend her inability to understand what he knew were simple concepts.

Night after night, he helped her with her homework and though there was some progress, it was very slow and frustrating for both of them. He tried to teach her the concept of money, how to count correct change, and the value of various coins. It was all to no avail. I also tried to help her but found it equally frustrating. I was too close to the situation, too eager to have her understand everything perfectly. The pressure on her was great: the last thing she wanted to do was disappoint me or Chuck, and she often ended up in tears, which made me feel so bad I too ended up in tears. This was not how homework was supposed to be.

It was evident that she needed somebody outside the family to help her. I found a wonderful tutor named Letty Buckley who lived nearby. In a surprising turn of events, Chuck eventually came to believe that Allegra did have a problem, whereas Letty never did. To this day, she believes that if Allegra had gone to a mainstream school she would have been fine.

"I taught in private schools and public schools for years," Letty remembers, "and I think I know children pretty well. I always felt there was nothing wrong with Allegra. I thought she should never have gone to a special school. Yes, she had trouble in math, but she could have had help for her math difficulties and been fine in all her other subjects. And with her great love of skating, I thought she could be an ice skating teacher and run a skating rink. I also never believed she would have trouble making it on her own as an independent adult."

It was so nice to hear such positive and firm pronouncements.

Apart from Chuck and Letty, there were not many others who believed so firmly in Allegra's potential. One who did, but showed this belief in a surprising way, was her older brother. And how did he show his belief? By treating her like she had no disability at all.

I wish I could say that Alessandro has sailed through life unaffected by Allegra's LD, but as with most such siblings, he has not always had an easy time of it. Children with a brother or sister with a learning disability often feel that more is expected of them (and often they are right). For Alessandro, the most difficult thing was his inability "to accept the fact that my sister was—and still is—unable to perform certain everyday activities that have become routine to me." When she was unable to read a book or do a simple math problem he used to ask me over and over again: "But *why* can't she do it?"

He was honestly trying to understand, and what was my response? "Because she can't." I underestimated his ability to understand. I am quite sure he would have understood her a lot better if I had taken the time to explain things to him as they were happening. Was I afraid? No. I didn't explain because I still didn't know what was going on myself. Before she was found to have LD, we were careening from diagnosis to diagnosis, back and forth between "perfectly fine" and "mentally retarded," and I found the prospect of explaining all that to a child close to impossible. I should have tried regardless, for I now know how vitally important it is to include the sibling in every step along the way.

In many families, failure to explain what's going on may create resentment among the nondisabled children. They may see that an "unfair" portion of time is focused on the interests of the child with LD, and most of the time they are right. It is nearly impossible not to focus on them. They have doctor's appointments, tutors to work with, schools that may be located at great distances, and homework that takes twice as long. Even the word "special" may cause resentment.

There is no more noble or generous impulse in our culture than our elevation of our disabled citizens to the level of special—special schools, special education, Special Olympics—but there is always the problem of our other children thinking they are somehow not as special. Alessandro once told me that he envied Allegra at times for having a "defined diagnosis." A failing grade for her was expected and accepted. For him, a failing grade meant personal failure.

In my family, a less than perfect report card was not unusual. My father went to summer school every single year of high school, and I wasn't a great student at all. Maybe Alessandro was simply following a family tradition when he didn't pull in straight A's, yet even now he searches for a more substantial reason. He recently went to an ophthalmologist and while he was in the waiting room he noticed a pamphlet that linked learning difficulties to vision problems. "A-ha!" he thought. "That's what my problem was!" But he quickly realized that wasn't the case. His vision has been bad only in the last few years.

His ability to treat Allegra as though she had no disability at all was one of his greatest gifts to his sister. He is a compassionate man and he has always been wise beyond his years. I often relied on that wisdom and have always been grateful it was there.

He never really understood why Allegra's contemporaries treated her so badly, especially in Southampton. She has nothing but good things to say about the girls who neglected her, but he still harbors some bitterness. I think their actions may have hurt him more than her. Alessandro has a heightened sense of compassion—he himself believes that having a sister with a disability "forced me into acceptance." That is true, though I wonder if "force" is the right word for it. He learned acceptance. He watched his sister struggle every day and watched my often futile attempts to make everything better, and he learned that we are all imperfect, all human, with failures and shortcomings, some of our own making and some not.

This is not to imply that he was superhuman or a saint—he and Allegra had as normal a brother/sister relationship as is possible. They fought all the time, there were little rivalries and jealousies, and sometimes they drove each other crazy.

Here is Alessandro trying to do his homework....The doorknob to his bedroom turns slowly. Allegra sticks her hand in the room, then shuts the door. He ignores it, but it happens again. And again. Finally he yells, "Will you get out of here?"

She retreats—he returns to his homework—a minute passes—the doorknob slowly turns, the door creaks opens.

"Allegra! I'm trying to do homework!"

The door closes.

Another minute passes. The doorknob slowly turns. This time Alessandro is ready. He's standing at the door. As soon as it opens, he pulls with all his might, Allegra topples against the door, bangs her head, and bursts into tears.

"Mom!" she cries. "Mom! Al hit me with a door!"

I arrive on the scene. "A door? You hit your sister with a *door*?!"

Alessandro, filled with righteous indignation, yells, "She keeps opening my door and closing it!"

I point out that opening and closing is a fairly common practice with doors, and then ask: "Is that any reason to hit her with it?"

"I *didn't* hit her!"

"I want you to go to your room."

"I'm in my room."

"Oh...well, go somewhere else then. And leave your sister alone!"

On it goes, the bickering and accusations, and I can't send Alessandro to his room because he's already in it, so I simply do what most mothers do—I throw up my hands and let them battle it out.

There were many scenes like that when they were young and a few when they were older, but there was never any real malice involved and never, ever, as the issue of a learning disability used against Allegra. (That's not to say it has never been used *by* Allegra. Once in a while she has pulled "But I have a learning disability" out of her hat as an excuse to get out of doing something she doesn't want to do. It doesn't work.)

Gateway buoyed Allegra up with positive reinforcement all during the school year, and then summer came and once again she entered a lonely, isolated world.

She could not ride her bike very well, so I was afraid to let her ride alone to the beach club. I either rode with her or drove her there. There was no group of friends for her except for the occasional weekend when my friends were invited and brought their children. Chuck also had two young children. She was five years older than they were. I thought the difference in their ages would work to our advantage, and that perhaps they would find they were on an equal level when it came to games.

They weren't.

On one occasion the children played Chutes and Ladders, a game known by many preschoolers. The object is to reach the top first by climbing the ladders and avoiding the bad luck of the chutes. Allegra flicked the spinner.

"Three."

She moved her piece forward, but by four or five places.

The children pointed this out. "That's five!"

"I moved it forward," Allegra said.

"You moved it five. Go back and move three."

There was no way she could do it. She went back, but not five, only three. Or she overshot her original position and became hopelessly confused.

The children could not understand. To them, Allegra was a "big kid," and naturally she would know how to play the game. They couldn't imagine that she didn't understand the rules. In the end, one accused her of cheating on purpose.

Allegra was shocked. Cheating was the last thing on her mind. She wanted to play! She wanted desperately to be able to understand and to be included. The children's accusations sent her from the room in tears and I had to intervene. They were sweet, good-hearted children and would never have hurt her intentionally. Once I explained that she couldn't understand the rules, they quickly called her back to play with them. The peace lasted until another misunderstood rule intruded and then the scene occurred all over again.

Sometimes it was left to Alessandro to bear the brunt of this. Allegra didn't have a group of her own so she would spend some afternoons pestering her brother. I was forever asking him to include her. He had his own friends and they played cops and robbers and "boy games." I don't think there is a brother since time began who has wanted to include his little sister in all of his games, but Alessandro tried.

I knew I had to find an alternative to Southampton. I heard about a summer camp for children with learning disabilities called Camp Northwood, run by a man named Jim Rien. Allegra and I went to his apartment and looked at pictures of the camp. "Oh, how lovely," I said, looking at photos of a rustic cabin, and thinking inside, "Oh my God."

I had never been to camp. I did not know what a camp looked like. I'm sure this one looked like every other camp, but to me it was a place I wanted to avoid. I am not, and never have been, good at "roughing it." Bugs, spiders, bears…no, thank you, not for me, and I could not imagine Allegra being in such a place.

In addition, I couldn't stand the idea of her going away.

She had never been away. Ever. She had never spent a night away from me in her life. She tried once to spend a night with a school friend in Brooklyn, but that lasted exactly the length of time it took for me to get from their apartment back to my own. The phone rang, and I was once again off to Brooklyn to bring her home.

I enrolled her in Camp Northwood, believing on some level that the experience would be good for her. I wasn't too worried about being separated from her because I was confident she would back out in the end. But to my surprise she agreed to go. I still didn't believe it would happen and didn't want her to feel uncomfortable about her eventual decision. I said: "Okay, here's the deal. You try it. If you don't like it, I'll come back to pick you up."

It was a five-hour drive but I would have done it twice in one day if that was what she wanted.

And so she went. She didn't want to at first, but she went. I expected her to have difficulty over our parting, but I never counted on *my* reaction. Embarrassing is hardly the word. When I put her on the bus I could not stop crying. This wasn't weepy crying. It was hysterics. Everyone stared at me like I was crazy. I could hardly see the bus leaving I was crying so hard, and after it was gone, I went back home and climbed into Allegra's bed and sobbed and sobbed. I drove to Southampton that afternoon, crying the entire way, and spent that night and the following night crying as if she had been taken from me forever.

I should have been ecstatic that she did not have to spend another summer in Southampton, but the separation was unbearable. It was painful—*physically* painful. I felt like my heart was breaking. I always knew we would have to be apart someday, but until it actually happened, I honestly believed that she could not exist without me.

This was a real lesson for me and one I often try to tell other parents of children with learning disabilities. It is important to understand that separation can be beneficial for both the child and the parent. This is easy advice to hand out but very difficult to accept. I understand how important it is now because I was so bad at doing it!

I wasn't allowed to talk to her the first couple of weeks. It was tough at first, but I understood the reason. Most of the children had never been separated from their parents, so it was reasonable to limit the conversations, thereby helping them ease into life at the camp. When I finally could call her, our conversations were timed. There was an egg-timer beside the phone and Allegra was so conscientious she ended the conversation the exact second the sand ran out. It didn't matter if we were in the middle of a sentence. The sand ran out and *click*. The phone went dead.

I went to see her on Parents Weekend. The camp was an extremely run-down collection of cabins beside a lake, with a small dining hall and an office—the same layout of most other camps. The difference between Camp Northwood and the others was the children. They were all disabled in some way, physically or mentally. And yet, on Parents Day it became immediately clear that, as at Gateway, Allegra finally had a place where she was happy. She had friends at camp: real, genuine friends. She had things to do, activities that kept her busy all day long, and her playmates turned out to be far more accepting than many she knew back home.

Allegra never came back to Southampton again, not in any real long-term sense. Oh, yes, she came out for a day, or for a family affair, but her heart—if it ever really had been there—was gone from the place.

In many ways, so was mine. The old magic was gone.

I began to spend more and more of my summers away from Southampton. Labor Day was the only time we all met out there, and even then Allegra usually wasn't able to make it. She always found a way to get out of coming to Southampton for any length of time. After years of believing she was unaware of what was going on and how she was treated, I came to realize that a part of her knew all along and was hiding it, putting on a brave front, being in control (as I had so diligently taught her to be). She never voiced her feelings and won't to this day. If someone asks, she'll tell them she loved it, that she had lots of friends, lots of things to do.

Eventually it became clear that the house itself was never going to be what it had been. It was a big old place that needed a lot of upkeep. I was no longer spending enough time out there to justify the expense of running it, so I sold it. Alessandro loved that place and will never completely forgive me for this, but I expect that he will buy his own house out there someday and that his children will begin the cycle of summer days that made him so happy as a child.

My niece Elena also sold her house. Only my sister Charlotte remains in Southampton and I wonder for how long.

Even the old McDonnell-Murray Compound is no longer there. The property was subdivided and sold out of the family. In the 1970s, a nor'easter storm struck Southampton. My grandmother and her sister stood and watched, terrified, as their stone house with enough rooms to house their combined twenty-eight children was taken by the storm. By morning, the two houses and the yard where we had played as children and where my mother and father were married had vanished into the sea.

Chapter 10
Graduation Day

*i know its hard but i'm with you . and i am with you all
the way throught.*

—E-mail from Allegra Ford

Allegra's five years at Gateway came to an end. Eventually the day
came when it was clear that the wonderful school on the fifth floor
had accomplished all it could and it was time to move on. Graduation was coming soon and I wondered who I should invite to come
along. Charlotte, for sure. I asked Chuck to come, but he was going to
be away on business that day. Alessandro was away at school. I
thought of my mother, but rejected the idea. I did so because never
once, in all of Allegra's five years at Gateway, did my mother ever visit
the school or even take an interest in it. This was not because she did
not love Allegra or take an interest in her life. I really do not know
why she never asked about the school, but I suspect that I may have
had something to do with it. I may have made any inquiry about my
daughter's school life a difficult subject to bring up. It may be that I
didn't want my mother or anyone else to see where Allegra spent her
days. I am not sure that my sister had ever been to Gateway either.

Mother knew of Allegra's disability, of course. I had told her
around the same time I broke the news to my father, back when Allegra was five.

She was a very kind, yet very stoic woman. Never once in my life
did I see her cry. Never. She faced life armed with a deep religious
faith and a firm belief that there was nothing she could not handle.
Still, I had been reluctant to tell her about Allegra's disability for the
first time. She had a group of friends she had lunch with nearly every
day, and I knew—*I knew*—she would tell them the very next day that
her granddaughter was different. This would have been done in the

kindest way, with the best of intentions; and her friends would have received the news in the same way, but the reaction would have been, "Poor Anne, I wonder if she can handle this," and I was unnerved by the idea of being pitied by my mother's friends. I didn't feel a need for pity and didn't believe my situation was particularly pitiful, and I hoped so much to avoid having to let my mother know.

But I couldn't avoid it, of course.

So one day, soon after I talked with my father, I told my mother. She listened dutifully, and then...nothing. She never said a word to her friends. I believe this was so because she truly did not understand what I was talking about. Like my father, she saw nothing out of the ordinary in Allegra's appearance or behavior. If anything, she may have thought I was exaggerating. She never again brought the subject up or expressed an interest in Gateway. For Mother, it was as if Allegra's disability did not exist at all.

But wait, I thought, it *does* exist. And why shouldn't Mother try to understand? This was her granddaughter after all, and I thought it was time she was confronted with the reality of our situation. It was also time for me to face a few realities—or at least, face them head-on with eyes wide open instead of the way I had before, as at Allegra's evaluation when I sat against the wall, as far from the action as possible.

A realization was gradually dawning on me. I found that I was actually proud of Allegra. She was graduating! Back in the days when no school would take her, the word "graduation" was nowhere close to being in my thoughts. But here she was, with five years of accomplishment behind her, ready to take her next step. Yes, I was proud of her, and I wanted Mother and Charlotte to be proud, too. It was not going to be any kind of graduation ceremony they were used to, but Allegra was ecstatic at the possibility they might attend. She couldn't wait to introduce her grandmother and her aunt to all her friends.

So they should be there, I decided. They should have their eyes opened and understand the reality of the situation. Mother and Charlotte agreed to join me at the ceremony, which took place on a lovely spring day in the large main room of the Gateway School. It wasn't until then that Mother really understood, for the first time, what we were dealing with. I could tell by her expression that she was shocked by her first visit to a "special school." It was one thing to be alone with Allegra and quite another to see her surrounded by all her classmates. Mother kept her feelings to herself but not long afterward, I began to notice new feelings emerge from her usually unruffled demeanor. She still did not express her views about the "special school," but she certainly began to express her feelings for Allegra. The day she went to Gateway was the beginning of an intensely close relationship. Mother began to take great interest in her school-life and all her activities from that moment on.

But on that day, I did not know things would turn out that way. I still didn't know what to expect. As we entered the school I told Mother and Charlotte, "Okay, you two. Don't be looking at your watch and asking me how long it's going to take."

"Of course not!" Charlotte replied, and mother echoed the sentiment. "We would never do that."

All the adults gathered in the back of the room, just as we had on Allegra's first day so long before. Most of the children were sitting on the floor in front of us while the seven graduates sat in chairs in the center of the room.

Nothing is rushed at Gateway. Each child stood and made a presentation, something they excelled at, whether telling a poem or singing a song. It went on and on and on....there was a bit of uncomfortable shifting in the chairs, the sound of an impatient sigh from somewhere behind me.

Allegra sat with the other children, smiling and radiant in a white dress with lace trim.

Suddenly—beside me—Mother looked at her watch just as Charlotte leaned over and asked softly, "How long is this graduation going to take?"

I immediately burst into tears, a response way out of proportion to the situation.

"I'm only asking," Charlotte whispered, shocked by my outburst.

"You just sit there," I hissed through gritted teeth. "Both of you!"

Allegra stood to give her presentation. It was a song. As she began to sing it, she too burst into tears. Maybe the realization that she was leaving Gateway struck her. Whatever the reason, she sobbed and sobbed as she tried to sing the song, which was, ironically, "Put on a Happy Face." So there we were: Allegra onstage crying her heart out and me doing the same in the audience.

Charlotte and Mother tried to comfort me, but I ignored them and continued to cry. It soon became clear that the tears were over more than a casual glance at a watch, yet I couldn't bring myself to tell them what was going on inside.

I was scared.

The future was so obscure. It was filled with questions and undefined fears.

The room was filled with parents who were so proud, and the ceremony was beautifully done. I was proud, too, but I looked at my daughter and I couldn't help wondering why she was the way that she was. Still! I was still wondering after all those years. Why did she have to have a learning disability? Why did she have to go to a special school?

My tears were selfish tears. I wanted everything to be safe and secure. I didn't want to have to find another school and face rejection again and again. I wanted Allegra to graduate from a school where my friends' children went.

I wanted the disability to *go away*!

Chapter 11
My Mother

mom im thinking of you on this day :)
as you look back 4 years agao today : (when your mom
was going to god. and i knew that when she going up that
god would make shour that she looked down @ you. its
funny how things go by so fast. but i know that today is the
day where we close our eyes and see granma and make shour
that she is doing well

—E-mail from Allegra Ford

When Allegra's isolation became too painful, and I decided to leave
our various circles of friends on family vacations, Alessandro never
once uttered a word of complaint. He gave up many happy days with
his friends but remained in high spirits and was always there to make
us laugh. We shared so much and spent so much time together, just
the three of us, that we created an unbreakable bond. There were a
few times when we had been apart, a few weeks at summer camp and
occasional visits to relatives, but it never lasted all that long.

And then the day came when Alessandro was to go away to Brooks
School in North Andover, Massachusetts.

I was happy that he had been accepted at Brooks, but as the day of
departure loomed closer, I began to dread the idea. He wasn't happy
about it either. Allegra was beside herself. The night before I dropped
him off we all stayed at a hotel in Boston. I decided it would be a
good thing for the three of us to stay in one room and to have room
service—anything to maximize our final hours together. Alessandro
and I slept in twin beds with Allegra on a cot beside me. I was so
happy to have the two people I loved most on either side of me. We
talked quietly and laughed and spoke of our dreams for the future,
Allegra as a skater, and Alessandro as a movie producer; when suddenly, in a fit of premature homesickness, Alessandro announced
that he would jump out the hotel window if I went through with the
next day's mission of leaving him at Brooks.

Of course he had no intention of doing anything so dramatic, but
my imagination compelled me to stay awake all night with my eyes

on the dimly lit square of window, worrying that I might see a shadowy figure open it and hurl himself to his death.

The next day was awful. We got to his dorm room very early so I could make his bed look exactly like his bed at home. I wept quietly as I covered his bureau with pictures of Allegra and me. A little extreme? Yes. In fact, Alessandro's new roommate was dropped off the same day: his father was so amazed by my actions that he asked if he could take pictures of me making up the bed.

When I finally got up the courage to leave, I said the words I was to say so often with my children: "Now listen. If you don't like it, call me and I'll come right back and get you!"

Allegra and I returned home. Alessandro didn't call. I waited and waited.

No call.

I thought that something must have gone wrong so I called him. "Are you all right?"

"I love it!" he cried, and I knew that once again he had immediately found a new circle of friends.

I had no intention of sending Allegra to a boarding school after she graduated from Gateway, so I needed to find something fairly close to home. I visited many schools in the New York City area, but it was one rejection after another, with the "We feel she doesn't belong here" routine rearing its ugly head once again. This time I wasn't quite as devastated: we get used to anything if it happens often enough.

I finally found a place in White Plains, New York, called The Windward School. Once again her evaluation scores were very low. They were reluctant to accept Allegra at first, but relented in the end with the standard condition that "If she can't make it, she'll have to go elsewhere." Once again it was to be semester by semester, without our ever really knowing if they would keep her or send her away the following year.

The commute was terrible. There were several children from New York City who went to Windward and all the parents took turns driving them there. It was an hour and forty-five minutes each way when traffic was bad, an hour each way on a good day.

Windward was good for Allegra and she loved it there, but I always viewed it as a transitional school and the uncertain "semester to semester" state was now compounded by the much deeper concern of, "What am I going to do when she's finished here?"

She made it through two full years there before the day came when

I received the phone call. To be fair, they recommended that Allegra move on at the end of her third year because they felt they could not help her any further, not because they were unwilling to keep her.

I received a transitional report in her final semester that gives a very accurate portrait of Allegra during these years. She was thirteen years old when the report was written.

Under strengths, they reported: "Allegra is a cheerful, friendly and polite young lady. She is quick to establish a rapport and engage in social conversation. She is highly motivated to perform well. At times, even when discouraged and appearing to derive no pleasure from academic activities, she continues to work extremely hard in apparent eagerness to please. Allegra's approach to learning suggests years of hard work and practice. She has a good self-image with a wonderful sense of humor. She prides herself on her ability to ice-skate and in her physical appearance."

Under weaknesses, they wrote that "Allegra becomes overexcited, engages in irrelevant speech and displays that may not be modulated. Her obvious difficulty sustaining focused attention and concentration is evident throughout interchange. Although persevering when tasks become difficult, she loses track of the task objective. Her perceptual analysis and synthesis skills are poor when stimulus material is abstract in design. She appears to have reached a plateau in terms of her general mathematical development. Allegra has a powerful need for attachment to others. Her desire to be accepted by her peers and have close friendships is very strong; however, she feels frustrated and unsuccessful in this area."

In summary, they wrote, "Allegra is a very likeable young lady with a pleasant interpersonal demeanor which is her significant asset for adults and older peers. Although it appears that she may have difficulty progressing beyond her current academic level, her reading and spelling skills suggest she is capable of continued achievement in these areas. Allegra would benefit most from a social skills and life skills orientation."

I found it a little difficult to believe that at thirteen years of age Allegra had reached the end of her ability to progress academically, but the phrase "social skills and life skills" resonated with me. I knew such skills were critical and that their importance would only grow as she got older. If there was a way to set Allegra on a course of independence and to help her handle the everyday ups and downs of life without my help or interference, I wanted to find it.

And so I began the search for yet another school.

The report from Windward suggested that I might want to look into a place called Riverview. I called the headmaster about it, and he told me that it was a boarding school on Cape Cod. I rebelled at once and barred all further thought of it. I was determined not to send her away to a boarding school, even if it meant letting her stay home for an entire year.

I have already described the hysterical scene at the bus stop when she went to summer camp. That happened twice for Camp Northwood, and again when she went to skating camp. The moment of release was unbearable for me each time, and our days apart were filled with constant worry and oppressive thoughts of "is she all right?" Mothers of children with learning disabilities often have an acute reluctance to separate from our children. Is it because we see how isolated they often are? Do we fear they may be easily taken advantage of if we're not around?

Those few weeks of separation when she went to summer camp were barely tolerable, and the idea of a longer period of time away from her was unthinkable.

I was convinced I could never send Allegra away to school and the idea of her becoming an adult and actually moving away from me was something I could not imagine. I refused to think about it. "That is way down the road," I reasoned, "something to worry about years from now." That was how I handled it, by pushing it off into the distant future.

As usual, I tried every school in New York, and as usual, none accepted her. I then started going further afield, hoping to come across another Windward, even if it meant driving two hours each way. But there was nothing. Finally, after a new round of rejections from the local schools and with a new sense of dread, I realized that what I thought was the distant future was upon us. It was clear that I had to find a school somewhere far from home. Riverview, on Cape Cod, had been recommended, but it was so far away. Alessandro was in Massachusetts, but he took the Boston shuttle or the train home whenever he wanted. Would Allegra ever be able to manage a journey such as that on her own? I didn't think so. In fact, I was convinced that she couldn't and probably never would.

But I decided to give Riverview a chance. One cold, rainy day I drove to Cape Cod and visited the small school in East Sandwich. I pulled into the main parking lot. A very attractive red brick building with white trim faced the road. It was a friendly looking place, and I found it was the same with the people who worked there. The headmistress then was a lady named Joanne Brooks, and she gave me a tour of the school grounds. The red brick of the main building gave way to a series of isolated buildings, each serving a separate function such as classroom, infirmary, or dining hall. The buildings were designed in typical Cape Cod style, with weathered shingles and clapboards—in the rain they looked particularly gray and not all that inviting, but it wasn't long before I understood that this might be the only place for Allegra. I didn't have much choice. The only other school under consideration was one that was primarily for children with severe mental retardation, and I couldn't bear to send her there.

Her academic transcripts and reports were reviewed and as always the school was reluctant to take her. I pleaded, and they finally agreed, but on the usual terms—she could stay for a semester. If it didn't work out, she would have to move on.

I was relieved, but my heart was still heavy at the thought of bringing her so far away to live. When I was given a rundown of the school rules, it was all I could do not to cry. Behind Mrs. Brooks, the window was wet with rain—the gray buildings in the distance were blurred. Everything was dark and gray, and the rules were so harsh...she could take phone calls only from me, and only once a week. Her activities were to be strictly controlled. There would be very little free time— what little there was would be spent in the presence of one of the elderly social workers who lived in the dorms with the students. On top of all this were rules which would allow her to go skating only on weekends.

I broke the news to Allegra the following day.

"What do you mean, go away?" she asked. "I'm not going to go away."

"It's a very nice school, Allegra. I think you'll love it there."

"Can I come home at night?"

"No, sweetheart. It's too far for that."

She began to cry. "I don't want to go!" On and on it went—she didn't want to go, she didn't want to leave me, and every time she said it, I felt like crying myself. But I couldn't. I had to make her understand it was for her own good.

"Look at Alessandro," I told her. "He didn't want to go to Brooks School, but now he loves it."

"Then why can't I go to Brooks like he did?"

"Allegra, that's not possible...."

"But why?"

"Riverview really could be fun for you. And I saw some really cute guys walking around...."

Even that didn't help.

This was the only time in Allegra's life when I remember her being truly upset for a long period of time. She simply could not understand why she couldn't go to the same school Alessandro was attending and no matter how much I tried to explain, it was no use. It was a constant refrain that summer—"But why can't I go to Brooks? I don't want to leave you. If I have to leave you, I want to be with Alessandro!"

Alessandro believes I was far too protective of Allegra and that I was overpowering in my need to keep her safe and by my side. To some extent, that may be true. I did let her walk to Gateway when she was old enough. It was only a few blocks away. New York City streets are not always noted for their safety, but still, I let her go on her own. I also allowed her to walk alone to her skating lessons at the Ice Studio. One day she was standing at a corner, her skates slung over her shoulder, waiting for the light to change. A deranged man came up from behind and pushed her into the street. She was cut and bruised and terribly frightened, but she merely brushed herself off and continued on to the Ice Studio. The owner of the studio called me immediately. I wanted to take her to the doctor, but she pleaded with me to allow her to take her lesson. Her love of skating overwhelmed everything.

It was the unknown that frightened me. When Allegra was about ten years old she went to a nearby store to buy a magazine. I gave her a $20 bill. She came back with no change. I asked her why and she said, "The lady told me there was none." Even after all those nights Chuck spent trying to teach her the difference between a nickel and a dime and that money had numerical value, she still did not understand at all. That shopkeeper was the sort of person I felt Allegra needed protection against. Who would protect her if I wasn't there?

I saw Allegra as too vulnerable for the world—a laughing, fragile being who needed someone to shield her from the hurt and pain that would inevitably come her way. Naturally, I was the only one who saw it that way. The laughing fragile being couldn't have cared less. She saw no danger, she saw nothing to be frightened of. To her, the lack of change from a $20 bill was correct and the man, though "bad," didn't really mean to push her into traffic. She was also becoming a young woman and I knew I had to face the issue of sexuality head-on. I never had the "birds and bees" discussion with Alessandro. I knew that had been taken care of in his school, which was fine with me because I admit I was a little embarrassed about it all.

With Allegra, I had questions and concerns far beyond mere embarrassment. Would, or even *could*, she get married? If she had children, would they be disabled? Would she be able to take care of them? I believed then and believe even more firmly now that she can indeed get married and have children. I also believe she would be a wonderful mother. But these were all unknowns back then and for once I decided not to attempt to go it alone. I went to see a psychiatrist—not for Allegra, but for me, to help me work through all this.

He was a warm personable man, and I felt comfortable discussing my concerns about my daughter's future. He listened for a while, apparently understanding everything I said, then he peered over his glasses at me and casually said, "You might want to consider getting your daughter sterilized."

Stunned silence.

"How...," I began, trying once again to come to terms with such unbelievable callousness in a professional, "How can you *possibly* say that?!"

Our session ended that moment. I left without another word.

I didn't know what to do. I didn't know how to effectively explain conception and contraception in a way she would take seriously. I knew she would either laugh it off or retreat into her own world, and I knew there was only one person she admired enough to hear a lecture from: her brother.

When he came home for summer vacation from Brooks, I asked him if he would talk to her, and without a hint of embarrassment, he said, "Sure. Now?"

Allegra and I sat at the kitchen table while Alessandro explained the mysteries of sex and childbirth to her. And while my daughter sat quietly and nodded to indicate she understood what he was saying and watched the whole condom and banana demonstration without smirking once; there I was, sitting beside her, utterly amazed.

I learned *so* much that day!

The summer of 1986 was excruciating. As each day went by, and June and July passed into August and August toward September, I became more anxious. Several times I nearly gave in to her fears and my most fervent desires and said, "All right. You can stay with me." But how could I do that? Could I possibly, in good conscience, tell her she didn't have to go to school and that she could remain where she was, completely dependent on me without ever having the opportunity to make it on her own? Yes, there was always the possibility that she wouldn't be able to make it—but she had to have the chance to find that out for herself.

The day to take Allegra to Riverview finally arrived. Alessandro had graduated from Brooks and was now attending Boston University. I was about to leave both of my children in Massachusetts, and I knew I couldn't handle it alone. I turned to my mother. I needed her stoicism, I needed her strength to help me get through it. She agreed, and so Mother, Alessandro, Allegra, and I set out for Boston.

I knew a car trip would be far too long a time to dwell on our parting, so I sent the luggage ahead to the school and arranged for the four of us to take the shuttle from LaGuardia to Logan Airport. I was already weepy and teary-eyed by the time we reached the airport.

My mother, who never cried at anything, was very supportive, though I'm sure she wondered what on earth I was so upset about. Allegra and Alessandro were subdued as we sat in the waiting area for our flight.

Mother, a little impatient with all the gloominess, stood up and said, "I'll be right back."

I looked at my watch. "It's almost time to board. Where are you going?"

"I have to use the ladies room," she whispered delicately.

"Okay, but hurry up."

Mother left, and we three remained behind, solemn and unsmiling....It was *so* depressing. We all knew what an enormous change this would be in our lives, and for once we seemed unable to find a way to express ourselves or even to find a redeeming shred of humor in the situation.

A voice came over the loudspeaker to announce our boarding call.

"Where's Gigi?" Allegra asked, using the name my children always called their grandmother.

"Oh, don't tell me!" I said irritably, thinking she was probably in the ladies room primping and preening, believing she had all the time in the world. "I'll be right back."

I went to the nearest ladies room. "Mother!" I called, glancing at the closed doors of the stalls. "We're boarding now."

Silence.

"Mother?"

She wasn't there.

I went back to our seats, now a little worried. I asked Allegra to see if there was another ladies room nearby. There was, and Allegra went off to see if my mother had gone there instead.

I returned to the first ladies room, hoping I had somehow missed her or that she didn't hear when I called. This time I knocked on one of the closed doors. "Mother? Are you in there?"

An irritated voice: "I'm not your mother."

"Oh, I beg your pardon." On to the next stall. "Mother?"

"I'm not either."

We couldn't find her anywhere. By now I was getting angry as well as worried. "I *told* her the flight was boarding soon. Why didn't she go somewhere nearby!?"

Then Alessandro pointed and said: "Look!"

We all turned in time to see my elegant mother, patron of the arts and voted one of the world's best-dressed women several years in a row, coming out of the men's room at LaGuardia, red-faced and laughing.

She had gone in unaware of her error, stepped into one of the stalls, closed the door, and only realized her mistake when she heard the deep voices of two men talking as they came into the men's room.

Once in, she didn't know how to get out without making a scene, so there she sat as man after man came in to use the facilities. I'm sure she heard the boarding call, and I'm sure she was frantic to figure a way out of her predicament. Most women would rush out of there as quickly as possible. My mother, conscious of all the rules of etiquette, simply could not come up with an exit that would in any way be considered graceful.

Finally—in a lull—this tiny 5'4" woman braced herself, threw back her shoulders, stepped out of the stall—probably said something like, "Good afternoon, gentlemen," and strode with great dignity out of the LaGuardia men's room.

I could still kiss her today for doing it. She broke the spell of gloom. We laughed so hard that we almost missed our plane. The flight was filled with our laughter—much more intense than it might have been, due to the tension that had lain beneath it for so long. Even the drive out to Cape Cod was punctuated by an occasional mention of the incident—Alessandro asking: "Didn't you wonder what those white things hanging on the walls were for?"—and we would all break down again.

But then we turned into the driveway of Riverview School and the laughter died.

This was it, I realized. This was the moment when my little girl and I would truly part for an extended period of time. I thought she would be away for the better part of four years, but perhaps I also realized, as most parents do, that a child who goes away to school will probably never live at home again. Whether this would be so for Allegra remained to be seen, but I knew she would not be with me in the way she had up until then.

I don't know when I started crying, but it was fairly soon after we arrived at Riverview. This was not my hiding-in-the-bathroom crying—no, this was something new. Mother was appalled. Alessandro says my tears at Riverview were surpassed only by those on the day I first dropped him off at Brooks.

I did not want to leave Allegra. I made things far worse for both of us. I thought she would be lonely, that she might not make friends, that she might be ignored by the other children. These thoughts were relieved somewhat by the sudden appearance of a charming girl around Allegra's age, who wore a Laura Ashley dress and spoke with a lovely Southern accent. Her name was Windy Harris, and she immediately took Allegra under her wing. It was Windy's first day there also, but she was so self-assured and so gracious she made us all feel welcome in this strange place. She took Allegra on a tour of the school and the dormitory while I followed behind like a mournful spirit, weeping quietly.

My mother, in an attempt to escape my hysterics, quickly bonded with the elderly social worker who would be supervising Allegra's dormitory. The lady was a smoker. My mother could not resist smokers. She had quit cold turkey but never lost the craving. She sought out people who still smoked or who had recently given up smoking, simply to talk about cigarettes. (She remained friends with the lady, and because the rules said that only I could talk to Allegra, Mother took it upon herself to call the social worker to discuss both her granddaughter and the number of cigarettes her new friend had smoked that day.)

When it came time for us to leave, I repeated the offer to Allegra that I had made so long before when she went to summer camp: "If you don't like it, call me. I'll come back and get you."

Mother eyed me suspiciously. We had planned to take the evening shuttle back to New York, and I'm sure she wondered how I was going to return to Riverview so easily. I announced that we weren't going to New York but would stay in a hotel in Boston that night...just to be sure.

I hugged Allegra goodbye, held her close, both of us crying, and then finally broke away, only to run back inside again. Then Allegra broke away, but followed me out to the car. The headmistress tried to part us, telling me, "Get out, get out, you're making it worse!" Poor Mother was beside herself in the car (having *never* seen a sight quite like it). It was awful!

Finally I managed to climb into, or was forced into, the car, and we were off. I was desolate, completely unhinged. I felt as if I had deliberately abandoned my daughter. I couldn't escape the image of her face and her tears as she held me at the car and begged me not to leave her there.

Mother and I drove Alessandro to his dorm at Boston University, then she and I went on to the hotel. That night was like a wake. I could not stop crying. Mother didn't know what to do. She made several phone calls to friends and relatives, telling each one in a subdued voice, "It's as though Allegra died. I've never seen anything like it." On and on it went, with phone call after phone call. "Anne's going through a mourning period. She's hysterical, and I don't know what to do with her."

I would have been better off in a room by myself.

I called Riverview several times that night and each time was reassured. "She's with Windy Harris, and they're getting along wonderfully."

On the last call I was told, "She's sleeping peacefully."

That was it. It was done. I finally realized she would be fine.

She had found a new home.

My reaction to our separation was extreme, but the sentiments underlying it were not uncommon. Many parents go through the same feelings. Grief and sorrow and fear at parting time are so common that Rick Lavoie, the present headmaster, now sets up a big banner at the end of the driveway aimed specifically at parents who are dropping off their children for the first time.

It is the last thing they see when they leave Riverview.

It reads: "Don't worry. We'll take good care of them."

Chapter 12
Riverview

*and then I went on to school on the cape called riverview I
had meet some really very specail staff members. and they
were rick lavoie and judy hafker. They both became very close
to me and I can recall always going to rick to talk.*

*I felt very close to both of them. So as my four years went
on I had also meet some great friends too.*

—E-mail from Allegra Ford

I hoped Allegra would fit in at Riverview and make new friends, and
by this I meant new friends her own age. Ever since she was a very
young child, Allegra had a tendency to befriend people who were
much older than she was—a teacher like Mary Zielenbach, or a parent
of a classmate. Even her friends Ali Halpern and Hilary Braverman
were both six years older. I was worried she would get to Riverview
and attach herself to a teacher or a social worker to the exclusion of
relationships with her peers.

She made it through the first night with no trouble at all, but I
wondered how long it would be before she called me in tears, beg-
ging to come home. I suspected that if she could last a full week she
might stand a good chance of translating that into a full year away
from home.

Before that first week was out, I received some terrible news.

My father had contracted Legionnaires' disease in a hotel in
Madrid and had to be flown from Europe to Detroit. He already had
a serious heart condition and the prognosis was not good. My sister
and I were told to come home immediately. By the time we joined
our brother Edsel at our father's bedside he had already slipped into
a coma from which he would never recover. I called my children and
arranged for them to be brought to Detroit. They were very close
to him, and his death came as a shock. Alessandro was fortunate
enough to have spent time with him in London a couple of weeks
before he died. He has often mentioned how grateful he was for that
short time together. As for Allegra, I didn't know how well she would

understand the concept of death (this was the first time she had lost anyone close). She took it hard, but handled her grief with dignity and maturity.

When she returned to Riverview a week or so later, there were no tears at our parting. I think we both knew and accepted that something had shifted in our lives. It was not only the death of my father, but the passing of Allegra's childhood. It was a bittersweet moment for me, realizing that my little girl was becoming a young woman and that we could never return to those early days. Yes, she would always be in my thoughts and we would remain as close as we always had been, but now there would be a distance between us. She would have friends I didn't know. She would go places without telling me first. I would not oversee every action and every movement in her life. She was beginning a new life as an independent adult. Riverview would be her home for the next few years, and we knew it was for the best.

I was initially disturbed by the school's strict routines and rigid structure but such things never bothered Allegra. She needed structure. She wanted structure. There is nothing so disconcerting for a child with LD than a lack of structure. Structure gives them boundaries and a sense of security. Without it, their lives are often filled with fear and confusion and feelings of inadequacy.

Allegra is supremely organized in her life and thrives in an environment of structure and routine. If she were to be suddenly immersed in a new, chaotic world, she would have a difficult time at first but would soon create routines to enable her to shape and define her place in that world. Such attempts to create order out of chaos are common in children with LD, although we may not always see it for what it is. Rick Lavoie told me of a boy whose homeroom class was on the ground floor of his school. The majority of his other classes were on the second or third floor. He was told on the first day to go from his homeroom to his next class when the bell rang. He did this dutifully, but after a week or two, his teachers noticed that he was coming to all his classes late and out of breath. Instead of reprimanding him, one of the teachers asked him why this was happening. It turned out he understood and retained one instruction from the first day of school: "Go from your homeroom to the next class when the bell rings." With that in mind, the boy returned to his homeroom *every* time the bell rang. If he had a class on the third floor, followed by another on the same floor, he walked all the way downstairs to his homeroom then back up the three flights to the next class. He did not understand that he was able to go to the next class directly. This may appear completely illogical, but for him it was not. It was a routine, and gave him guidelines to follow.

Only after the teacher sat down and plotted out the way for him to go from class to class in a structured manner was the boy able to find his way through the school.

Allegra needed structure and was comfortable within a structured setting, but paradoxically was uncomfortable in any setting that appeared to be *too* rigid. Structure was fine as long as it didn't look like structure.

"What do you remember about Riverview?" I recently asked her.

"That I couldn't skate."

"Why couldn't you skate?"

"It was some rule about skating only on weekends. I wanted to go during the week, but I couldn't because of the rules."

She didn't understand the rule, therefore, in her mind, the rule had no value.

It wasn't long after Allegra's arrival at Riverview that my concerns about her attaching herself to an adult became a reality. She met a dorm mother named Judy Hafker, a petite attractive woman with blonde hair in her early thirties. Allegra gravitated toward her at once.

Allegra had always bonded closely with one adult, no matter which school or summer camp she was in, but it was at Riverview that I saw how strong this need for an older friend could be.

Adolescence is a difficult time for everyone. Friendships can often be problematic, especially for children with LD. Allegra needed and wanted friends, but she was far more comfortable with adults than with others her own age. I suppose the reason was that she spent so much time with my friends and me and she learned very early in life how to deal with older people. This was easy to understand—if you have been ignored and excluded by children your own age, why not put your best foot forward and go where it's safe and easy?

Allegra was never a classic adolescent. She was never moody. If anything, she carried her childhood enthusiasms into early adulthood and always seemed less mature than others her age. She looked younger, too. She was a bit of a tomboy in those years and always wore her hair back in a ponytail and she favored loose-fitting casual clothes, usually jeans and sneakers and sweatshirts. But I never had to deal with my child being "embarrassed" by her mother. I never had to deal with teenage rebellion. I never even had to listen to heavy metal music because Allegra never lost her love for *Annie* and *The Sound of Music*. When she went to a concert it was never a cause for concern because she only went with Judy Hafker and the only singer she truly wanted to see was Anne Murray.

Judy was married and had a family of her own, yet she was able to find the time for Allegra. They went to concerts and Judy listened with endless patience to Allegra's daily concerns. During lunch Allegra sat with Judy or the teachers instead of with the other children. This happened during the first three years she was at Riverview. She was so charming that the adults fell into the trap and happily allowed her to stay with them. When Rick Lavoie took over as headmaster in 1990, her fourth and final year, he saw what she was doing and knew it was a problem.

"When Allegra was growing up she didn't spend much time with other children," Rick says, "so she learned social skills not as a child but as an adult. She also learned how to use those skills with adults. Many kids with learning disabilities will try to establish relationships with adults because if you make a social mistake with an adult, the adult is not going to say, 'You're so stupid,' which another child might say. What often saved Allegra's self-esteem was her ability to establish relationships with adults because they weren't going to make fun of her when she made a mistake. But this is not a good thing in the end. In the real world she would be forced to deal with others her own age, and we had to find a way to help her with this. We came up with a list of things I found appealing about her, and I said, 'Allegra, don't you understand that these things will work with kids, too? They want a friend who is loyal like you are. They want someone who is sweet. They want someone who is generous and kind and all the things that you are with me. You can take those skills you have learned with adults and use them with other kids.'"

And she began to do it. Rick remembers that it was painful for her and that it took great courage, but she did begin to try to use her social skills with other children. He insisted that she sit with her peers in the dining room and not spend so much time with the teachers. One teacher told Rick, "Oh, I just love Allegra. She stays inside with me at recess and helps me clean my desk." He pointed out that staying inside with an adult instead of being outside interacting with the students was not what Allegra needed to be doing.

He says, "The problem is that Allegra makes people feel so good. I've had an opportunity to meet political people and one thing they have in common is that they are very good listeners. When you talk to them it's as if you are the only person in the room. Allegra has that gift. When I've talked with her I feel good about myself, I feel good about what I do for a living, I feel good about our relationship. She's very good at that, but she was afraid to use those skills with people her own age. She was afraid of rejection. One of the saddest things about children with LD is the feeling that they somehow deserve all the isolation and rejection. Their self-esteem is so low that they think it's fine if someone makes fun of them. They say it doesn't bother them. They think it is their lot in life to be someone that others pick on in order to make themselves feel better. I tell them it's not fine. I tell them 'God didn't put you on this planet to be a punching bag for someone.'

"Allegra's self-esteem wasn't low, but she had difficulty breaking away from her adult friendships. For someone who never had an age-appropriate friend before, giving a child a friend like that is like giving an inexperienced woodworker a fancy piece of equipment. They don't know how to use it. It was also very difficult for us to help her. We came close to closing the door on her and saying, 'Allegra, we can't have lunch with you every day.' No one had the heart to do that, of course, so we continued to work with her and gently ease her into groups of her peers. We knew it had to be done. She had no trouble with thirty-five-year-olds, but it was time for her to be with fifteen-year-olds.

"It was then that she started to make the classic mistakes. All the children at Riverview make some or all of these mistakes. The first we call 'putting out the candle.' She became so possessive of any new friend and so afraid of losing them that if she was having a conversation with a girl named Susan, for example, and the next day she saw Susan talking to somebody else, there would be a huge crisis. She might come to my office and say 'Susan doesn't like me anymore. She's talking to someone else.'

"We call that 'putting out the candle' because they light the candle of friendship and then put it out by being overly possessive. They don't want to share their friend. They find it threatening if the friend talks to someone else. They think they are going to lose the friendship.

"Another problem Allegra had with friendships is what we call 'timing and pacing.' Relationships develop. For example, if a new kid moves into a neighborhood, most kids might say, 'Hi, I was wondering if you'd like to go to the mall with us.' If the new kid says no, then that's that. It's fine. Children with LD will walk up to the new kid and say, 'Let's go to the mall because we're going to be best friends, and I'll give you my bike, and come over to my house tomorrow and we'll watch TV and I want you to come to my birthday, and on and on and on.' They want the product of a friendship. They want a best friend.

But they overwhelm the person. They often don't understand that relationships are a process.

"Allegra also had some difficulty with recuperative strategies.
These are among the toughest social skills to learn, even for those of
us without learning disabilities. When you've done something
wrong, when you've damaged a relationship in some way, how do
you get it back? How do you work it around so that the relationship
can be rekindled? That is a recuperative strategy and as I said, it is a
very difficult skill for all of us to learn. Allegra might make a small
mistake and suddenly say: 'Susan hates me, she'll never talk to me
again. Will you fix it, Mr. Lavoie? Will you talk to her for me?'

"'No, I won't,' I'd tell her, 'but I'm going to give you a strategy to go
out there and take care of it yourself.'

"'Oh, I know what I'll do,' she might say. 'I'll go ask Bill to tell
Susan that....'

"'No, no, Allegra. You can't do that. You need to talk to Susan
yourself.'

"It was hard for her—the natural impulse in many LD kids is to
avoid Susan for the rest of their lives. But in the end, Allegra found
the courage to face Susan and apologize."

I pointed out to Rick that one of Allegra's old school reports mentioned that she often apologized in the event of a dispute, even if she
was not the one at fault. He told me this is also very common. He
called it "generalizing conflict." Anytime there is a conflict in the
room the child assumes it is her fault. If there is tension, they take it
on themselves. This is one reason why children with LD often have a
difficult time with divorce in the home.

Allegra viewed every relationship as being very fragile, as if the
least little thing would end it. She had difficulty seeing gradation in
relationships. She didn't understand that if we love someone and
they hurt us, we don't immediately go from love to hate. We move
down a little bit, then move back up again. Allegra didn't see it that
way. There was so much fear of losing the relationship that she
thought the least little thing was going to make it go away. Rick used
to say to her, "These kids are your friends. They like you. You are
going to make mistakes and they are going to make mistakes, and
you are all going to be able to bounce back from them."

These are all examples of social skills, and the importance of learning them cannot be overstated. The ultimate success of these children
as adults is determined not by their academic skills, but by their social skills. As Rick says, "No parent has ever come into my office cry-

Anne with Allegra at her
christening in 1972

Alessandro with
his sister, Allegra

Anne with Allegra at five months

Alessandro teases
his little sister.

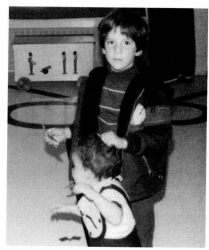

Allegra learns to
buckle her shoe.

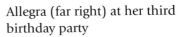

Allegra (far right) at her third
birthday party

Allegra examines the
puppets at her party.

Hugh Carey reads with Allegra.

Hugh Carey backstage with Andrea McArdle who played "Annie."

Allegra as "Annie."

Allegra off by herself
at the Madison Avenue
Presbyterian Day School.

Allegra learns to swim in Southampton.

Allegra with the alligator her grandfather gave her

Henry Ford II on vacation with his grandchildren: Alessandro, Allegra (on his shoulder), and Elena

The three musketeers: Alessandro, Anne, and Allegra

Allegra, center, with Archie Walker, left, and other skaters after a performance at the Ice Studio

Anne with Allegra, Alessandro, and their grandmother, Anne Ford Johnston

Best friends Allegra and Alessandro

Allegra and Anne at a
National Center for Learning
Disabilities benefit

Allegra at the U.S. Figure Skating
Association's Adult Nationals
in New York

Allegra at her final
skating competition.

ing because of low math scores. It is the lack of friends, the isolation, the loneliness of the child that breaks our hearts."

Many of the routines and rules of Allegra's first three years were changed when Rick took over at Riverview. They weren't eliminated but were altered to fit the realities and needs of the students. Sports is a good example. Many children with LD excel in sports, both team sports and individual sports. However, many children with LD do *not* excel in sports, and were threatened by competition. Riverview had no sports program at all. Rick instituted one, but it was one in which the students did not compete with each other. It accommodated those who wanted to play sports and was designed to build self-esteem, not to shatter it.

It was perfect for Allegra. She never liked competition and did not do well when confronted with it—neither in sports nor in life. Figure skating was her one and only sport and the competition involved was directed more toward competing against herself instead of against others. Skating is such an individual activity and does not rely on teams like so many other sports. Even when she participated in national competitions, she did it by herself, alone in the spotlight on the ice. The self-esteem this gave her would have been diminished or perhaps destroyed if she had been forced to compete as part of a group.

Rick explains his views on rules and routines this way: "A school needs to have a philosophy. Once you have a philosophy, you need to have policies that support the philosophy. And then to make your policies work, you need to have procedures. But the philosophy should always be first. What happened here was that there was a philosophy that said that the kids should feel like they are at home. Nice philosophy. The policy that supported the philosophy then became—the dorm should be clean and neat, like home. Good. But the procedure became, you can't put posters on the wall because you're ruining the walls with thumbtacks. So you've set up a procedure that cancels out your philosophy because if a student is here from Chicago, he ought to be able to put his Bulls poster on the wall. When I first came, I made up a list of things that made up the philosophy of the school. And if the school is philosophically driven, it makes decisions so easy. For instance, one of our philosophies is that we're noncompetitive. We don't have the kids compete against each other. So if a teacher comes to me and says I want to do a school-wide spelling bee, I would say, 'I like spelling bees and I like you, but we're not going to do it because it doesn't fit the philosophy.'

"The first philosophical point I made when I came here—I got up in front of the staff on the first day and said, for thirty years we have dealt with 'learning disabled adolescents.' From now on we're dealing with 'adolescents with learning disabilities.' That sounds like a simple thing, but it is very different. A kid shouldn't have to sacrifice his adolescence at the altar of learning disabilities. Why shouldn't they be able to play sports, or like Allegra, go skating? Why shouldn't they have a prom?

"When you tell them they can't have a prom or a first-class graduation ceremony, you are telling them they are somehow not deserving of one. When we were in high school, our parents told us that those were the best years of our lives. Of course we hoped they were wrong, but the reality is that for many of the kids at Riverview that happens to be the truth, and we should make it as memorable and special as possible."

Allegra and her friends thought they had died and gone to heaven when they heard they were going to have a prom. She told me, "Not only are we having a dance this year, but we're going to have a graduation that will be just like Al's when he graduated from Brooks!"

How wonderful it was that she could see no difference. And how wonderful it was that Rick understood that a prom and first-class graduation ceremony would stand out as true highlights in the lives of these children.

Allegra's happiest memories of Rick center around his decision to let her go skating more often. I also was very happy about this, but even then the realities of living with learning disabilities forced their way into our lives.

There was a skating rink about ten minutes away from the school. I was given the name of a skating instructor, and I called her to set up skating lessons for Allegra. The woman was very happy to speak with me and was interested in Allegra's skating history, but then I told her some things might be difficult for Allegra to grasp, such as knowing her right from her left. When she asked what I meant I told her Allegra was attending Riverview.

"Oh, I don't coach those kids."

"What do you mean?"

"I don't coach the kids from that school. And I wish you had told me all this at the beginning instead of wasting my time."

Once again, shocked silence from me, and once again I ended the conversation without an appropriately angry response. This time I wrote a letter. I was furious but held my emotions in check. I believed it was far better to explain that learning disabilities are not a communicable disease and that teaching children with LD how to skate was not going to result in her or any of her students coming down with dyslexia.

I mailed the letter and received a response the following week, the gist of which was, "I don't think your daughter is learning disabled—I think *you* are!"

Needless to say, Allegra did not get the coaching she hoped for. Still she persevered, as usual, and was often found skating on the large rink in Hyannisport, the only one out on the ice.

On a beautiful weekend in May, Riverview held its prom and graduation for the class of 1991, or "Allegra's Class."

Most of her family was there—Charlotte and her daughter Elena, Alessandro, my mother, and I. Even her father showed up.

The prom was held the evening before graduation and it was a beautiful event. The weather cooperated nicely—it was a perfect spring night. Soft breezes passed through a huge open tent set up on the school grounds. Flowers and ribbons and candles were everywhere. A DJ played records and parents danced while their children gathered outside for their entrance.

There was a lot of fanfare. Everyone left the dance floor. All eyes turned to an arbor set up at the entrance to the tent as the Class of 1991 entered. Each student's name was called out as he or she passed beneath the arbor and stepped into the light. There was wild applause from the families for all these wonderful students with learning disabilities, dressed in their tuxedos and ball gowns, huge smiles on their faces and pride in their eyes.

Allegra's name was called. She appeared in a black and white strapless sequined dress, and was beaming as she walked under the arbor with her escort. She was so beautiful that night. For once her hair was not tied back in her usual ponytail but hung straight to her shoulders, and every trace of tomboy and girlish awkwardness seemed to have vanished. Up until then I had always thought of Allegra as a child, sweet and innocent, and completely dependent on me. But that was no child walking across the dance floor in the candlelight. For the first time I saw my daughter as a lovely young woman, still sweet and in some ways still innocent, but by no means completely dependent on me. She was ready to go out into the world.

This was the first prom I had ever seen and it was extremely moving. My mother stood by my side, and I saw that she too was moved. All around me mothers and fathers and brothers and sisters looked on with tears in their eyes as the students filed into the room. What was it about these children that moved us so? Their courage? Their simple and honest pride? Many had physical disabilities and weren't able to dance, but they still went out on the dance floor and had fun. I have rarely been to an event so deeply touching or so satisfying. Fears and insecurities and memories of isolation and rejection were banished for a while. Self-esteem and pride took their place and for once—for once!—these children found themselves the total center of attention.

Allegra was crowned Prom Princess and it was then that I saw how well she had learned Rick's lessons, and how successfully she had overcome her difficulties with making friends. When her name was announced the tent filled with cheers and applause, which grew louder and more boisterous when Rick took her by the hand and led her onto the dance floor.

The graduation ceremony took place the following day. Once again, the weather was stunning. It was all sunshine and irises and daisies on Cape Cod, and the tent was given a more formal appearance with rows of seats and a stage. The students filed in to a recording of "Pomp and Circumstance." There were awards, there were diplomas, there were speeches, and best of all, there was an address by Rick Lavoie. He praised the students' progress, he told us how courageous and special they were. He gave the graduates words of wisdom to carry with them through life: "I wish two things for you," he told them. "I wish you the two words that appear on our letterhead, and on your diploma and on the flag in front of the school. Those words are 'courage' and 'honor.' If I could wish one thing for you, it's a lifetime filled with both. What does honor mean? It means being honest. Giving back. It is important to do well, but it is more important to do good. We can't change the world but we can take one small part of it and try to change it. You have been helped and you've been guided. You've been given assistance through your lives and now it's your turn to return that assistance to those who are younger and weaker than you are. Be someone's hero. The second thing I wish for you is courage. Many people don't understand courage. I had a group of seniors in my office the other day and I asked them what courage meant. Invariably they said, 'Courage means not being afraid.' But that's not what it means at all. Courage means being afraid and doing it anyway."

Alessandro was acting as a producer that day and videotaped the entire event. As I sat down to write this I thought my memory might be helped by watching the video, and it was. I once again saw the candles on the tables at the prom, and Allegra's wide grin as she entered the tent with her date. I saw her white cap and gown and listened once more to the sound of wind passing over the microphone as Rick spoke with such simplicity and such eloquence. I saw the parents seated in the folding chairs, programs rolled up in their hands, craning their necks to catch a glimpse of their child. Charlotte was there, and Elena and Mother and Gianni. But where was I?

Alessandro suddenly panned the camera away from the audience. I wondered why and sat back with a bit of a shock when it came to rest on me.

I wasn't with the other parents. I wasn't with my family.

I was by myself outside the tent, wearing sunglasses, standing all alone while watching the ceremony.

I can tell that I saw the camera come my way, and it looks like I'm about to make an attempt to say something witty...but I don't. Or can't.

I look calm and composed, but seeing myself like that brings back another memory of that day that I had forgotten. The fact that I had forgotten it is a bit surprising—it is the same memory I have of every graduation ceremony, of every moment of change in my daughter's life.

I see my serene unruffled exterior, but I know full well that inside I was churning with fear and once again asking, "What now? What now?"

I wanted to go off on my own, much farther from the tent, somewhere I could be by myself and give vent to those feelings I could never seem to shake—insecurity, uncertainty, fear of the future—all brought on by that everlasting question: "What is going to happen to my daughter?"

As I stand there, motionless, another figure enters the video frame. She comes up beside me without a word, wraps my arm in hers and stands beside me to watch the ceremony unfold.

It is my mother.

Chapter 13
Threshold

after that I went to a program called lesley in boston
and the program was for young adults with learing disabilite.
I meet 2 very special staff members and they are jane carol
and ms. Arlyn roffman. I became close to them both. I
Had graduated in '93.

—E-mail from Allegra Ford

Many people were surprised that Allegra wanted to go to college. They seemed shocked by the notion—"She's going to *college*?" My answer always gave them pause.

"Why shouldn't she?"

Neither Allegra nor I saw any reason to end her education at high school.

We looked at several colleges and universities with programs for adults with learning disabilities. We knew of a two-year program called Threshold, which was based at Lesley College (now Lesley University) in Cambridge, Massachusetts, but Allegra didn't think she wanted to go there. Many of her Riverview classmates were planning to attend Threshold but Allegra—bravely, I thought—felt she wanted a complete break with the past. She wanted to start a new life in a school where she didn't know anyone. At least, that's what she thought she wanted. We went to Chicago to look at a program at Pace University. Once she saw how far from home she would be, she changed her mind. She then thought she might try to find something a little closer to New York.

I believed Threshold was a better choice because she already knew some of the students who would be there. She wouldn't have to go through the difficult ordeal of stepping into a new environment with no familiar faces. So without her knowledge, I sent her transcripts to Arlyn Roffman, the director. Arlyn had specific criteria for admitting students to the program. In general, they have reading and writing skills ranging from the fourth to seventh grade levels. Math skills are usually somewhat lower. Most students fall into the low-average range on the IQ tests. They were also looking for emotional stability in the students. They determined this through references and through a series of questions asked in the evaluation.

But what about a student who tested even lower than most of the applicants? Would they still take the time for a personal meeting and evaluation even though it is clear there was no way the student would be qualified? Allegra's case put their admissions process to the test.

On the basis of the transcripts alone, Arlyn's initial negative response was justified. "Allegra tested lower than most of the others," she told me, "and I'm genuinely worried that she would be too challenged here and become frustrated. I'm sure you understand that we don't want anyone to walk away from Threshold with a sense of failure."

"Yes, I understand that. I really do. But will you please meet her? I understand that you meet all the applicants."

"No, we only meet those applicants who we feel are best suited for our program. It's all based on the transcripts."

Arlyn was trying to be as diplomatic and gentle as possible, but I couldn't give in. "I understand your concerns," I said, "and I appreciate them. Her transcripts tell one story, but if you meet her you'll see that she can do it. I know she can."

"Her academic skills are very low."

"Yes, I understand that, too. But even so, I hope you'll give her a chance. If you meet her, you'll know she can do it."

I now faced the prospect of convincing Arlyn to accept Allegra, and Allegra to accept Threshold. There was a great deal of discussion between myself and Allegra, with her almost saying yes, then saying no, then telling me she would think about it, and finally agreeing to give it a chance.

Now for Arlyn. I set up an appointment to bring Allegra to Threshold, and when she walked into Arlyn's office she poured on the charm. "Oh, I love that dress," she told Arlyn and asked her where she got it. It was all very comfortable and lighthearted. Without realizing it, Allegra was doing what she knew how to do best. She had tremendous social skills and a presence about her, and most of all, she was extremely motivated.

After the interview Arlyn agreed to accept Allegra into the program but on a probationary basis. "We'll give her until Christmas," she said. "If there isn't any improvement, or if she is obviously not able to keep up, it really would be unfair to her to allow her to stay."

I grabbed at the chance. Allegra and I had experienced this situation before. Each time she surpassed all expectations. I was sure she would do it here as well.

"Thank you, Arlyn," I said, greatly relieved, though I knew she still had very serious reservations.

So now we knew what was in store for us the following autumn. But what about the summer? By this time, at age nineteen, she was well beyond Camp Northwood and had spent a summer at a skating camp in Pennsylvania. I thought she might want to return there this year, but she had heard of a new summer skating program in upstate New York. I called and asked for the brochures and a list of skating coaches. There were over twenty coaches to choose from. I randomly chose the name of Tammy Lalande and called her to inquire about the program.

"My daughter is a figure skater," I told her, "and she's very interested in your summer skating camp. Would you be interested in coaching her?"

"How experienced is she?" Tammy asked.

I gave her a brief history of Allegra's training and accomplishments and then said, "But there's something you need to know up front. Allegra has learning disabilities."

"That's fine," she said casually, and I knew that she had no real idea what a learning disability was. Like most people, Tammy's first and only thought was of dyslexia, and she couldn't imagine how reversing letters when reading could possible affect a person's skating. Once Tammy agreed to be her coach, I made arrangements for Allegra to live with a group of skaters in a house owned by Michael James, another skating coach at the camp. I loved the idea of skating camp. Allegra was certainly used to living away from me by this time, and I thought it would be a wonderful way for her to be around friends and others with similar interests. There was no longer any point in hoping for the same from Southampton.

I took her up to the small town in the mountains. Michael's house was enormous, but it still proved to be a little small for his needs. It could easily have housed ten skaters, but he took on about thirty that year. As usual, I was the only one distressed about the living conditions. There was only one bathroom for thirty girls! Allegra didn't mind. She assured me she was going to love it there, but as I got in the car to leave, the usual parting scene took place. Crying on both sides. Promises to call every day, every night. Astonishingly, this *never* got any easier.

We finally calmed down and separated, and I promised to come see her as soon as I could.

Little did we know how soon that would be.

I received a call from Tammy the following day. Of course, I assumed she called to tell me that "Allegra tries very hard, *but...*" and I was surprised that it was coming so quickly. They hadn't even had a full day together.

But that wasn't what the call was about. That morning Tammy and Allegra met on the ice for her first time. Several skaters were already on the rink doing warm-ups before class. Allegra joined them for her practice sessions. A girl skated toward her, backward, preparing for a jump. Allegra tried to get out of her way. The girl didn't see her. She leaped and turned—Allegra called out, but it was too late.

The girl came down. Her skate caught Allegra on the knee. It was one of the worst cuts Tammy had ever seen.

Allegra was rushed to the hospital. She had to have 148 stitches in her knee.

Her summer at the skating school came to an end. She promised Tammy she would return that season, but it wasn't meant to be. She would not be back for a full year. She spent the rest of the summer recuperating in New York and, on occasion, out in Southampton. Time flew by and before we knew it, she was off to the Threshold Program at Lesley College.

Allegra's academic weaknesses were counterbalanced by her social and emotional strengths. Emotional stability was important at Threshold. Working toward independence is very exciting for a young person with learning disabilities, but it can also be very stressful. Threshold was looking for students who could come into the program without falling apart.

Allegra was still very naïve and somewhat young in her psychological development. She looked years younger than her actual age. Her thinking was very black and white, especially when it came to relationships with her peers. These were some of the same challenges she had faced at Riverview—the tendency to gravitate toward an older person and difficulties connecting in a meaningful way with others her own age.

In her first year she took an overview of the two vocational courses offered back then: early childhood studies and human services. These were accompanied by courses in independent living skills, which included classes in apartment living, adult sexuality, personal finance, consumer education, and current events. Other courses focused on social and psychological development, including social skills, and one course was specifically designed for students to understand their own learning disabilities.

Her first year went by without a hitch. She fell right into the new pattern of living and very quickly found a new adult to replace Judy Hafker and Rick Lavoie. This was Jane Carroll, a teacher of independent living skills. Allegra became very attached to Jane, and the pattern of establishing a close bond with an older adult was continued.

In her second year, she signed up to be part of a group called the speakers bureau. Jane was convinced that most people did not understand what a learning disability was and she felt the best people to explain it were those with LD themselves. The students talked about the Threshold Program, their own disabilities, and how they viewed their connection to the main campus at Lesley College. It could not have been easy for those students to get up in front of a group of strangers and talk about themselves in such an open, honest way. Jane made it easy by asking the first questions. The students were free to answer or not answer, depending on their comfort level. The audience was then free to ask any question they wanted, always with the understanding that the student did not have to answer. The presentations began on the Lesley campus, then moved on to Boston University, and eventually out into the wider community to students in public schools.

At one event in a public school in Framingham, Massachusetts, Allegra stood up and talked about her skating. She always talked about skating and was obviously very proud of her accomplishments. She was comfortable with her audiences and was even able to joke with them. After the speech, Jane asked the audience members to write to Threshold to share their thoughts about what they learned. One little girl sent a letter addressed to Allegra. Inside was a drawing of a skater. Allegra kept the picture for many years.

After the two years at Threshold, her teachers and I decided that Allegra really wasn't ready to live on her own. She entered Threshold's Bridge program, which was designed for graduates who need to strengthen their vocational or social skills prior to making the move to their own apartment and career. I was relieved: it gave me an additional year before I had to deal with the "Now what?" ordeal, especially since there really was no further educational path we could follow. This was the end of the line for structured living. After Threshold, she would be on her own and the thought of that terrified me.

During the Bridge year, Allegra still lived on campus, but her main focus was on her position as a teacher's aide in a day care center.

Jane Carroll and Carol Noveck, the coordinator of career services, worked very closely with Allegra that year. "It was her internal sense of self that I remember most," Carol told me. "Whatever she did, she carried herself with grace. It was feminine, but she was not a weak little girl. It was a sense of herself as a growing young woman. She was so gentle and so delicate, though she was physically very strong. There was also a delicacy about her interactions with people and with children. She was so kind and patient and gentle."

It was clear to everyone that Allegra was best suited to working with small children. Most of the sites used for the Bridge program had a great deal of exposure to Threshold students. Carol cultivated them over the years and everyone involved knew what to expect. It was different for Allegra. Her site was a new one, untried and untested. The director was Rosemary O'Neil, and Carol felt that placing Allegra with her would be a good personal match.

The center was in a church basement. Rosemary had no real understanding of learning disabilities. She had taught a few children through the years with learning problems, but had no experience with an adult with LD. But she agreed to take Allegra on and, as was true at all the sites, agreed to treat her as another member of the staff. In the beginning, Allegra was unsure of herself and had to be supervised quite closely. Her first jobs were simple maintenance jobs, setting up cups for juice or getting the paints organized, but even here she was unsure of her abilities. She wanted to do everything perfectly. Carol explained to Rosemary that Allegra was a very hard worker but needed a lot of direction. "You can't say 'Okay, go do the project.' It has to be broken down into small bits, and each one has to be explained clearly." Allegra reviewed each step, convinced herself she could do it, and it wasn't long before she was perfectly capable of performing whatever job she was given.

When the time came for her to work closely with the children she was much more confident. She had a wonderful rapport with them. All the students at Threshold are taught to let the children come to them, to not rush in. On Allegra's first day at the center she sat down by herself at a table and one little boy marched right over and sat down beside her. She was thrilled by that. Carol says, "Allegra has a terrific ability to hold back and wait. She is appealing and soft looking, and her voice is soft, so they never felt overwhelmed by her. She also has a nice feel for playing with them, but she was never childish. She never became one of the kids. Unfortunately some of our other students did that. The only trouble was that she didn't like to set limits. She had some difficulty with very rowdy children. Our students aren't taught to say, 'No,' but to redirect the child by saying something like, 'How about playing with this instead?'

"Allegra had some trouble with that, but she did really well working with children who were complicated in other ways. She was able to relate to and draw out children who were less overt, less assertive, or the shy child who needed a little extra attention."

When the year ended, there was a great deal of discussion about Allegra staying on for a fourth Transition Year. I wanted her to. Jane and Carol wanted her to. So did Arlyn who, by this time, had become one of Allegra's greatest champions and exhibited great faith in her abilities. They all believed she could benefit by living in an apartment with some supervision, and Carol was quite certain the day care center would hire her. But Allegra's newfound independence asserted itself.

She wanted to return to the ice, where she was happiest.

Arlyn was concerned that she would backslide a bit, that she would rely too much on her skating coach and not be quite as socially independent. I listened to what Arlyn said. Her advice to me was always accurate, and I trusted her completely. She was an extremely wise woman and always had Allegra's best interest at heart.

Still, the fact was that self-determination was what we had been struggling for all along. I was convinced that Allegra had to take a large role in planning her own future.

She knew what made her happy and she knew where she could find it.

At the graduation ceremony, she stood before a large crowd to give a speech she had worked on for weeks.

She stepped up to the microphone, but she couldn't do it. It was exactly like her graduation at Gateway so many years before when she couldn't get through "Put on a Happy Face." She began to cry after saying only a few words, and then cried so hard she couldn't finish the speech at all. She knew she was leaving school for the very last time and was stepping into the real world. I'm sure she had mixed feelings about all of this. For Allegra, the two worst aspects of every school she attended was her reluctance to go there in the first place, followed years later by her greater reluctance to leave.

As always, she is still in contact with her teachers. I asked Arlyn what lasting impression she has of Allegra, and she said, "I learned a lot from her. She taught me a lot about determination, and how it can make a big difference. In the beginning, I felt that she was limited based on the numbers and tests. Because of her motivation, though, she plodded right along and absorbed much more than I expected. I'll even go so far as to say Allegra changed my thinking about certain things. We recently had a student come to us with really low numbers and her mother said, 'I want you to meet her.' We said, 'The numbers indicate she is a young woman with mental retardation, and we think it is a mistake to let her come here.' Her mother insisted that we at least meet her, and I thought back to Allegra and how we very nearly made the wrong decision with her. I met with the young woman, and once again, saw that the test results were no longer the only appropriate criteria for acceptance into Threshold. We learned that from Allegra, and from that day on we have changed our way of thinking. We have learned to look beyond the numbers."

Allegra also looked beyond and wondered where her life would go from there. At Threshold, she had an organized life, something I cherished for her, but it was once again time to move on. The unfortunate thing was that there were no more programs for her to attend. Most young adults and their parents view the end of college with some apprehension—there is excitement, of course, and a sense of endless possibility; but there is also some fear about going it alone, of flying without a net for the first time. Imagine what it is like for a young adult with LD, and what visions they have for their future. Structures that supported them most of their lives are now to be taken away. So much will depend on them alone. Some wonder if they can do it. Others leap forward with the same optimism and sense of possibility we see in others who have no disability.

Allegra was a member of the second category.

Arlyn recommended, and felt very strongly, that Allegra should stay in the Boston area. She could find a job there and be with her classmates and remain close to a support network made up of friends and former teachers. I wanted the same. Nearly everyone recommended that she stay in Boston and continue on without a break in the life that was formed for her.

The only person who did not feel this way was Allegra.

Chapter 14
Ice

*my mom called about a pro skating coach named Tammy
and said my daughter is willing to take lessons from you. So
off we went and the next day I meet my pro tammy. We
talked as the ice was being cleaned and she asked me what
are you working on? So I said spins, jumps, so tammy said ok
lets see what you can do and ill take it from there.*

—E-mail from Allegra Ford

"Can she do this?" I asked myself over and over again. "Can she live
on her own, without teachers, without longtime friends, and without
me?" Sometimes my answer was a resounding "Yes," but then my optimism would be undercut by doubts and fears that were too in-
grained to be easily dismissed.

I spent so many years believing that Allegra was limited in some
way (even as I fought against those same beliefs), and I found it very
difficult to change my thinking overnight. I longed to believe she was
perfectly equipped to handle life as an independent adult. And I
wanted to believe this easily and naturally, as though I had no reason
in the world to doubt the truth behind it.

I would have loved to tell people that she was living in upstate
New York, implying, "And she is happy, and has a great job, and will
someday be married with children." Instead, my tone betrayed my
fears: "She's living upstate," I would say, but the thought behind the
words was, "but I'm worried about her because I don't know if she'll
be able to get by on her own, and I don't know if she has friends,"
and on and on.

She went to the skating camp that summer and moved back in
with Michael James, one of her skating coaches. When the summer
was over, she got her first real job. Her advisors at Threshold were
very helpful. They advised her to build on the skills she learned at the
day care center in Boston. She began a part time job as a teacher's as-
sistant at a parochial kindergarten, and would stay in that job for two
years.

She also stayed on at Michael's house after all the summer skaters returned home. Michael traveled a lot so Allegra spent a great deal of time alone in that rambling house. That bothered me more than anything else: I used to lie in bed in New York, thinking of her all by herself in that huge house. I was worried about fire, worried about someone breaking in. Allegra, as always, didn't mind it at all, but to please her distraught mother, she agreed to move into a small apartment. She decorated this new apartment on her own, picked out the colors, the furniture, the pictures on the walls. It was lovely, very close to a beautiful lake, and within walking distance to town. I also hoped she would find a roommate. It wasn't long before one of her coworkers at the kindergarten showed an interest and moved in with her.

Now we were both happy. Allegra was where she wanted to be and was living in a way that made me comfortable. But I wondered: will I ever truly get over these worries? Will there ever be a day when I do not think of her and wonder if she is all right? As the years pass, I realize the answer to those questions is "no." I will never have another day when I do not wonder and think about Allegra's future.

One of the truly comforting facts of her life outside of school was that she surrounded herself with people who cared about her. Her coach, Tammy Lalande, has become like a sister to her. It hasn't always been easy for Tammy. She was the first teacher Allegra ever had who'd had no experience with learning disabilities. And why should she? She was a skating coach. Every other teacher, from Gateway through Windward, Riverview, and Threshold, was an expert in LD and understood what it meant to have LD. For Tammy, this was a new, sometimes distressing, experience. She could easily have given up. I think of the skating coach in Hyannis who told me, "Oh, I don't coach those people." It's such an easy way out. Tammy was open-minded enough to give her a chance.

That summer, when they met on the ice for the first time since Allegra's accident, Tammy had almost forgotten our initial conversation when I told her about the learning disabilities. She was unaware of the many ways LD can be defined and affect a person so, as she says, "I gave it little attention." Allegra was asked to set goals for the four weeks of the skating program. She decided her goals were to learn new skating skills and incorporate them into a two-minute program. She also wanted to perform the program in a recital at the end of the four weeks.

"I thought this was reasonable," Tammy remembers. "I still didn't know her that well. I only had that one day with her before she was cut so badly by the other skater, and still did not realize the extent and severity of her learning disabilities. I thought we would have no problem achieving her goals. I began to choreograph a program to music that Allegra chose for herself. Within a few minutes I realized that her goal and my job were to be far more challenging than I ever could have imagined."

That first lesson went very slowly. Allegra couldn't seem to understand Tammy's instructions. "Why isn't this working?" Tammy wondered, still not putting it down to a learning disability. Allegra listened politely to every instruction, but it was obvious that Tammy wasn't reaching her, either through her words or her visual demonstrations, and her frustration began to mount. "I felt incompetent," she says. "My ego was bruised. As we parted, I remember thinking 'I can't do this.' And I'm embarrassed to admit it now, but I believed that my coaching skills and time would be best spent with my competitive skaters."

Tammy even considered making a phone call that evening to give me her version of The Inevitable But.

Instead, she chose to accept the challenge. As she says, "There is no doubt that Allegra's learning disability tested my patience, my competence as a professional, and worse, my pride. Still, I felt I had made a commitment, and I decided to bite the bullet and finish the four weeks. Allegra's challenges became mine. I felt that her inability to learn was because of my failure as a coach. I felt threatened by her learning disability. And I realized that for me to give up on her would have been to give in to my own fears and sense of inadequacy."

Off the ice they enjoyed their time together very much. Tammy began to appreciate Allegra's sense of humor. "I could always rely on her infectious smile and laugh," she says. Allegra began to send her cards, complimenting her on coaching. I don't know if Allegra sensed Tammy's need for reassurance but whatever the reason, the compliments, the cards, and the smiles all served to help Tammy feel better.

"It was ironic," she says. "It was supposed to be my job to help her gain confidence and build her self-esteem, yet every time we met on the ice I found that she was doing the same for me. When I realized this, I decided Allegra would have the best possible skating experience my coaching skills could offer. I was mentally and emotionally committed to Allegra's success at attaining her goals."

Tammy found herself in the position I was always in. Worrying, wondering if things would turn out all right. And if they didn't, how could she help Allegra move on with confidence to the next challenge?

Those challenges continued. Allegra left her job at the kindergarten and began to work at a local Head Start. She continued with her skating and rose to a level where she was able to compete at an adult national level of competition. Even more impressive, she now coaches young hopefuls on her own. The children love her and she is able to show the same patience and caring that so many others have shown her. She is living the life that Rick Lavoie advocated at that graduation ceremony so long ago: "Be someone's hero. You have been given assistance through your lives and now it is your turn to return that assistance to those who are younger and weaker than you are."

Allegra's family continues to be supportive in every way. Charlotte speaks to her by phone nearly every day. Edsel has a robust e-mail correspondence with her. Melinda is untiring in her support and love. And Alessandro is...well, he is Alessandro: wise and compassionate, a brother, a friend, a confidant, the center of her life and mine.

The last time we were together for a family trip we went to Austria for Christmas, the three of us back together again. I thought it would be a wonderful experience and was horrified when we reached London and Allegra's first words were, "I want to go home."

"But we're not even there yet!"

I could barely hide my irritation. Once we arrived in Vienna things became worse. She started to cry for no reason. We went to see Placido Domingo sing in a Christmas concert at the town hall. It was magnificent and moving, yet there sat Allegra between Alessandro and myself, her arms folded, her mind a million miles away, completely uninterested in all that was happening onstage. I looked over her at Alessandro and gestured with my eyes, "What are we going to do!?"

We went to Christmas Mass and heard the Vienna Boys' Choir sing—it didn't help.

After all those years, Alessandro and I still were taken by surprise. We were angry. We could not understand why she was so wholly and resolutely intent on remaining miserable.

"Maybe we should go home," I suggested, but Alessandro would have none of it.

"I'll talk to her," he said, and when he did, Allegra began to cry. Somehow he was able to look inside those tears and realize something I did not: she missed her home and her friends, yes; but he saw that it was much more than that. She was frightened. She didn't understand the language, the customs, the currency. Nothing was familiar. Nothing reminded her of home. She had left a fairly structured

universe behind and was thrust into a chaotic world, filled with confusion and unfamiliar things.

Alessandro pulled her back from that place. He talked to her,
stayed with her, made her laugh, and little by little, she eased her way
into Vienna. She was once again the laughing Allegra we hoped for.
We visited Salzburg and took the *Sound of Music* tour, and when the
time came to leave Austria, she turned to me and said, "Mom, that
was the best trip ever!"

It was, and it was due entirely to my son.

His feelings about Allegra were summed up in a speech he gave at
the annual dinner for the National Center for Learning Disabilities. I
can do nothing to improve upon his words: "When all is said and
done, I am truly blessed," he said. "I cannot say enough about my
sister. Of course, we have our little secrets, the same as any brother
and sister, but everything that comes out of that golden girl's mouth
is straight from the heart and smothered in love. What a better place
this whole world would be if we were all that way."

Allegra is an aunt now. Alessandro married a wonderful girl
named Kimm and they have a baby daughter, Eleanor, named after
Granny Ford who hid behind the same set of curtains every time
Charlotte and I came over to play hide-and-seek.

Allegra also has wonderful friends. Whenever she comes to New
York, the first person she calls is Ali Halpern, her old friend from the
neighborhood. Ali has stuck by her side through all these years. She
comes to every competition in the city with a bouquet of flowers,
and is always there with a smile and hug at the end of Allegra's routine. And Tammy has gone beyond being a coach. As she says, "The
typical rapport between coach and skater has metamorphosed into
an unbreakable bond of friendship. Allegra is my best friend. It is because of her that I feel such conviction in teaching my students that
you can accomplish whatever you set your sights on. Allegra continues to be the best role model for my skaters and myself. She has
proven against all the odds that she could do what some professionals did not believe was possible."

As for me, I found myself faced with a dilemma when Allegra first
moved away. Could I now return to the life I had led before my
daughter's struggles? My own struggles had changed me in ways I had
not even realized, for I found it nearly impossible to stay away from
the issue of learning disabilities. I translated my experiences, my worries, my pain as a mother into a hope that I might somehow find a
way to be of some help to the hundreds of thousands of others in Allegra's situation.

I was asked to become chairman of the National Center for Learning Disabilities in the spring of 1989. Since then, I have watched the organization grow from a small foundation to the most influential learning disabilities organization in the nation. We have led thousands of parents to the information they need. We have funded and helped guide new research. We have influenced legislation on Capitol Hill. My involvement and my passion would not have been possible were it not for the years I spent trying to help my daughter find her way.

Allegra has continued her life of independence and achievement. She is now thirty, and has decided the time has come to hang up her skates—at least in the competitive arena. She will now skate for the pure joy it brings her.

This past spring she skated in her last formal competition. She was very nervous and excited, hoping to make this final effort her very best. Tammy was also anxious. Would she remember her routine? It was the most complex one she'd ever attempted and was to be the culmination of years of practice and perseverance. To give an idea of just how difficult this was, bear in mind that Allegra was still unable to tell her left from her right. But she practiced her routine over and over and over until the moves came as naturally as breathing. Now it was time for her to perform in front of hundreds of people. Would she be so overwhelmed that she would forget all she had learned?

And now here we are. Sitting in the bleachers, waiting for Allegra to step onto the ice. Today I feel like every other mother. I am nervous and worried, but not over the things I worried about in the past. My worries now are about high marks on her routine, not if she'll find friends or a job or have a happy life.

I have learned to have faith in Allegra herself. She has had a great deal of help along the way, yes, but it would be a sad mistake not to give credit where credit is due. Her dignity, her resolve, and most of all, her endless optimism have been the keys to her finding a happy and fulfilling life.

The music begins. The spotlight hits her. She stands tall and beautiful and full of confidence, almost as if she is telling the world that she has finally made it; and I thank God for giving me Allegra and allowing me the deep satisfaction and pleasure of watching her reach beyond what I once thought was possible.

"How many people have thought you incapable of this?" I wonder as I watch her skate across the arena. "Yet how many have learned from you, Allegra? How many have had their opinions changed and their outlook broadened? We'll never really be able to tell. But this we do know—it is all due to you."

For two full minutes she jumps, she glides with speed and elegance across the ice. The music reaches its climax and Allegra spins into the light. Ice chips fly, and we leap to our feet, applauding, as she ends her routine and lifts her arms in triumph.

An Epilogue:
It Can Be Done

you are the best from the west and dont ever forget that
annie —legs [Anne's nickname for Allegra]
—E-mail from Allegra Ford

In 1989, after Allegra went away to Riverview School, I found myself alone in my apartment for the first time. My interests, my passions, my entire life (whether I liked it or not) had been consumed by the long slow journey from denial to acceptance of my daughter's learning disabilities. I was a changed person and would never again be able to live a day without being affected by my experience. The question then was, "What shall I do now?"

It was then that I was asked to join the board of directors of the National Center for Learning Disabilities. Within months I was elected to serve as chairman of that board. I had the honor to serve in that capacity for twelve years.

During that time I was inspired in so many ways by the countless people I met who are as passionate about the issue of learning disabilities as I am. There have been controversies, there have been struggles, but overall, I doubt that there is a more committed group of people than the army of teachers, researchers, public policy experts, and, most importantly, concerned parents who fight daily for the millions of children with learning disabilities.

So much has happened over the last decade, with so many advances in all areas from public awareness to new research, and it is heartening to me to know that young parents today have so many more resources available to them.

One difficulty that remains however, and the main reason that I decided to write this book, is that many parents are still reluctant to seek out help. That resistance, coupled with the still prevalent stigma attached to LD, is a stumbling block for many and often stands in the way of a child receiving the help needed.

The resources are there, the structure is there, the caring people are there: everything is ready to go for the parent who reaches out. There is no shortage of parents who take an active role in their child's education, but there is also no shortage of parents who do not realize that help is available. These are parents who still do not understand LD, who may believe the school-yard taunts that their child is simply lazy or stupid. They may know something is wrong, but they do not have the first clue about what to do. They stand beside their child and see with their own eyes that there is a problem, but they are so frightened by what they see that their ability to accept truth for what it is breaks down completely. They need to be led to acceptance before they will ever see the need for help.

Allegra's entire life has been exposed in these pages. I struggled with that reality and wondered how fair it was to document every difficulty and failure she had as a child. But I realized that every difficulty and every failure has been balanced by determination and success, and I knew that Allegra, in all her complexity, embodies so many of the issues and concerns faced by every child with LD. By telling her story, I hoped I could tell the story of so many others.

I would never have done this without her full cooperation. In the beginning, when we first discussed the idea of a book, she was understandably reluctant. I decided not to go ahead with the project, and when I told her that, she sat back and thought for a moment, then said, "Mom, do you think a book would help people?"

"That's what I hope, Allegra. You remember what we went through. I think our book might help some people avoid all those problems."

"Then I think you should do it," she said.

How brave my daughter is!

I have come to realize that such bravery is a common attribute of people with learning disabilities. Our culture is filled with images that tell us what is means to be "brave." We have superheroes. We have lone defenders of truth and justice. We have a hundred different idols to show us how courageous we are as a country and a society. But for quiet bravery, the day-to-day bravery of living in a complex world, my vote goes to people with learning disabilities.

I now understand Rick Lavoie's concept that the definition of courage is being afraid to face your challenges but facing them anyway. Children with learning disabilities go to school day after day, knowing they are entering an arena filled with language and numbers and abstract concepts they may not understand, but they do it anyway. Adults with LD understand the challenges they face simply by going from one part of a city to another, yet they go out and face those challenges. When I watch Allegra speed across the ice and take a quick turn and suddenly become airborne, I can't help but admire the determination and bravery that are present in every leap.

Parents can take their cue from their own children. Our sons and daughters are examples for us all. Yes, there are school bureaucracies to deal with. Yes, there are neighbors and friends who will not understand. Yes, there are endless visits to doctors and testing facilities and, yes, there are walls of denial within ourselves and pain so deep and profound we cannot imagine a way out of it. But it can be done. With help, with guidance from professionals, and most of all, with the love of a committed parent, every child can break through the challenges of LD and live a happy and productive life.

But parents must reach out. They must be vigilant at all times. They must go to bat for their child. It is a long struggle, sometimes made bearable only by the realization that you are not alone and that your efforts will make a difference. Children with learning disabilities are not doomed to a life of defeat and failure. Parents can make an enormous difference in their lives.

I have taken to heart the expression: "God may steer the boat, but He expects us to row." You, the parent, have the oars now. The help is there: People who understand you are there. All you have to do is row.

It *can* be done.

PART II

Questions Parents Ask

Your First Questions

I do not know the exact questions on the mind of every parent, but I am certain I understand the feelings that lie beneath them all. I had a special chair in the living room of the apartment where I lived when Allegra was first diagnosed with learning disabilities. I used to sit in it and stare out the window at 71st Street, looking at the building across the street, at the trees below, at the sidewalks, but I saw none of these things. I was so caught up in my questions and in my confusion over the questions, that time passed without my realizing it. I could think and daydream and worry and not know if I had been there for five minutes or five hours.

I was afraid to ask most of my questions: "They are too dumb," I thought, "or they are unanswerable." Consequently, I kept quiet for far too long. Parents today are more likely to reach out for answers due to the greater openness about LD and the wealth of information to be found on the Internet. Yet some of their questions still have no answers, or have answers that are so vague that they lead to more confusion and more questions.

One most basic question of all still has no answer. It is also one I have never heard asked out loud yet I know it's there, for to be a human being with thoughts and feelings and strengths and weaknesses seems to lead directly, at some point, to this unavoidable question: **"Why me?"**

I asked it. Sometimes while I was sitting in that chair, the question came with great force, often accompanied by tidal waves of self-pity: "Why did *I* have to have a child with disabilities? What did *I* do to deserve this?" Of course, the answers to such questions (if there are any) are known only to powers greater than myself.

I used to be a little envious of my sister Charlotte. Her daughter Elena was smart and successful. Why did Charlotte have Elena while I had Allegra? What a lovely sight I must have been, curled up in that chair, feeling sorry for myself and wondering what I had done wrong to be tested in this way. All I can say is that whether or not it was a test, those feelings did not last long. I love and admire Elena, but having a daughter who is *not* Allegra is inconceivable to me now.

There are no prizes given for raising a child with learning disabilities. No one is going to come to you and give you a "Best Parent" award. There aren't going to be many term papers hanging from a magnet on the refrigerator, with "A+" scrawled on the top. There are no awards from spelling bees, no academic trophies, and there are very few moments of complete serenity. But when your love runs so deep and so pure, you soon find that simply having her was reward enough; and the question, "Why me?" is somehow transformed over the years into a quiet, reflective: "Thank you, God."

There are other questions, of course, and most are not so profound and impossible to answer. Every day letters come in to the National Center for Learning Disabilities from parents asking for basic information. I was Chairman of NCLD for nearly twelve years, and though I have been immersed in the subject and have met every leading professional in the field, I still believe my role as Allegra's mother has given me the most insight. It is in my role as a mother that I sit down to write my responses to those in need. I leave the hard facts for the professionals. The best I can do is to hold someone's hand and say, "Yes, I remember. I felt that way, too...."

Following are some excerpts from letters I have received, each containing a question common to most parents of children with learning disabilities.

Q: *My ten-year-old son was recently diagnosed with learning disabilities. My husband and I are having a difficult time accepting this. One of the problems is that I can't seem to explain what a learning disability is to my family and friends. I've read some books but I can't remember the definition. It's so difficult to tell people what is going on when I can't tell them what a learning disability is!*

A: I asked this question, too. Every parent asks it, and every person I share Allegra's story with asks it. Even last week, a new acquaintance asked me: "What is Allegra's learning disability?" and my first unspoken response was, as always, "I don't know." I was able to come up with an explanation, but how satisfactory that explanation was, I cannot say. Anyone newly exposed to learning disabilities asks the question and I *still* have difficulty coming up with an answer. The reason is that there are so many ways to answer. The best, most recent, definition I heard begins with something that seems close to an anti-definition. Dr. Sheldon Horowitz, Director of Professional Services at NCLD, told me that the one unchanging fact of learning disabilities is that they are "unexpected and unexplained."

I am attracted to the phrase "unexpected and unexplained" because it perfectly encapsulates the difficulties inherent in any definition of a learning disability.

Dyslexia has managed to stick in the minds of the general public. Almost everyone who hears the phrase "learning disability" conjures up an image of someone reversing letters when they read. It is a concrete image. It has a frame of reference. People understand it. They know what letters are supposed to look like and what they look like when reversed. But what about a cognitive learning disability? How do you explain an inability to understand an abstract concept?

There is no single definition of a learning disability. The only way to accurately define it is to explain the full range of problems encompassed by the term, and then explain that the possibility of accurately describing any specific combination of learning disabilities is next to impossible.

The reason is this: every learning disability is unique. No two individuals have the exact same learning disability.

There is no way to sit down with a parent and *explain* exactly what the child is experiencing. But it is important to tell them something they can hold onto and understand. This is what I came to realize about my situation with Allegra, and what I held onto when I sat in that chair, faced with all the other questions that crowded into my mind.

I needed to know, clearly and simply, what was going on with my daughter.

I was told that a learning disability affects a person's ability to interpret what they see and hear or their ability to link information from different parts of the brain, because their brain is "wired" a little differently. These differences can show up as specific difficulties with spoken and written language, with coordination, self-control, or with paying attention. People can have learning disabilities in reading, writing, math, and processing information. Allegra had difficulties in every one of these areas. Most children with LD can read words, but comprehension may be another matter entirely. Some may be able to read and solve math problems, but they may also need special types of teaching to help them keep up with their peers. Learning disabilities can reach out of the classroom into personal relationships. They can involve social skills and cause difficulty in common, everyday interactions with others.

Learning disabilities are not confined to childhood or to classrooms. They continue throughout a person's lifetime and touch upon every aspect of their lives, from school to jobs to relationships with family and friends. They touch upon them, but they do not irrevocably lead to failure in any of them. Children with LD *can and do* succeed in school. Adults with LD *can and do* succeed in the workplace. And children and adults *can and do* have successful relationships throughout their lives.

One side effect of a learning disability that must be carefully tended to is low self-image. At its core, a learning disability is intimately linked to repeated failure. Repeated failure may be what triggers the diagnosis in the first place, or at least a realization that something may not be right.

Nearly every checklist of signs to look for include the words: "inability," "having trouble," "difficulties," or "failure." Any one of these, if ever-present in a person's life, can lead to a poor self-image. I believe low self-esteem should be included on every checklist for LD. It is far more widespread than the reversal of letters we associate with dyslexia and can create more social problems than the actual disability itself.

Allegra has been able to achieve so much in skating that her self-image is pretty high. Academic failures were offset by her ability to overcome challenges on the ice. Parents should always be on the lookout for something that a child excels at. Sports, art, music—anything. Give the child every opportunity to achieve in those activities.

Another way of describing a learning disability is to say what it is *not*.
"Is my child retarded?"
    No.
"Is a learning disability the same as autism?"
    No.
"Are learning disabilities curable?"
    No.
"Do learning disabilities ever just go away?"
    No.

"Is there any hope?"

Yes. Oh, yes. There is no cure, and LD does not simply disappear (still one of my deepest wishes), but there is great cause for hope. LD can be treated successfully, and children with LD can go on to live happy, normal lives.

Q: *My child was diagnosed with auditory processing disorder and with dyslexia. Are these both learning disabilities? How many types of learning disabilities are there?*

A: Yes, these are both learning disabilities. Learning disabilities are unique to each individual and there are as many different types of learning disabilities as there are people who have them. But broadly speaking, there are three main categories of learning disabilities. Within each are found some of the disorders that may be diagnosed with some degree of accuracy.

The three categories are:

- Developmental Speech and Language Disorder
- Academic Skills Disorder
- Other (My favorite, so typical of the LD field)

They could easily be called: *Concern, Panic,* and *Pain.* Here is a brief overview of these categories.

CONCERN: DEVELOPMENTAL SPEECH AND LANGUAGE DISORDER

Problems with speech and language are often the earliest indications of a learning disability. Linking these problems to a learning disability brings its own set of difficulties, as most speech and language problems disappear on their own or are outgrown. Even persistent ones can be treated with a high rate of success by a speech therapist. Children with this disorder may have difficulty producing some sounds, using spoken language to communicate, or understanding what other people are saying. In this category we find three further sub-groups:

- Developmental Articulation Disorder
- Developmental Expressive Language Disorder
- Developmental Receptive Language Disorder

The first, Developmental Articulation Disorder, is very common. We all know young children who talk too fast or have a little trouble learning to make certain speech sounds. It used to be called "Baby Talk" in my circle of friends, referring to the child who continued to say "crewdriver" instead of "screwdriver" long after the other children got it right.

Developmental Expressive Language Disorder refers to children who have problems expressing themselves. This is the child who speaks in one word sentences or who can't seem to answer simple questions. Again, many of these types of disorders disappear on their own.

Developmental Receptive Language Disorder refers to an inability to understand certain aspects of speech. Young children with this form of LD may consistently misunderstand the simplest instructions. For example, if you ask a child to put the blue pencil back in the pencil case, they may not understand the words pencil case. Adults with this disability may be repeatedly unable to follow a simple set of verbal instructions. There is nothing wrong with their hearing, but certain sounds or words simply make no sense to them.

Allegra had trouble with all three—articulation, expression, and reception. On the surface, she appears to have no difficulty with language, especially verbal expression. But much of her language is on autopilot. She had early problems with articulation, with speaking too fast and mispronouncing words, but much of that disappeared on its own. Expressing herself and understanding others have presented greater challenges. One of her most persistent language traits has been the repetition of slogans or sayings. The official word for this is perseveration. She would fixate on a phrase and often repeat it to the point of driving me, and everyone else, crazy. One was "Sprinkle a little pixie dust." Another was "Attention Kmart Shoppers." Rick Lavoie remembers the phrase almost as a secret code between himself and Allegra, and I understand what he means. I, too, learned to look beyond my initial irritation at hearing the same phrase repeated over and over and came to view it as a way to reach Allegra when other methods failed.

For some reason the film *National Lampoon's European Vacation* struck a chord with her. Chevy Chase played a character named Jack, and for years, whenever I was away from Allegra, she would call and ask, "Have you found Jack?" It was always the same question: "Have you found Jack?"

Once, when I was in Europe and we were missing each other, I was able to break through her tears by saying, "Allegra, I'm still looking for Jack." She stopped crying enough to laugh, which helped the situation enormously. To this day, if I am away from her and she calls in tears, I have only to bring up Jack's name and we immediately reach an understanding and she calms down. Good old Jack is so important to us—if I never find him, we can continue to use his character for many years.

My advice to parents who have a child who repeats phrases like Allegra did is to let them do it. Yes, it can be annoying and even embarrassing at times, but it has the potential to become part of a secret code between parent and child. This can be very comforting. Many conversations between Allegra and myself consist of words, phrases, and concepts that would bewilder any listener.

Allegra did not outgrow some of her language disorders, but most children do.

Key words to remember when you are wondering if a child has these developmental speech and language disorders are *consistent* and *repeatedly*. Every child makes mistakes with language. This is cause for concern, but parents should not panic over an occasional mispronounced word or misunderstood direction. It is the *repeated* pattern of confusion or failure to understand that is the main indicator for learning disabilities.

PANIC: ACADEMIC SKILLS DISORDERS

This category includes the most well-known learning disabilities, such as dyslexia. These are the disabilities of the classroom, the ones that lead to the call from the teacher. While the speech and language disorders cause concern, the academic disorders are the ones that can truly cause panic in a parent. They involve the three Rs—Reading, 'riting, and 'rithmetic—and are so clearly at the heart of academic success that difficulties in any one of them ring alarm bells in any parent's mind. They are:

- Developmental Reading Disorder
- Developmental Writing Disorder
- Developmental Arithmetic Disorder

The first, Developmental Reading Disorder, may be the most prevalent of all learning disabilities. This is where dyslexia is found. In fact, most people do not realize that dyslexia refers to *all* reading disorders, not only the reversal of letters we hear about. Recent research ties reading to the ability to sort out the sounds of the spoken words (which shows how interwoven learning disabilities can be. Reading disorders may result from speech and language disorders which in turn may lead to writing disorders, and so on). Allegra had difficulty rhyming words. She understood the concept of rhyming, but she seemed unable to confine her rhymes to real words. Dog rhymes with fog, but Allegra would also say dog rhymes with gog or pog. She could come up with a rhyme, but not always one that made sense.

She was also unable to sound out words phonetically. What she saw on a page had no verbal meaning for her. When she saw the letter *F*, she did not hear, in her mind, the sound *Effffffff*. She saw a straight line, with two shorter lines sticking out from it. *F* existed as an actual, literal thing—it was not seen as a symbol for a sound or component of a word. *F* was a piece of abstract art, open to any sort of interpretation. Imagine putting several of these "things" together. F U N. D O G. B A L L. We read those letters and know what the words mean. But what if you did not know how to associate a sound with the letter? What if each letter stood out as a thing, an object in itself, unrelated to the word it is describing?

I have often looked at anagrams, where letters are jumbled together in random order with the object being to sort them out and construct a real word, and I have wondered if that was how Allegra first experienced reading. We all did in our earliest years, but what must it be like as an older child to pick up a book called *Great Expectations* and see something as meaningless as "EATRG CXAEPT- TNSOIE"? With help and patience, the letters do become meaningful as symbols of sounds, and the sounds string together to form words, and understanding comes—at least a recognition of a word might come. But what does the word mean? What sort of idea does the word convey? Those are also part of reading, and can be a stumbling block for many.

I have heard that many reading disabilities do not show up until the fourth grade. Before then, children are learning to recognize words and to read simple sentences. "The dog is happy." In fourth grade, the focus shifts from word recognition to comprehension. "The dog is happy because he chases the ball." Allegra could read that sentence out loud to me, but if I asked, "Why is the dog happy?" she would not be able to answer. At that stage it was enough for her to say each word as a separate entity and to be proud of herself for doing so. And why not? It had been a constant struggle to get to that point, and now she was asked to string words together in her mind as she was reading them to come up with an answer to a question far more complex than, "What does D-O-G spell?"

Think about this. As you read this sentence, your brain is doing several things at once. You are visually focusing on these words. You are recognizing the sounds associated with each word, and you are understanding the entire word and then the sentence. For children with reading disabilities, each of these steps is arduous and initially incomprehensible. For them, the various components collide, cancel each other out, compete for attention, and cause chaos. There are ways to teach them how to master this complex task called reading, but for some whose disabilities go undetected, the problem is never addressed. Many rebel and assume they will *never* be able to read. They will give up. For them, the road leads to functional illiteracy. Words will always remain a mystery, *Great Expectations* will gather dust on a shelf, and a life of hopeful possibilities will remain elusive.

What can a parent do?

Children with reading disabilities most often benefit from teaching that recognizes the importance of phonological awareness as a prerequisite to learning to read, which is what is meant when the teacher or parent says, "Sound it out," but there is nothing easy about this. The sounds are blended together to form words. Whatever method of instruction is used, this is a skill that children need to be able to read. Some children seem to master this skill effortlessly, and sometimes even without formal instruction.

Allegra was taught with the phonic system. She still has problems reading, but she would not be reading at all if she had been taught through another system such as the whole language method of teaching. In whole language, the child essentially learns to read in a holistic natural manner with little or no explicit instruction in phonics and the rules of spelling. I know that this never would have worked for Allegra.

There are accommodations that can be provided for the child with reading disabilities. It is helpful for them to use other senses when learning to read: hearing, writing, speaking. An example is to use visual examples or handouts to provide practice and to reinforce instruction. Some children find books-on-tape useful, and parents have shared that they are good ways to build vocabulary.

Finally, the parent can create an atmosphere that tells the child that reading is not a chore. It is not something that leads to boredom. What interests your child? If the child loves dinosaurs, fill your house with books on dinosaurs. Read to your child. Let your child read to you. Use your imagination and create a dinosaur zoo. Make it fun so they'll realize that the best way to satisfy their interest and excitement about dinosaurs is to open up a book.

Developmental Writing Disorder (dysgraphia) is intimately linked to reading disorders and expressive language disorders (another example of the complex web of LD). To write, we must be able to coordinate memory, word comprehension, grammar and vocabulary, and the motor skills to handle a pencil. Problems in any of these areas may result in an inability to compose grammatically correct sentences.

There are many strategies with which to help the child with dysgraphia. Many children benefit from learning specific skills required to produce a written work, such as a book report or term paper. Checklists that outline all the steps in the writing process can be used. Some teachers will allow students to give oral reports rather than or in addition to written reports.

The use of computers, even within the classroom, can help many with writing problems. Spell check and grammar check are extremely helpful—even for those of us who don't have a writing disability.

Many children with LD are highly creative. If the child is faced with a writing project, you might suggest that they talk about it first into a tape recorder. They can collect their thoughts that way, and write them down later. Another method is to let them draw or paint their ideas first. Creativity clarifies the ideas and helps them formulate them in their mind before they touch the pen to paper.

Finally, it is useful to let the child help with household writing such as lists for the grocery store and letters to family and friends. Take home forms from the bank or doctors' offices, or tear them out of magazines, and let the child fill them in. It doesn't matter what they say—let them have fun. The point is to get them to write, write, write.

That is the best strategy, but sometimes it simply doesn't work. Allegra never really mastered this, but found a way to compensate for her inability to express herself in writing. She buys endless amounts of Hallmark cards and uses them to express the emotions she is unable to put into words. I realize a lot of people do this at Mother's Day or other special occasions, but Allegra does it constantly all through the year. If she wants to express her love for me or for anyone else she will pore over all the cards in the store until she finds the words she wants to say. It's a little excessive (some people get a card a week!), but it's also a very clever way to get around her difficulties.

The last disorder in this category, Developmental Arithmetic Disorder, is something more than a lack of proficiency in mathematics. It refers to an inability to associate actual numbers and their values. Math is full of symbols and abstractions. It is no wonder that so many of us have difficulties. For some, like Allegra, the difficulties have been insurmountable. Math will remain elusive for her. She has learned that $3.95 is less than $5.00, but that has been after years of trying. She cannot handle anything more complicated than that.

Parents can help by making numbers real. Many children do not realize that math is a part of everyday life, and that a phrase like "two pieces of cake" is based in math. Give them opportunities to count as often as possible. "How many forks are on the table? How many more chairs do we need for our dinner guests?"

It sounds simple, but it works. Sometimes the knowledge that numbers are not "out there" but are a part of the child's life can make a real difference.

These academic disorders often overlap. That is why some people can be diagnosed with more than one specific learning disability. Reading, writing, listening, speaking, comprehending, adding, subtracting: what a jumbled mix of skills we must acquire! It is amazing any of us can do them all. It almost makes the possibility of a learning disability understandable.

PAIN: "OTHER"

Finally, there is the last category of learning disabilities: "Other" It is the one I also call "pain."

These "others" are problems that lead to academic or social failure, but do not meet the criteria for a specific learning disability. They are the epitome of "unexpected and unexplained."

These are the problems with social skills, the ones that cause the most suffering, and the ones that are most in evidence throughout a person's life.

These are the questions a child asks over and over again when playing a game, until the other children have lost all patience and move elsewhere.

These are the standing-too-close-when-they-speak problems. The inappropriate-response problems. The talking-too-loud problems. The "loose cannon" qualities, as Alessandro calls them, that lead you to always be on the edge, never quite knowing what will be said or what the reaction to it will be. Allegra still says things that have no meaning (except for me—they may be part of our secret code). This does not mean they do not make me cringe at times. When I am engaged in a three-way conversation with Allegra and someone who has never met her, I am always on edge, waiting for her to say something that completely bewilders the other person. "So are you going to paint your office?" she asked someone the other day. It would have been appropriate and relevant had we been discussing either paint or offices, but we weren't. I don't know why she said it: she had obviously made some connection between something said earlier in the conversation and the need for painting an office. I couldn't see the connection, but I have no doubt it was there.

Some of these "other" learning disabilities may be problems that arise, not because a child has a neurological difference but because they have lost all faith in their ability to do anything correctly. How many times does a child fail before the failure becomes a part of their assumed nature? If two plus two has led to ridicule and accusations of laziness or stupidity, how much real effort is going to be put into three plus three? Does the sense of futility these children feel fit into the category of a disability? In a clinical sense, no. But in the everyday world of a child who cannot understand why the dog is happy, I think it does.

Q: My daughter is having difficulty in school, but I can't tell if she has a learning disability or if it's a behavioral problem. What should I be looking for?

A: There are early warning signs, but watching your child's every move and gathering information about every word they misuse and every question they don't understand is a double-edged sword. Early intervention can make a substantial difference for children with LD, yet there is also the danger of mislabeling a child as having a learning disability when, in fact, they are following normal patterns of development. Nearly every warning sign for a learning disability is exhibited at some point or another by nearly every child. Once again, consistent patterns and repetition are the things to watch for.

It's a matter of paying attention. At different ages, the signs of LD are different. But most parents will be the first to notice that something is not quite right. I say "most" parents, knowing full well that I was not among them. There was very little public awareness of learning disabilities when Allegra was a child. My own lack of awareness, coupled with my refusal to believe that something was wrong, led to many serious problems. My hope is that today's parent can find a middle path between panicking over every minor incident and willfully ignoring the obvious ones. I also hope that increased public awareness and the fact that the term "learning disability" is in common use will help parents settle into acceptance more readily than in the days when no one ever heard of such a thing.

Children with LD often have trouble doing things we think they should be able to do, especially when their peers appear to be doing them better. They start to avoid certain kinds of activities, and may be seen as having a behavior problem. They may even "tune out" and seem a bit "spacey," and may be thought to have attention problems.

Here are some warning signs for preschool and elementary school children that may indicate trouble ahead.

PRESCHOOL CHILDREN

Is the child having difficulty or delayed development:
- Learning the alphabet or connecting sounds and letters?
- Rhyming words and being able to tell stories?
- Counting and learning numbers?
- Learning the meaning of new words (vocabulary)?
- Remembering things that they have recently learned?
- Using scissors, crayons, and paints?
- Being understood when speaking to a stranger?
- Staying on task and paying attention?
- Walking forward or up and down stairs?
- Remembering the names of colors?
- Playing with other children?
- Following routines and simple directions?
- Dressing without assistance?
- Self-esteem issues?

ELEMENTARY SCHOOL CHILDREN

Is the child having difficulty:
- Sounding out words and understanding what is being read?
- Learning new vocabulary?
- Speaking in full sentences and understanding the rules of conversation?
- Retelling stories?
- Holding a pencil?
- Writing with good handwriting, good spelling, and good information?
- Playing with peers?
- Moving from one activity to another?
- Expressing thoughts orally or in writing?
- Computing math problems at his or her grade level?
- Studying and remembering material for tests?

- Remembering routines?
- Understanding what is read?
- Remembering left/right and telling time (and estimating time)?
- Modulating voice (may speak too loudly or in a monotone)?
- Understanding how to play age-appropriate board games?
- Making and keeping friends?
- Self-esteem issues?

If any of these items on the checklists strike a chord, the parent may want to consider medical issues that may have led to a learning disability. First of all: heredity. Learning disabilities often run in families. It is not unusual to discover that a child with learning disabilities comes from a family in which other family members have similar difficulties. Problems before and during birth should be taken into consideration. Substance abuse by the mother, and possibly by the father, have also been implicated. Low birth weight, problems during pregnancy, or lack of oxygen at birth have all been associated with early language and learning disorders. Children who have eaten lead-based paint are at significant risk for serious learning problems.

Finally—and possibly most importantly—there is often no specific reason why a child has a learning disability. Looking back at the medical history of the child is useful only insofar as it may help with a diagnosis, not because it will lead to a cure. I have mentioned this before, but it always bears repeating: regardless of the reason, there is no positive outcome gained by feeling guilty or obsessively wondering if the disabilities could have been prevented.

Q: I suspect my child has a learning disability. Now what do I do?

A: Speak to your teacher and pediatrician and be open about your concerns. Ask if the teacher has noticed anything going on in the classroom. Gather information from your own observations and those of the teacher and anyone else who comes in regular contact with your child. The information should include the child's strengths and weaknesses, both in the school and in other settings. Any strategy that you have provided that have promoted success, whether by accident or design, should be noted. By accommodations I mean things you have done that seemed to help your child learn when the usual methods failed. I'm thinking here of Allegra's inability to listen to a bedtime story until I hit upon the idea of making up stories about her. Another example might be an unorthodox game you made up to help your child remember colors or numbers. You should also meet with professionals who know about testing and evaluation and can advise you on the next step. These include pediatricians, school guidance counselors, school psychologists, teachers, school administrators, and learning disabilities organizations. If the person you approach doesn't seem to know about LD or the evaluation process, go to someone else. Go to *everyone* until you find the answers you are looking for. And don't be shy! You must ask questions, and you must keep asking them over and over again until they are answered.

Another thing every parent should do is use the Internet and organizations such as the National Center for Learning Disabilities (www.ld.org) and resources such as LD Online (www.ldonline.org). There is a wealth of information online.

Once your suspicions have been confirmed and you have found someone who can advise you, you should arrange for an evaluation. These evaluations can only take place with your written consent and are meant to help identify areas of relative strength and difficulty and to determine whether the student is eligible for specialized assistance in school. Once you and the school personnel agree that an evaluation is warranted, the public school system *must* provide an evaluation to determine if a student is entitled to special education services. These evaluations can be arranged through the public school system (at no cost) or through private clinics, private evaluators, hospital clinics, or university clinics.

As for the evaluation itself, it is simply a series of tests administered by a trained professional. Allegra went through test after test, and though the testing may seem excessive or repetitive at times, it is important to realize that the more information there is about your child's capabilities, the better the chances of academic success.

Bear in mind that you may not always agree with the findings or consent to the recommendations. Many parents have told me that they didn't think the tests went far enough, that the evaluation didn't touch upon certain areas of learning difficulties. In that case, request further evaluation or a period of trial teaching and progress monitoring.

Once the testing is completed, school personnel and parents must meet to discuss the results and, if appropriate, come up with an Individualized Education Program or IEP.

And what if the school refuses to do so?

That is the time when you must learn to become a "difficult" parent.

Your Legal Rights:
Learning How to Become a "Difficult" Parent

Q: My child was diagnosed with LD, but his school refuses to recognize the problem. What do I do now?

A: When I first went on the board of NCLD, I used to go into their small offices in midtown Manhattan and help answer mail and phone calls from distraught parents. I was always struck by how much I had in common with so many mothers, but I remember one phone call that really shook me up. It wasn't the common bond that affected me, but the opposite. I'm sure the mother was as loving as any parent, but unlike most, she was completely upfront and honest about her lack of interest in fighting for her child.

I could tell from her voice that she was frustrated and worn down. She was having problems with the school. They weren't giving her child the accommodations she needed. I talked to her about her legal rights and she listened for a while, then suddenly she stopped and said, "It sounds like a lot of work."

What was running through my mind the entire time was that she might have a learning disability herself and not understand what the word "accommodations" means. If she didn't understand that, how could she possibly know what her legal rights were and what she could do to help her child?

"Yes, it is work," I said. "But you really are the only one who can help your son."

"I guess so," she said in a tone of resignation or disinterest—I honestly couldn't tell which. "But I really don't know where to begin."

"If you don't do it, no one else will," I told her.

"I don't have the time," she said. "I work all day, race home and fix dinner, help with the homework for my other three children, and my husband will not accept that one of my kids has LD. He's never attended a school meeting. He won't help with the homework, and always has an excuse why he can't make a doctor's appointment. Why should I have to do it all?"

The conversation ended soon afterwards. Nothing I said changed her mind and when I hung up the phone, it was a long time before I could get her words out of my mind. I was frustrated, thinking I had not been able to help her or give her any concrete answers. I hoped I had said the right things to her. I spoke with one of the directors at the center, and he assured me that some parents simply are not equipped to deal with the problems caused by learning disabilities.

I try to keep that in mind now. It is not easy, particularly when you are passionate about trying to make people understand that they are the last best defense their child has against a life of frustration and disappointment. But the truth is that much of the frustration and disappointment lifted off a child's shoulders through the work of a committed parent, ends up falling on the parent's own shoulders. Navigating through the system sometimes requires a great deal of strength and patience, but it can be done.

Obviously, when I suggest a person become a "difficult parent," I do not mean being an unpleasant stubborn hothead. Remember this: Schools and teachers are not the enemy, and it does no good at all to barge into an IEP meeting like a gunslinger entering a saloon, armed with accusations and unrealistic demands. The difficult parent realizes this and becomes difficult only in situations where their child's education is threatened. Even then, reasoned argument, facts and level-headed determination are the best tools to use in handling such a situation. I sometimes think of this parent as the one that a school administrator whispers about when she is seen in the hall— "Oh no, it's *her* again"—not because she is an unreasonable nightmare, but because she is relentless. These are the mothers who go to the school, willing and ready to listen to advice and teachers' insights, but who are also equipped with evaluation results and forms and doctors reports and who are persistent in their efforts to help their child.

LEGAL RIGHTS

Over the past twenty years, federal laws have been passed to protect the rights of people with disabilities, including learning disabilities. Each state is responsible for implementing the law, and states choose to provide the needed services in various ways. It is important to find out how your state delivers these services.

As always with legal issues, there are many complexities involved and a lot of words and phrases that few people outside the legal profession understand, but essentially the laws protecting children with learning disabilities boil down to two things:

1. *Identification of the Disability.* You have the right to have your child evaluated free of charge by the public school.
2. *Special Education Services.* If the evaluation proves that your child has a learning disability, special education services must be provided at public expense.

Let's look at each of these in a little more depth:

Identifying the Disability

You, the parent, have the right to request that a comprehensive evaluation be conducted by the school system at no cost.

You have the right to have your child tested in all the areas you suspect may be giving the child difficulties. Bear in mind that *identification* of the learning disability and *eligibility* for special education services are two separate issues. Identification is only one step in the process. Eligibility for special education services is determined by a team that may include a school psychologist, speech and language pathologist, or a remedial reading teacher. At least one teacher must be included on the evaluation team.

You have the right to look at all of your child's records and to receive copies of the evaluation results. You also have the right to have the results explained to you in language that is clearly understood. If you do not agree with the evaluation results, you may request an independent evaluation at public expense. Be sure to check with your school district regarding policies for reimbursement.

You have the right to have the school evaluation team consider all the findings from the independent evaluation.

You have the right to request a complete reevaluation every three years, or more frequently, if needed.

Special Education Services

If your child is found to be eligible for special education services under the Individuals with Disabilities Act (or IDEA), you have the right to have your child receive these special education services at public expense. These services are paid for with state education dollars and not by private insurance carriers.

- You have the right to have an Individualized Education Program (IEP) in effect within thirty school days of the date when eligibility for special services was determined.
- You have the right to participate in all meetings regarding the development, revision, and review of the IEP. You also have the right to have meetings scheduled at times that are mutually convenient for you and school personnel.
- You have the right to have an advocate or someone of your choice accompany you to all IEP meetings.
- You have the right to have an interpreter present at the meetings if you are hearing impaired or if your native language is other than English.
- You have the right to receive a copy of your child's IEP.
- You have the right to withhold consent to a proposed placement or program.
- You have the right to have your child receive services that are educationally appropriate and that are delivered in the least restrictive environment. Least restrictive environment (or LRE) means that, to the greatest extent possible, students with learning disabilities must be educated alongside peers who do not have disabilities (such as in a mainstream classroom). This applies to private schools as well as public schools.
- You have the right to request a reevaluation if you feel that your child's educational needs have changed.
- You have the right to be informed of your child's ongoing progress.

I have included a list of organizations that help with Legal Rights in the Resource Guide at the back of the book. I have found that the most comprehensive and up-to-date source of information on legal and advocacy issues is a Website run by Pete and Pam Wright. It is called Wrightslaw and can be found online at www.wrightslaw.com. It is particularly helpful for parents new to the process. Such parents can download two guides, "Advocating for Your Child—Getting Started" and "Wrightslaw Game Plan for New Parents."

TALKING TO THE PROS

How many of us can sit with a group of professionals in any field and speak with confidence or even more, disagree, on the subject of their expertise? If I were to meet with a group of construction engineers I doubt I would dare take issue with their choice of steel girders. It is the same with teachers and education experts. Many of us feel ill-equipped to tell them what we feel is right for our child.

But our children are not steel girders. We know them better than any other person on earth. We know what their interests are, what bores them, what makes them happy, sad, excited, or distracted. We know their strengths and, though more difficult to admit, their weaknesses.

When meeting with teachers or education professionals, give them their due—they truly are professionals and the overwhelming majority are committed to the child's best interests. What they are not, however, is *the* expert on your particular child.

The true expert in the room is you, and it is your responsibility to bring your expertise to bear on the discussion. This does not mean you should dismiss their observations without consideration (another version of the difficult parent is one who refuses to accept reality, including the fact that the child may be having trouble in school), but it does mean you can be an active partner in the decisions that affect your child.

The legal rights I listed before illustrate that the Individuals with Disabilities Education Act (IDEA) gives parents a great deal of input and influence in their child's education. The law is filled with rules requiring schools to accept your consent, to keep you apprised of progress and to provide documentation when requested. But note the words *consent, request,* and *apprised,* all of which imply continued vigilance by the parent. It is the rights vs. responsibilities argument. Yes, the rights are there, but there is no one in the school or legal system who will force you to use these rights to your best and full advantage. The reality is that it is far easier and involves far less paperwork and inconvenience for the school to do as little as possible. But this is not because they are lazy or negligent. Most schools have limited time and finite resources and often are overwhelmed by the needs of their students. Bearing such realities in mind may not be easy, particularly when a parent feels their child's education is at serious risk, but it goes a long way toward helping your child. How? By allowing the parent to help create an environment where the child has the full attention of the professionals on the evaluation team. To do so the parent must be insistent, but respectful; persevering, but not annoying; and willing to inform and collaborate rather than intimidate. It is up to the parent to request or give consent or ensure they are included in every step along the way. Don't rely on a school administrator to call you up to tell you that you should request copies of the IEP or to offer to rearrange everyone's schedule to suit yours.

Emerson K. Dickman, Esq., an expert in legal issues and LD, gives this advice: "Remember that an advocate, whether a parent or a professional, is someone whose purpose is to fight *for* something, not *against*. The most effective parent advocates fight for the child and for an understanding of LD, and they do this to convey an understanding of the child and the child's needs to those with the resources to help."

The best way to do this is to share your own observations about your child's habits and behavior patterns. If your child has trouble understanding your verbal instructions at home, there is a good chance the same is happening in the classroom. Let the teacher know any strategies you have come up with to help your child in problem areas.

A teacher who does not know your child's unique behavior patterns will tend to expect the same work product and rate of learning from your child as they do all the children in the class. For a child with learning disabilities such expectations may be unfair, and the teacher should not be faulted for keeping expectations high.

It is also extremely important to stay in contact with teachers throughout your child's school years. Situations change, skill levels fall and rise, new challenges appear just as old challenges seem to fade: Remember that learning disabilities are with the child for life.

And remember this too: Schools are not the enemy. The chances are great that your first and most effective ally in your fight to help your child will be a teacher.

PART III

A Mother's Perspective

The Power of Words:
Words Should Be Weighed, Not Counted

"The word is half his that speaks, and his that hears it."
—Montaigne

I was recently asked to speak to a group of pediatricians, parents, teachers, and medical personnel, all associated with a renowned local hospital. I agreed before I really thought about it, and once I did think about it, my nervousness kicked in, and I thought, "What on earth will I say? How can I speak to pediatricians? What can I possibly say that they don't already know?"

Yes, I was affiliated with a well-respected LD organization, but that did not automatically guarantee an ability to come up with sparkling insight and profound concepts never before considered by these professionals. I decided at once to steer clear of their special areas of expertise, such as the latest method of detecting LD or strategies for teaching children. I thought the best, most logical, thing I could do was to stress the importance of something that should be self-evident, but often isn't. And that is the importance of kindness and understandable language when a doctor is explaining a child's problems to a parent. Academic jargon is impressive, but the fact is, many of us hear only what we can understand.

The power of words is there at the moment of diagnosis, or even before. It may be an offhand remark made by a teacher or a relative. Parents may already suspect something is not quite right, but may not have the ability to put their concerns into words. For others, like myself, the possibility that *anything* might be wrong comes as a shock. Either way, the first professional opinion a parent hears may sound like this: "Your child suffers from Minimal Chronic Brain Syndrome." (This is only one term, used as an example. There are many others, all of which have been used to indicate a learning disability.)

The parent, especially the one who had no clue there was a problem, immediately panics. "What is that?" they ask. At this point the professional has an overabundance of words to use as an answer, many of them as frightening as minimal chronic brain syndrome. Sally Smith, director of The Lab School in Washington, in her book *No Easy Answers*, lists forty-six different terms used by professionals to replace the words "learning disabilities." Some of them, such as dyscalculia or dysgraphia, describe specific types of learning disabilities. Others such as conceptually handicapped, diffuse brain damage, association deficit pathology, and neurophysiological dyssynchrony seem designed specifically to scare parents or to create a reputation for originality for the inventor of the term. Regardless of the intent, every one of these terms can send a parent into a tailspin of panic.

We all use words every day, and I believe that most professionals choose their words carefully and are sensitive to the concerns of a parent's first exposure to the reality of their child's disability. The trick is to keep that sensitivity in the forefront at all times and to remember that words—both positive and negative—have enormous impact for years to come.

I wrote earlier of the prominent pediatric psychiatrist who told me that, "Allegra is borderline retarded and I think it best for her and for your family to put her in an institution," which was followed up with, "I wish I could help you, but I'm too busy."

I still shudder when I remember those cold, impersonal words from so long ago. They were words. That's all. But think of the power they had!

Professionals need a wake-up call. They are there to help parents understand the truth about their child's disability. Why is it still so difficult for a parent to find someone—anyone—who can explain in simple, clear words what is going on with their child? How many parents hear the term "unspecified"? What on earth does that mean? And what about "borderline"? How close to the border are they, what measurements are being used to tell how far behind they are, and what can be done about it? Even the words "developmentally delayed" confused me. I did not know what they meant. At first I believed she hadn't developed physically. Then there is "borderline unspecified pervasive developmental disorder."

How can a parent break through this wall of words to arrive at a simple understanding?

Words should not frighten parents, or cause confusion, or be so harsh that they shatter all hopes and dreams for the child. Words should provide hope. They should bring on a sigh of relief and help the parent to understand that something can be done to make things better. Words as serious as "Your child is having trouble in school" can bring a smile to a parent's face *if* the rest of the sentence is "and there's something we can do about it to make it better."

Professionals often take it for granted that parents immediately understand what the names and words mean. It's not true and, like me, they may be too shy or embarrassed to ask for an explanation. And it isn't only parents. A couple of years ago a noted LD expert was asked to speak on learning disabilities at the World Economic Conference in Davos, Switzerland. In her speech, she focused on the importance of providing accommodations for students with learning disabilities. During the question and answer period, a prominent businessman asked if accommodations meant "a place to stay." The expert had been referring to special methods of instruction. The man's question showed her the difficulties raised when one assumes that everyone understands the meaning of words.

Parents, educators, doctors, speech therapists—everyone who touches the life of a child—needs to share a common vocabulary. We must use words to agree on what has to be done and we must use the same words to be sure that everyone is working together for the same common goal.

It is such a simple idea, but so hard to do in real life.

Parents are extremely vulnerable when it comes to a diagnosis of learning disabilities. Patience, sensitivity, and clarity cannot be emphasized enough. Learning disabilities run in families. The parents trying to understand this new challenge may also be suffering from learning disabilities themselves. There is also the difficulty some have accepting that anything is wrong at all. I went to doctor after doctor hoping one would tell me she would be all right. After I accepted the reality that Allegra had a disability, I faced the problem of trying to understand the disability itself. I needed words to explain my daughter's pain. Words I could understand and could live with. Words to help me believe my daughter had a bright future.

Many parents welcome the specific diagnosis of a learning disability. For them, the realization that there is an actual term for what has been going on is a great relief. But once again it is the balance of explanation and sensitivity that helps them through this difficult moment in their lives. Professionals often forget or are not aware of the cascading emotions that flood a parent's mind when they discover their child has a learning disability. Unlike chicken pox or measles, there is no cure. A comprehensive understanding of the specific type of disability is often impossible and, as I've noted, many of the terms used to describe it are frightening and vague. There may not always be comforting answers for a parent, but that does not eliminate the need for comfort.

Guilt, anxiety, feelings of incompetence or failure, depression, helplessness, and despair are common emotions at this difficult time. There is extreme frustration and exasperation, often with the medical community or the school, and sometimes with the child. Most of all there is fear for the child's future. This fear is oppressive and long-lasting, and lies at the root of all the other emotions.

Professionals need to dive right in and confront those fears and alleviate them as much as possible. They must not leave parents hanging. They must not be offhand or flippant. Yes, it can be draining to deal with distraught parents day after day, but it is so important to remember that every one of those parents is an individual with a child who is an individual; and what is said at that moment is critical to their future.

If the neurologist who told me that Allegra should be institutionalized had thought for a moment before making that pronouncement, I would have been spared *years* of psychological pain. The fear would be there always, but at least I would have been spared that hideous "What if he's right?" notion that repeatedly intruded into my thoughts.

I presented my speech before the professionals. When I had finished, I wondered if I was too presumptuous. After all, most professionals are caring and sensitive and already understand the importance of comforting a parent. Then one of the doctors came up to me as soon as I stepped away from the podium and said, "When my daughter was born, she had severe jaundice. I'm a doctor and knew what that meant, but I'll never forget my feelings when one of my colleagues approached my wife and said: 'Your daughter won't die, but she'll probably be retarded.' He turned and walked away from us without another word. All my medical training went out the window. I wasn't a doctor anymore. I was a father and I was devastated."

It can happen to anyone.

For parents, it is so important to listen to the professionals, but also to remember you have the option to get a second opinion. It's an option that parents should not be reluctant to act upon. If the words of one professional frightens or confuses you, go to another. It won't be long before you will find someone who can cut through all the complicated scientific words to tell you, in your own language and at your own level, what is wrong.

There is also the Internet. Today, this is the primary source of information about everything, especially learning disabilities.

And parents should always remember this: Even when the outlook is confusing or bleak and the words of the professionals have confounded and confused you to no end, you still have the ability to exercise your own power of words.

There are quiet moments, even in the storm, when all the jargon is cast aside and all the frightening pronouncements are laid to rest. They no longer matter in the quiet moments. Their power is diminished in the light of a parent's words to a child. These words, more than any other, have the greatest impact.

Sit with your child, talk to your child, listen to your child. Forget the terminology, forget the diagnosis, and all the big labels. Speak from your heart, for the words you use to comfort a lonely child or calm a frightened child are the ones that truly matter. They are the most enduring, most powerful words of all.

Homework:
The Battle Zone

Q: I am having so much trouble at home, especially when it comes time for homework. I have two children who do not have learning disabilities, and they feel neglected because I spend so much time working with my son who does have LD. At the same time, I get frustrated working with my LD son and sometimes feel I may not be helping him at all. Homework is turning into a battle zone in my house! What can I do?

A: The word homework often conjures up the image of a mother or father sitting at a kitchen table with a studious child, a Norman Rockwell portrait of domestic harmony and progress.

I have no idea where such an image came from because "battle zone" is a perfect way to describe the reality of most homework sessions, especially when learning disabilities are involved. Homework is one of the few times when home life and school life collide, and the results can be distressing. Few things led to as much personal guilt and distress as my attempts to work with Allegra on homework. She felt inadequate and so did I. Alessandro felt left out at times, oppressed by my unrealistic expectations. My second husband, Chuck, was frustrated by Allegra's lack of progress and my insistence that he go easy on her, even though I myself had given her a difficult time.

I made countless attempts to work with Allegra. I sat down with her at the kitchen table, determined to help her get through her lesson. I knew she had learning disabilities, I knew she would have difficulty, yet I still went in fully expecting to be able to help her. And when she couldn't do a simple assignment or couldn't seem to retain the information she had just learned, I often could not hide my frustration.

If there was a simple math problem, she might not be able to come up with the answer. I gave the suggestion (rightly or wrongly, I don't know) that she should count on her fingers. Allegra counted on her fingers, but then might count the same finger two or three times, which never led her to the correct answer. I then felt compelled to try to teach her how to count on her fingers, and we spent so much time doing that, that the original math problem was abandoned. When we finally returned to it, she might then forget what she just learned about counting on her fingers and we would be back at square one.

But now she would feel she had disappointed me. She hadn't, but my frustration showed, and she read it as personal disapproval. The tears would start then, and I would feel so bad for her and so guilty that I had brought her to this point that I would start crying. At the next homework session, she wouldn't try at all. Rather than disappoint me, she would simply give up before she started, and I could do nothing to change the situation. I wanted her to understand, but she couldn't. The more I pressed her, the more evident it became that there was something that was stopping her from even trying to learn. When Allegra was confronted with difficult situations, she was able to erect a wall that was impossible for me or anyone else to penetrate. It soon became difficult for me to determine if she was having trouble learning a particular skill or if she didn't want to learn. Eventually, I would give up altogether. We went for long periods when I couldn't and didn't help her with her homework. Chuck might try, or a tutor, or a family friend; and they, too, would eventually run into the wall. Then I would take over once again, determined this time to break through and help my daughter learn.

Ironically, as I retreated from Allegra's homework problems, my focus shifted away from Alessandro, and his homework suffered as well. I cannot improve on the words he wrote in an article for the National Center for Learning Disabilities.

"My mother is the Chairman of the National Center for Learning Disabilities or NCLD. Sometimes I imagine myself as Chairman of NCSPLDWDNNHLDT, or National Center for Siblings of People with Learning Disabilities Who Do Not Necessarily Have LD Themselves. Our mission would be to teach parents and teachers of children with LD how to cope with their children who do not have learning disabilities.

"In reaction to the limitations faced by their children with LD, parents of LD children should be wary of expecting too much from their children who do not have LD. I always felt that because Allegra could not perform as a regular student, the weight of scholastic achievement rested on my shoulders. I think I even envied Allegra at times; she had a diagnosis, but what was my reason? In hindsight I wonder if my poor grades were an attempt to divert attention away from Allegra to myself.

"It is extremely important to educate siblings of children with LD as to exactly what their brothers or sisters are experiencing. It was very hard for me to understand why Allegra could learn to become an expert figure skater but met with constant frustration with her reading, writing, or math skills. I saw my mother's heart sink and Allegra's teachers become resigned to their lack of success in helping her to learn. I did not buy that for one minute. But then again, I did not know what a lot of parents and teachers know. So while I was punished for bad grades, I saw Allegra getting comforted. While I was pushed to do better, Allegra was allowed to move on and sidestep the problems arising from her education. To all parents, I cannot stress enough how important it is to allow your other children to share in what you are learning about LD. If I knew then what I know now, everything would have been a lot clearer."

So there it is. This is one area where I must admit that I did not do the best job I could have. My inability to deal with Allegra's homework difficulties was so pronounced I could never overcome it. This, in turn, led to Alessandro's lingering feelings of academic inadequacy. No matter how well he did, I turned all my hopes and expectations—both real and unrealistic—upon him.

This need not happen in other families.

Parents should be involved in their children's homework, no matter how daunting the prospect may be. One way to look at it is to realize you are helping the child learn study skills as opposed to just learning the task at hand.

The first thing to do—as is so often the case with LD—is to throw out all of your preconceived notions of what homework is "supposed" to be. If you have an image of yourself and your child working at the table in a quiet kitchen, but that environment proves to be difficult for the child—be flexible and willing to change your image. Maybe your child is more comfortable spreading out books and papers on the bedroom floor. That's fine. The point is to learn, not to learn at a table. Doing homework needs to be seen as a positive experience, something filled with fun and gentle control.

What is gentle control? It is fighting down the urge to see the child "get it" immediately. It is realizing that your expectations may be unrealistic—don't lower your hopes, but realize that it may take more time and patience than you ever could have expected to see results, and that the results may not be what you expected in the first place.

Sometimes simply finishing the homework is a worthy goal. Try to view completing the homework as a goal—not completing it perfectly.

In addition, parents need to do a bit of homework themselves. Some of their ideas about reading and math may be in conflict with methods used to teach the child. Parents need to speak to the child's teacher to understand homework expectations.

The National Center for Learning Disabilities offers the following advice for parents who want to help their children:

- Show an interest in your child's homework. Ask about the subjects and the work to be done, then follow up the next day.
- Coach your child with an unknown word or difficult problem, but let the child do the work.
- Learn the nature of the approach to reading and spelling that your child is being taught, so your coaching can be maximized.
- Encourage your child to establish a regular time to do homework, and eliminate as many distractions as possible during study time. In other words, turn off the TV.
- Depending on the type of learning disability, consider what is available to help: computers, calculators, spell checkers, books on tape, tutors, etc.
- Try to relate the homework to your child's everyday life. For instance, if fractions and measurements are being studied, have your child prepare a favorite food using the different measurements.
- Make sure your child has an organized bookbag or backpack so that completed homework can be placed inside and not forgotten at home.

Finally, I urge all parents to praise their children for their effort as well as for successfully completing a homework assignment. It is a very simple thing to do, but it is invaluable. Nothing builds self-esteem like praise from parents.

Mothers and Fathers:
Understanding Each Other

Imagine this: you—a mother—have been up since 6:00 a.m., fixing breakfast and the children's lunch, getting them off to school, plus looking after your husband. One of your four children, a son, has learning disabilities. The scene is chaotic. Nothing is in order, there are schoolbooks and papers scattered everywhere, there is food on the table, dishes in the sink, the dog is barking. The children must be out the door in three minutes, and you can't find your son. This is yet another morning where all your attention (which should be divided amongst your four children) is centered solely on him. You can't help but pay more attention to him: he needs help organizing everything. His homework assignment is missing, he doesn't have the right book in his bookbag, he left his jacket upstairs, and now you can't find him. Your other children see this go on day after day and feel you are neglecting them. On top of all of this, today your son is to be taken in for another evaluation. You spoke to your husband about it, but he was distracted. This morning, on his way out the door, he didn't ask a single question about the upcoming evaluation. If you confront him and express your fears, he'll say, "Don't worry about it, he'll be fine." He can barely hide his irritation. Later, on the drive to the doctor's office, your worries about your child are joined by feelings of anger toward your husband. "Why doesn't he understand what we're going through?" you ask yourself. "Doesn't he care?"

This is the man you've lived with for years, who shares your likes and dislikes, or, if he doesn't share them, at least knows what they are. He knows and values your opinions. He knows what you are thinking about most subjects. It is the same for you. Above all, he loves each and every one of his children. There is very little he can do that will surprise you.

Until now.

With the other children, he has always been there, always ready to help with homework or join you at a teacher conference. But ever since your son was diagnosed with LD, you have noticed a certain distance, a reluctance to talk openly about the problem. When you panicked, he could not understand why. When you were in despair, the shoulder you always leaned on was suddenly unavailable. When you went to the one person in the world who knew how to listen to you, he suddenly changed the subject or told you versions of the truth you knew to be false. "There's nothing wrong with him," he would say, and you know in your heart that he can't possibly believe it.

Resentments build. Rifts develop. The relationship can suffer.

Learning disabilities affect the entire family. Rick Lavoie calls it "The Waterbed" and explains the term this way: If an entire family is lying on a waterbed and one person makes a sudden move, the ripples are felt by everyone. No one escapes its effects, especially the parents. When one is up, the other is down. When one feels hope, the other is in despair.

Every mother and father goes through a series of emotions when a child is first diagnosed with LD. I have listed them earlier: anger, disappointment, hope, despair. These varying feelings may be a bit easier to handle if both parents go through them at the same time, but that rarely happens. The mother may be in a panic, determined to do all she can to find the right expert to help her child, while the father is in the middle of a denial phase. He may come home from work and she says, "Get in the car, we're going to New Jersey for a consultation with a reading specialist." He turns around and says, "There is nothing wrong with our son. You are inventing this problem." The harder she pushes, the more he resists. Her determination works against his denial. Or maybe the father is in a grudging phase of acceptance while the mother is lashing out in anger. "Why weren't you there when I needed you?" she may think.

Sometimes a mother is so accustomed to her role as defender of the child, that she is unwilling to give it up. She may not even be aware of this behavior. She may fall into a pattern of thought that tells her that she is the only one who really understands her child's needs. Now when her husband appears at her side, she views it as an intrusion upon her territory. To her surprise, she finds the one thing she has been asking for—his support—is now a threat to her relationship with her child. The father now feels left out, and may retaliate by becoming even more detached or demanding.

What a terrible cycle of misunderstanding and miscommunication! There are no longer ripples on the waterbed, but large, threatening waves. When the couple discusses the child, it is as though they are talking about two different children. Neither sees the problem in the same light, at the same time. It may be the first time in their married life that they are looking at a life altering situation in two completely different ways.

It is phenomenally difficult to come to terms with the fact that a learning disability has entered your life. I went through my own journey with denial—I know how painful it is, how isolating, and how it leads to endless problems down the road. It is easy for me to give advice on communication and acceptance, but would I have listened to similar advice back then? I don't know. I was a single parent from the time Allegra was a year old, so every decision about school, tutors, and summer camp was mine alone. This was all well and good, but there were times when I needed someone else to lean on for advice and support. I went to school weekends at Riverview by myself, year after year, and that was difficult. Unlike most schools, where parents attend football games or plays or concerts, Riverview parents' weekends focused on confronting problems. There were many meetings with teachers. At Alessandro's school, I knew so many of the parents. A good percentage of them came from New York and were parents of boys Alessandro had grown up with. At Riverview, I knew very few parents. It was a difficult time for all of us. At the beginning of these weekends, I was always overwhelmed by the sight of the varying levels of disability. Many of the children were physically handicapped, and all of them had challenges with learning and social skills. In Allegra's first year, I saw that the mothers visited the classrooms and usually dove right in and confronted all the issues. Some of the fathers, on the other hand, remained outside talking. Four years later, at graduation, I was so happy to see mothers and fathers sitting together, proud of their child's accomplishments. It is possible that for once the ripples on the waterbed were calm.

Those weekends are when I really would have loved to have someone to lean on.

It would have been great to have someone to talk to because the answer to so many of these problems is communication. Talk to each other. Talk to experts. Talk to school personnel. Talk to a marriage counselor if it comes to that. Talk to everyone. And most of all, talk to your child, honestly and openly.

And remember this—talking openly and honestly does not mean talking endlessly. It is all too easy to fall into an obsessive state about your child's disability, where every thought revolves around that one issue. Don't forget the other qualities of your child, the sweet disposition, the ability to sing, the love of music—whatever it is. Balance your concern with appreciation for the blessings your child brings into your lives.

On Their Own:
Challenges of Life

I would have loved to give Allegra a party when she turned twenty-one, not only to celebrate her entry into adulthood but also to celebrate her passing successfully through all the difficulties of a childhood with learning disabilities. At the party we would have raised our glasses and said, "Well done, Allegra. It's over now, you have left all your problems behind." But as always with LD, such dreams are only dreams: The reality is that learning disabilities are never cured. They are lifelong challenges. For adults with LD there is comfort in knowing that the often-tortured days of school and homework are over, but now they are faced with new, sometimes greater challenges involving work, independent living, transportation, and relationships.

Parents of young men and women with LD may find the transitional period from childhood to independent adulthood a time filled with concern. The parents were always there for the child, able to protect them from those who did not understand. Now, as the young adult moves out of the house and maybe to a different city, worries flood in upon those left behind. How will they get by? How will they get around? Will they live a happy life? Will they meet someone special in their life? Will they get married? *Can* they get married?

I have had every one of these concerns. I have heard every one of them from other parents.

They begin when the child is very young, as questions in the back of the mind. "I wonder how it will be?" they ask themselves, but the child is still a child. Those concerns can wait. Then the child becomes a teenager, and the future is bearing down. Soon the child is a young adult ready to leave the nest. For the parent, there is no escape. Concerns are now realities, and for many, this is the first time they feel utterly helpless. What was once seen as welcome protection by the child with LD, may now be seen as intrusion. What was once advice, may now be considered nagging. Parents often feel helpless when they hear their adult child talk of difficulties at work or in a relationship. They want to help, they know they can help, but they also realize that their help may actually be harmful—there is a lot to be said for allowing people to learn how to handle problems on their own. At the same time, it is extremely difficult to stand by and watch someone in distress, knowing you have the power to change the situation by reaching out with information or a helping hand.

I still struggle with this on a daily basis. Should I intervene in Allegra's personal life? What is the appropriate amount of help? Am I going beyond simple advice, or am I doing too much, thereby preventing her from learning to handle day to day problems?

Each situation calls for a realistic assessment of how much the parent should do. The level of disability must also be considered. Some adults with mild learning disabilities may need no help or guidance at all. Others like Allegra may need much more outside help.

I have discovered through both observation and research that there are certain basic elements involved with so many issues faced by adults with LD. They are threads woven through a life, sometimes prominent, other times hidden below the surface; but one or more of them seem to find their way into every difficult situation.

They are:

- *Impulsivity.* By this I do not mean the occasional spontaneous purchase or decision to go to the movies, but a constant inability to gauge the effects of an action taken. For instance, many people with difficulties in math may never really know how much money they have in their bank account, yet will continue to buy things at the spur of the moment, mindless of the detrimental effect on their personal finances. Allegra recently booked two nights in a hotel where she would only be staying for one night. She didn't do this because she is a reckless spendthrift, but because the hotel said they only book a two-night minimum stay. Instead of looking for another hotel, Allegra impulsively agreed to the terms. Consequences are often overlooked or never considered at all.

- *Time Management* is another challenge. An inability to judge the time it will take to get from one place to another or when to pay bills or when to meet a friend, can lead to endless difficulties. We all have situations where we are late for an event, but many people with LD have a chronic inability to show up on time. Sometimes this is a matter of organizational difficulties, other times they simply "forget" they were supposed to be somewhere.
- *Lack of Judgment* is another thread that runs through many lives of adults with LD. By this I mean an apparent inability to understand the reality of certain situations; for instance, whether a friend is really a friend or simply an acquaintance, or if the person is actually someone who may be harmful.
- *Openness and Honesty.* The last and most important thread is also the most positive. It is not something that comes automatically with LD. Being forthright about learning disabilities can be the key to solving so many of the difficulties presented by the threads of impulsivity, time management, and lack of judgment. Nearly every problem can be alleviated if the person without LD is made aware of the learning disability. Instead of being irritated, they will usually go out of their way to be accommodating. Instead of growing distant from a friend who constantly shows up late, they will make allowances and even help come up with ways to improve the situation.

With this in mind, I offer lessons I have learned about how parents and their young adult children can learn to deal with the challenges of life. The next four chapters address how these challenges affect the ability of the adult with LD to get around by car or public transportation, manage finances, gain employment, and create and maintain healthy relationships.

From Here to There:
The Challenges of Getting Around

Think of a time when you have taken a wrong turn, or a wrong exit off a freeway, confident in your ability to find your way back. Then suddenly you ask, "Do I take a left here? Or a right?" Before you know it, you are lost. It is a disconcerting situation, and thankfully it doesn't happen all that often.

Unless you have learning disabilities.

That feeling of being turned around, unable to find your way, confused about the direction you should take is a daily occurrence for those with LD. Cars, buses, taxis, and trains present a bewildering set of challenges. A map of a new town might as well be a guide to an unexplored planet. A simple walk down an unfamiliar street leads to confusion.

Over the years I have wondered if Allegra would ever be able to drive a car. For most people it is a necessity, especially for those who do not live in a city, but driving can be a difficult challenge for people with LD. The skills and coordination required seem to be a distillation of all the problems associated with LD: spatial problems, poor hand/eye coordination, perceptual problems, time management, and reading difficulties.

When Allegra was very young, I used to let her sit on my lap and "drive" on the back roads of Southampton. She loved it, as most children do. By the time she was sixteen and ready to get her license, the idea of getting behind a wheel terrified her. I tried to allay her fears by teaching her how to drive in our driveway, but she had trouble coordinating her hands and feet, and became even more frightened.

Allegra was overwhelmed by her own sense of inadequacy. Back then, it was clear that she would never be a driver.

So what to do? I tried to look forward and consider her life without the independence of mobility. How would she get by? Most of us take it for granted that we can simply get from here to there without a problem. But what is it like for a person who can't drive? Who can't understand directions? Who can't read a map?

In New York City, it is easy to avoid driving. When Allegra moved to her new home in the Adirondacks, it was also easy to be without a car. Everything was within walking distance. In her continuing quest for routine and structure, Allegra got in the habit of walking to a small bakery every morning for coffee and a bagel. No matter what the weather, rain, or shine, she had to have her coffee and bagel. It was part of the set pattern of her life.

And it doesn't matter where she is. If we're traveling, and the coffee shop is miles away, she will take a taxi or find some other way to get there. I was with her on one of those mornings. "Allegra, why don't you buy some bagels and coffee and make them at home?"

"I like the way they do it at the coffee shop."

"But it's so inconvenient."

That doesn't matter. It is part of the routine, and she insists on following it, regardless of the inconvenience.

Eventually she realized that the best way to handle situations like this was to overcome her fears and get behind the wheel of a car and go on her own. When she told me this, my own fears surfaced. I was always comforted by the idea that Allegra was not driving. Yes, driving means freedom, and yes, it makes life easier; but it is also one more thing to worry about.

"Mom, I think it's time I got a car and learned to drive." That's how she told me one evening over the phone. Her words were met by silence from my end.

"Mom? Don't you think I should learn to drive?"

I wanted to say, "No way!" I was in one of those difficult situations common to parents of adults with LD. So many years had been spent preparing for Allegra to live an independent life. Now she was reaching out to exercise some of that independence, and my reaction was to prevent it from happening, to protect her. It is still my deepest desire and it is in constant conflict with my desire to see her living happy and free.

"All right," I said quietly, "let's give it a try."

I was oppressed by my fears but tried very hard not to let her know I had any fears at all.

We searched around until we found a suitable driving instructor. I called and explained the situation, hoping I wouldn't run into the situation I had with the skating coach on Cape Cod who told me, "I don't teach those people."

That was not the case at all. The instructor understood perfectly, and continues to work patiently with Allegra, trying to teach her all the skills necessary to drive a car.

On my last visit, I went out with Allegra and the instructor for a drive. It was a lovely August afternoon, and I settled into the back seat, perfectly at ease as my daughter drove me over the narrow country roads of rural New York. Stopping, starting, left, right, foot on the gas, foot on the brake: all the small complexities were pulled off without a hitch, and Allegra was delighted.

"Want to go get a bagel and coffee, Mom?" she asked.

"Sounds good," I said, so proud of her I could have burst.

Allegra has not yet passed the written test, but she has not given up.

As always with LD, there are varying levels of ability. Some people can learn to drive quickly. Others may never learn. Learning disabilities come into play throughout the driving experience. Manual transmissions can present a host of problems, as they can for most of us. People with LD may find it particularly difficult to coordinate the clutch, brake, and shift. There are also simpler issues that many of us take for granted but which may become insurmountable obstacles for a new driver with LD. They may have difficulty judging the response of the steering wheel. Parallel parking can be a hopeless undertaking.

Rearview mirrors may present problems for those with visual perception difficulties. What are they seeing in the mirror? Another car, yes, but is it behind them, in front of them, how fast is it going? There are road signs to read, sometimes requiring quick decisions based on the information presented. They may have trouble judging distance between themselves and another car. Directions using left vs. right or east vs. west can be difficult. Road maps may be incomprehensible. If they have problems with abstract concepts, they may have problems with speed. The numbers on the speedometer may be as meaningless as those on the posted speed limit signs.

These are all daunting realities, but the larger reality is that the vast majority of LD adults are capable and safe drivers. Many understand their difficulties and have found ways to compensate for them. They may go out of their way to avoid distractions by not, for example, driving during rush hour or using cell phones in their cars. They may only drive to familiar locations. If they are lost, they do not panic. Instead, they do the simplest thing of all: They stop, roll down their window, and ask someone for directions.

Getting around involves more than driving a car. In New York City, we have the option of taking a bus, a subway, or a taxi. That option is easier than driving, but has its own set of problems. In each case, money and financial transactions are involved. Simple, yes, but not for someone who has difficulty counting change. There are also transfers and maps and unexpected service or route changes; all of which can make the experience of going from point A to point B a demanding ordeal. People with poor time management skills may have a particularly difficult time with public transportation. They may be late due to their inability to conceptualize how long it will take to get to their destination, or an inability to compensate for the unexpected, such as detours or changes in the schedule.

Letty Buckley, one of Allegra's tutors, helped overcome the challenge of taxis. "I used to give her little tricks to help her along," Letty remembers. "She didn't know how much to tip a cab driver. I said, if you're getting nervous because the meter is high, give the driver a dollar. If it's not a large amount, give him seventy-five cents. Try to make it simple."

Letty also encouraged Allegra to take a cab on her own for the first time. She had never been in a cab by herself, and she was so nervous. But I told her over the phone, "You can do it." She got in the cab, and then Letty called me and said: "She's on her way!" I met Allegra at the other end. She was nervous, but she made it.

Allegra has often taken the train from New York City to Albany, New York. She has never had a problem, though I must admit I went to Penn Station with her every time. I stayed with her through the boarding announcement, and helped her find the right gate. I do believe she could have done this without me, but my overprotective nature and my desire to see her off prevented her from trying.

There was one incident when Allegra was left entirely on her own. There was panic involved, but it was mostly at my end. She was taking a plane from Florida to Albany. A blizzard moved in from Canada that morning, and her flight was diverted to Ohio. Once she was there, the airport was shut down and she was stranded with no flight out and nowhere to stay. She called to tell me the news.

"Oh, my God," I thought. "She's lost in the snow." I started making phone calls, as if that would help. I don't know what I was thinking. I knew someone who knew someone who was connected with the airline, and I hoped they could find Allegra and help her get through this. But I couldn't reach anyone. Meanwhile, as I was frantically trying to find someone to change the weather and get the flight to Albany up and running, Allegra took matters into her own hands.

She went to the airline personnel and told them that she had a learning disability and was having difficulty understanding what she should do. The situation was chaotic. Every plane in Cincinnati was grounded and thousands of people were stranded and looking for a place to stay. Here was a young girl approaching the ticket agent to tell her she had a disability and didn't know what to do. The ticket agent looked at her blankly, probably because he had no idea what a learning disability was. A kind-hearted passenger overheard the conversation and offered to help.

They banded together and managed to find a hotel room, and the next day they boarded the same plane for Albany. Everything worked out fine. Naturally, Allegra befriended the lady who helped her and is *still* friends with her, several years after the episode!

In that situation, as in almost all situations involving getting around, the best plan of action was the one Allegra followed: When in doubt or in trouble, ask someone for help.

Finances:
The Challenges of Money

Wouldn't it be wonderful if we all believed our American Express or Visa cards were simple pieces of plastic that magically paid for everything we wanted with no strings attached? Wouldn't it be great to insert your ATM card into the bank machine and out would come money that was completely unconnected to anything like a checking or savings account? That's like having Christmas every day! Problems only arise when the ATM doesn't give back or the credit card is rejected; but of course, the rejection isn't because there aren't enough funds to cover the withdrawal, but because the machine or card is somehow "broken."

This is Allegra.

Her inability to grasp certain abstract concepts led to a great deal of trouble. Banking transactions, bill paying, credit card disputes: all can be minefields for someone with a learning disability. Technology such as ATM machines and debit cards only add to the confusion. Allegra simply could not understand the connection between a bank deposit and an ATM withdrawal. She had the withdrawal part down fine. She took $80 out of the machine every single time, whether she needed that amount or not. If she needed more, she took $80 out twice. Once in a while, the machine would print out figures to show she had insufficient funds to withdraw $80. Instead of taking out a smaller amount, she assumed the ATM was broken.

I equate Allegra's inability to understand the ATM process to my inability to understand certain technological advances. It's a different level of understanding, but I couldn't possibly tell you what fiber optics do, or how, exactly, we get electricity. These things just happen. I turn on a switch and the light goes on. I click my mouse and I'm connected to the Internet. I have no idea if fiber optics are involved in either of these processes. It is the same for Allegra and the ATM. She puts in her card and money comes out. This seemingly has no connection to the money she deposited in her account the week before.

The most common financial difficulty for people with LD, and one which can literally cause panic in some, involves check writing—especially when having to write out a check in front of someone. Writing the numeric value, first in numbers then as words, and spelling the name of the recipient correctly creates a great deal of anxiety. If at all possible, it is preferable to avoid that situation. Have the check written out in advance. If that is not practical, there is no law that requires anyone to write out a check while another person stares at them. Go to another desk or move to a nearby private area. Do anything to avoid the obviously disconcerting situation of public check writing.

Bill-paying is another difficult issue. Some who have time management problems are chronically late paying their bills. Others may skip a month completely.

Managing money can be a true challenge. Some people with LD are impulsive and spend far too much on an item they don't need, only to find they no longer have enough for rent or the utilities bill. Others may spend money needlessly. Arlyn Roffman, former Director of the Threshold Program, in her book *Meeting the Challenge of Learning Disabilities in Adulthood* tells of one young man who did not understand the letters CR on a bill meant Credit. He paid the CR amount over and over, not understanding why it went up each time he received a bill. Before long, he was spending most of his money on that one bill while neglecting others.

Once again, the answer to so many of these problems is honesty and openness. Anyone with a learning disability who is having trouble should go to the bank, ask to speak to the manager, and be very candid about the disability. The chances are extremely good that people who work in the bank will go out of their way to accommodate the needs of someone with LD.

I made the phone calls on Allegra's behalf. When I spoke to the manager, she expressed surprise. Allegra had taught this woman's daughter how to skate and she couldn't imagine she had a disability of any kind. That is often the root of the problem: so many people with LD do not appear to have a problem, and it is difficult for bank tellers to understand why they can't manage their money. Once they understand the disability, they are generally very helpful.

Employment
Challenges in the Workplace

The issue of financial challenges brings up the larger issue of challenges on the job.

Many people with learning disabilities find that some of the difficulties they faced in school do not end with graduation from high school or college, but stay with them through the job search, the job interview, and into the workplace. For many, employment issues become the greatest challenge of their lives. They are no longer surrounded by teachers who understand LD or friends and classmates who share many of the same difficulties. Now they are in the real world, with employers who may have no exposure to LD and coworkers who expect them to carry their own weight. Some may be unable to find challenging and satisfying jobs that help them reach what they perceive to be their true potential. Others may find that their learning disabilities interfere with job performance in frustrating, sometimes infuriating ways.

Most jobs require some degree of reading skills or basic math skills. Many jobs that used to be somewhat removed from technology now require some proficiency with a computer or other device. Waiters now place orders through computers. Federal Express and UPS delivery personnel use small computers to track packages. The world of technology is closing in everywhere and it is getting harder and harder to escape it. In many ways, this is not a bad thing. Many children with LD are very proficient in the use of computers.

There is no question that individuals with LD can and often do succeed in the workplace—indeed, many top corporate CEOs have been quite open in acknowledging their own LD. But for most people with a learning disability, there are pitfalls and challenges as daunting as those they once faced in the classroom.

When Allegra left the Threshold Program at Lesley College she knew she wanted to work with young children. She was good at it. She liked them. They liked her. She felt comfortable working with them. These were strengths, and she was confident in her abilities. When she moved to upstate New York, she applied for a job at a parochial school as a teacher's aide. She was hired right away and was very happy. They were very young children, and because of her sunny disposition, they got along wonderfully.

She eventually moved on from the parochial school to work in a Head Start program, once again as a teacher's aide.

Allegra never had to face many of the daunting issues common to most first time job seekers. The Bridge Program at Threshold gave her the skills and confidence to work with young children, and for her, finding and keeping a job was relatively easy. If she ever decides to change jobs or, for some reason, loses her present position and has to look for a new one, my advice to her would be the same as it is for anyone else. And for the parent reading this book now—if your child is an adult looking for work for the first time, it may be helpful to read this section and to pass on some or all of my suggestions to your son or daughter. I know, I know—it can be awkward sometimes. Your child is an adult now and may resent your "intrusion." It is a delicate balance, but there is no harm in letting them know you are there to help. If they are absolutely intent on doing it all alone, let them. And if things don't work out at first, do not say, "I told you so!" One thing a parent could do is to go over all the suggestions on the best ways to find and keep a job, and then pass them on to their child.

There are some practical matters that should be considered when a young person with LD is seeking employment, especially when they are joining the workplace for the first time.

Disclosure becomes an issue. The workplace is the one area where my standing rule about honesty and openness must be tempered somewhat by practical realities. It is entirely appropriate for any prospective employee to be a little guarded about their disability. It's not a good idea for any job-seeker to barge into the office and announce that he or she has multiple learning disabilities before being offered the job. There are ways to handle this issue in a sensible, constructive manner. How?

First, let's talk about finding a job in the first place. Creating a résumé is often a challenge, even for people without disabilities. It is important for job candidates to present themselves in a positive light. But it is also important to be honest. Employers rely on résumés to assess a person's skills. For example, people who have *no* computer skills should never say they do. This may seem like an obvious rule, but it is surprising how many do not follow it. I know of one young woman with LD who had a great deal of difficulty keeping a job, though she never seemed to have trouble finding one. When she came to me for advice, I asked to see her résumé. It certainly was impressive. In fact, it was suspiciously impressive. Whatever well-meaning soul helped her create that résumé seemed to have mixed her up with a corporate vice president, listing skills and qualifications she very forthrightly admitted she did not possess. My advice to her was to redo her résumé in a professional manner and to be honest and thorough in her self-analysis. Many people are shy or have trouble blowing their own horn, so another invaluable addition to a résumé is a collection of references. They are a very good way to gauge how others see us, and many employers rely on them for information on our work habits and personality.

A list of people who can be used as references should be created. These may be former or current employers, teachers, school counselors, or others who may have knowledge of your abilities. Parents, family members, or friends should not be included. Each name on the list should also include the person's title, work address, and phone number. Each one should also be alerted to the fact that they have been included on a reference list. Most people will be more than happy to help. Written references gathered beforehand can also be a big plus, especially if brought along on the job interview. For some job openings, the candidate may be required to fill out an application. This can be a challenge in itself, especially for those with a disability in reading or writing. To make the process easier, especially in remembering important information, the applicant should bring a driver's license (if one has been issued), a copy of their social security number, and a résumé. And don't forget to bring a pen! This may seem like a small detail, but job interviews are made up of small details: how the candidate looks, how organized he or she appears to be, how well questions are handled, and so on.

The application should be read all the way through and all the required information filled in. Once again, honesty is extremely important. The résumé can be used to complete the section asking for employment history—this helps ensure that all company and employer names are spelled correctly. No sections of the application should be left blank. If the question does not apply, the letters "N/A" (for "not applicable") can be written in the space.

Now the application has been filled in and the candidate has been asked to come in for an interview. This is one of those times when the importance of social skills comes to the forefront. There are some basic suggestions, which again, may seem obvious but often are neglected or ignored by job applicants.

Before the interview, the candidate should try to find out as much information about the company as possible. This can be done through ordering brochures or any other printed material that is available or doing research on the company through the Internet or library. It is very helpful to have some idea of what type of company the applicant is hoping to work for and what opportunities may be available within the company.

Another helpful suggestion is for the candidate to write down a list of possible questions the interviewer might ask and then to practice them with a friend or family member asking the questions. These are some questions typically asked in an interview:

- What are your reasons for applying to this company?
- What are your career goals?
- What do you consider to be your greatest strengths and weaknesses?
- What is your work history? Why did you leave your last job?
- What salary are you hoping for?
- What other experiences have you had that have prepared you for this job?

These may not be all the questions asked, but most of them will be included in the interview. Some employers may ask questions that are unexpected. The candidate should ask for clarification, listen for important words in the question, ask for an example, and try to understand what specific detail the person is looking for. It is also helpful to bring a résumé, social security number, and driver's license to the interview. That way, instead of saying "I don't know" when asked how long they worked for a particular company, they can refer to the résumé for the answer.

Finally, the candidate should dress and act appropriately for the interview. This is the one chance to make an impression. Jeans and shorts and T-shirts are not a good idea. Neither is chewing gum or smoking. The jobseekers should arrive early, allowing plenty of time to deal with traffic, weather, and other unexpected difficulties. They should always remember to smile and make eye contact and shake hands with the person who is doing the interviewing. And always maintain a positive attitude! This includes finding something positive to say about former employers and coworkers, even if they parted on bad terms. An interview is not the time to vent old resentments.

Now that the application process and interview have been passed with success, we come to the challenge of disclosing a learning disability to an employer. Thanks to the Americans with Disabilities Act (ADA), it is illegal for any prospective employer to ask if the candidate has a disability during the interview process. For this reason, the decision on whether or not to tell about your learning disability is entirely up to each person. Even then, the employer cannot refuse to hire someone because of the disability (though admittedly it would be difficult to prove if they did). The first thing to realize is that there may not be a need to disclose at all. If a learning disability has no impact on the work, there does not seem to be much point in telling a supervisor about the disability. Even if the disability does affect the work, there may be ways to set up accommodations without disclosure. For example, if a person finds she cannot easily follow verbal instructions, she should ask her supervisor to give them to her in writing. Most will be happy to do this, especially when they see how this simple action improves the work.

If the situation is such that the learning disability must be disclosed, it is best to do this first with the personnel manager or immediate supervisor. This should be done in person, not in a phone call or e-mail or through a third party. The employee should explain how it affects job performance and especially how the work can be improved. The employee can then present a list of strategies or accommodations devised to compensate for the disability. Finally, the employer should be asked to provide periodic performance evaluations. Most employers will appreciate the sincere effort, and the evaluations will be very helpful in the job.

It important to continue those efforts because getting a job is only half the battle. The other half is keeping it.

These are some examples of what employers look for in an employee:

- Dependability. Do you arrive on time? Do you work well with others? Do you complete your work on time?
- Attitude. Do you maintain a positive attitude in the workplace?

Do you interact well with coworkers and customers? Do you accept criticism well? Do you show initiative and willingness to learn? Are you honest?

- Job Skills. Do you follow directions well? Are you effective in your job? Do you provide good customer service? Are you able to solve problems? Do you communicate effectively?

Difficulties with any of these may require accommodations of some kind. And again, this does not necessarily mean public disclosure of the learning disability. Chronic tardiness, for example, can be handled by leaving the house earlier. Other problems such as an inability to follow directions may require a change in the way the directions are given.

Finally, for the young man or woman with LD, especially when joining the workforce for the first time, it is important to remember that a job should not be an ordeal or simply a continuation of difficulties encountered in school. It is an opportunity to express talents and interests. Most young adults with LD have a basic knowledge of their strengths and weaknesses. These should be taken into account when looking for a job. People with severe deficits in math should not be looking for a position as accountants. They should look for positions for which they have the abilities and skills required by the employer. Once these are found, it should be fairly easy to describe their strengths to their prospective employer, and there is no need to dodge the truth—if a creative person is applying for a creative position, she should focus on her creative abilities. There is little reason to go on and on about her difficulties with math.

Getting Along:
The Challenges of Relationships

Most have us have met someone who seemed to be just fine on the surface, but suddenly said or did something we thought was peculiar. Maybe it was a comment that made no sense or a response completely unrelated to whatever question was asked. Maybe they made no eye contact at all, or suddenly shifted the conversation inappropriately, or simply walked away. Our first reaction may be to think the person is strange or rude, and we may conclude that it is better to avoid this person in the future.

Those of us familiar with learning disabilities see this scenario all the time. Learning disabilities usually have no visual cues: strangers have no idea they are speaking with someone who has trouble processing information or has no ability to understand the subtleties of social interaction. I have written so much about the importance of social skills in Allegra's story, but I keep coming back to the subject again and again.

All of us live in a constantly shifting world of social interaction. Every day we deal with family members, coworkers, friends and business associates, the lady who works in the laundromat, the man who delivers the mail. Every one of these dealings is made possible by the complex weaving of skills we learned as children: smiles, handshakes, nods, listening, reacting, small talk. It is how we get by.

Difficulties with social skills often lead to isolation and ridicule in childhood. Sometimes this isolation is carried on into adulthood, and is usually self-imposed. Adults with LD sometimes feel their difficulties are so insurmountable they feel comfortable only when alone.

Friendship is challenging for people with LD. Allegra has had friends, but with one or two exceptions, they have always been much older, and often have been teachers. It is sometimes surprising that she hasn't made more friends her own age. The taunts and small cruelties of childhood are gone, and I believe she would find far more acceptance within a world of adults than she did with children. Her present difficulties stem more from her own insecurities than from any slights or insults from others. Allegra needs to feel completely comfortable with someone before she becomes the fun-loving extrovert most of us know.

Ali Halpern has been a friend since Allegra was a small child. When they are together, Allegra is as funny and charming as she is with older adults. Ali knows Allegra has LD, but has never had a problem with it. "I love hanging out with her," Ali told me. "Once I brought a friend to meet Allegra. I told the friend ahead of time that Allegra had a disability, and sometimes you see it and sometimes you can't. Later my friend said she didn't see it at all. Sometimes it comes up—she might not understand distance or which direction to go. She won't be able to tell if something is five blocks away or ten blocks, even if she's been there many times. But that's not a problem. Who cares if she doesn't know? She also used to have problems understanding money, but now she uses a credit card and a little calculator to figure out the tip, and everything is fine. Her learning disability never causes any problems in our friendship."

Any friendship has challenges. There is always some work involved in making and keeping friends. Still, there are always open-hearted people who embody Ali's attitude of "Who cares if she doesn't know?" They, like Ali, are very special people who look beyond the disability and understand the shortcomings.

Adults with LD often have the same social skill deficits they had as children. The same problems they had understanding the rules of a game like Monopoly have evolved into difficulty understanding the rules of the workplace. They may have perceptual problems and be unable to understand certain aspects of social interaction such as facial expressions or the subtleties of language. A simple handshake can lead to all sorts of problems. Imagine meeting someone for the first time. He has learning disabilities, but you do not know this. You hold out your hand in greeting, and he ignores the fact that your hand is held out. You wait, he pays no attention, and finally you lower your hand awkwardly—embarrassed or irritated. Now imagine that you are an employer interviewing this man who just ignored your handshake. Or maybe you are a bank manager and he has come into your office to secure a loan. It seems unlikely that the ignored handshake will be forgotten when you make a final judgment about the person's abilities.

Problems do not arise only in situations involving employers or bankers. Friendships and dating relationships are a made up of complex interactions, most of them unconscious and natural. Human beings are born to be social creatures, but these complex interactions have to be learned.

One concern many parents have is the "quality" of friendships. The potential for disaster is ever-present. Take for example, a young woman at a party who finds the first man who speaks to her to be attractive. So many people with LD have lonely lives, and they may gravitate toward anyone who pays the least bit of attention to them. The need to be liked is so strong that judgment is impaired. I know of one young woman who met a friendly waiter and fell head over heels in love with him. They ended up getting married. On the face of it, there is nothing wrong with the situation. He was extremely attractive, polite, and seemed to be well educated. But what lay beneath the surface and was completely unknown to the young woman and her parents was that he was both a heavy drug user and a drug dealer. It wasn't long before the young woman was pulled into a terrible spiral of drug abuse and domestic violence.

Of course, this can happen to any unlucky person whether they have learning disabilities or not, but the situation was exacerbated by the young woman's LD. Other people picked up small cues that she missed. Long after it was obvious to all that there were serious problems, she was unable to see the situation clearly. This was not a "love is blind" situation. Her inability to judge his character and motive was not a result of her love for him—she simply could not see him as others did.

Another, common example of this is a group of girls in a bar who see a very attractive man, yet they all instinctively sense that he is not right for them. They all agree, "He's cute, but what a loser." How do they know this? By his attitude, a look, something he says. The women pick up on subtle clues to the man's character. Someone with LD may not see these cues, or may completely misunderstand them.

At Riverview School, the administrators and teachers were always on the lookout for predatory adults who might be hanging around the school. There was also concern about cults. Young adults with a strong need to belong are easy targets for groups who are looking for new members. Allegra would have joined—I know she would have, but once the concepts of cults or con artists are explained to her, she understands the situation perfectly. For Allegra, it often comes down to very stark, simple choices. Good and bad. She will usually assume anyone and everyone is "good," but is able to turn that assumption to "bad" if she finds out that drugs or other problems are involved.

I do not want to alarm parents needlessly. These situations are few and far between. Still, if something does happen, it isn't easy or even advisable for a parent to step in and end a friendship by force. But it *is* advisable to sit down with your child and explain your concerns.

There are other difficulties involving friendship that are far less sinister than those outlined above. One of these is the self-centeredness often found in LD adults. I do not mean selfishness, but there may be an egocentric need for attention beyond what most people require. Adults with learning disabilities may remember their childhood as lonely and painful, yes, but also one where the disability was a central issue in the household. Allegra had no idea that her disability was a central issue, but she could not help being aware that the *effects* of her disability were a central issue. The focus was always on her, rather than on Alessandro. I spent far more time with her than I did with Alessandro, not by choice, but of necessity. When one child has many friends and the second child has few, there isn't much choice in the matter. And then there was my own obsession with her learning disability: first in my struggle to deny it while simultaneously searching for an answer, then in my seemingly endless pursuit of the right doctor, the right school, the best plan of action to ensure a successful future for my child. The relentless focus of a committed parent advocate can be so strong that the disability may be seen as the defining aspect of the child's life. When the child becomes an adult, they may expect the same sort of constant focus, and when it isn't forthcoming, they feel lost and confused. They were the center of attention as children and feel the situation should be the same when they are an adult. They may even expect a friend to be as interested in their disability as their mother was, and express disappointment if that isn't the case. This is not a selfish need for ego fulfillment, but a pattern that they have unknowingly come to expect.

Such behavior does not ensure long-lasting relationships.

There are other patterns that can lead to difficulties, some of which we have seen before, such as poor time management. Difficulties with time can lead to situations where the person is always late or forgets to show up at all. After a while, friends may stop asking to get together. Why should they, if they are always left waiting?

Distractibility is another difficult issue in relationships. People with LD often cannot pay attention in a conversation. Their mind may wander, they may be poor listeners, they may react in ways that confuse the speaker.

Another communication challenge for some people with learning disabilites involves humor. The meaning of a sarcastic phrase, a pun, or a play on words may not come through.

There are often problems with social immaturity. Adults with LD may lag behind their peers understanding current events, abstract or theoretical concepts, and especially issues related to relationships. While her peers may be dating and meeting boys, a girl with LD may still be focused on childhood dolls. When others are getting married, she may still be hoping for her first date.

Allegra always appears to be much younger than she is, not only because of her attitude and the way she acts, but because she actually looks younger than her true age. Because of this, many of our acquaintances and friends have asked me, "Will she be able to get married?"

My answer? "Of course she can!"

Learning disabilities can affect a partnership in ways that may not always be obvious at first. In the case where only one of the partners has LD, it is important for both to understand the situation completely. The person with LD needs to clearly explain how the disabilities will affect the ability to communicate or process information or interfere with day-to-day living. Self-awareness is vital: If a person has trouble accepting the disability or tries to justify problems caused by LD by blaming others, there could be trouble ahead. There is no need to feel guilty if special accommodations are required, and there is no need to make excuses—if everyone is upfront and honest about the learning disabilities, problems can be minimized.

At the same time, the partner without LD should try to understand the disability as much as possible. People with LD may not do things in a "logical" way, may need more time to finish what others might think is an easy task, or may have trouble concentrating or explaining themselves. There are so many ways the LD can manifest itself and the partner who understands and accepts this will go a long way in ensuring a strong, healthy marriage.

Of course, problems will develop, but understanding is the key to overcoming difficulties in any relationship, whether friendship, a romantic attachment, or a marriage. Being upfront about learning disabilities takes the power away from the disability. So much time and energy is wasted and so many misunderstandings develop when we try to keep learning disabilities in a dark corner and view them as something to be ashamed of or guilty about.

Sometimes both partners have learning disabilities. Communication gaps can be profound, and there is often a need for each person to talk about the difficulties they are experiencing. They may want to talk to a parent, but in this instance, my recommendation to parents is to try to find a third party who understands issues of both learning disabilities and relationships.

And everyone—family, friends, coworkers—must remember that some people do not view the world as we do.

When I Am Gone:
A Parent's Final Challenge

One of the great unspoken questions of every parent of a child with learning disabilities is also the most mysterious: "What will happen when I am gone?"

Our own death is difficult to contemplate, but the difficulties are magnified when you know you are leaving behind a dependent child. Most people realize that by the time they leave this life, their children will be happily out on their own, with families of their own, perfectly capable of living a long life of their own. Parents of children with a disability—any disability—are often haunted by fears of leaving the child without that firm support they themselves have always provided, regardless of the age of the child.

Are there siblings who can stand in for you? Is there another support system that can be relied on?

Allegra has Alessandro and many other family members who will always be there for her as long as she needs them. But as long as I live, I will never fully escape that awesome question of how she will fare after I am gone. Even so, there are many comforts to be found.

Allegra has dealt with death before in her life. Her grandmother and grandfather, her godfather Philip, and several family friends have passed away. When my mother died, I tried to explain what had happened. Without realizing it, I went back to our earliest days together, when I used to make up bedtime stories for her. "Grandma isn't really gone," I told her. "No, she's up in heaven, having a great time, just as she always did when she went to lunch with her friends." That was the starting point and from there I could always get her to laugh when I described what was going on at that corner table in heaven. Even today, if someone close to the family dies, Allegra is comforted when we enter into our personal vision of the afterlife. Grief is there, but it is tempered with our discussions of who is sitting beside whom and what is being said.

Allegra is deeply affected by anyone's death. Part of this is her fear of the day when I end up joining the lunch crowd. That is understandable. The bond forged between a parent and child with LD is formidable, and the idea that it will one day be severed is more than a little frightening for both.

Still, as I say, there are some comforts.

Apart from the grief and period of mourning that follows, I have no doubt that Allegra will be fine.

That is the very best, the most comforting thing of all: the realization that she will be fine.

The years have passed and difficulties have been faced—some successfully, others not so successfully—and Allegra's life as an independent adult is well underway. Sometimes I find out from a third party that she is thinking or feeling something that she hasn't told me. The first time it happened, I was a bit alarmed. "But I know everything," I told myself. "She has always confided in me, we don't have any secrets. Why didn't she talk to me about it?"

I was confused and maybe even a little hurt, wondering why she was pulling away from me. But isn't that what she is supposed to do? Isn't this what I have ultimately worked for over the past thirty years? I now find it reassuring to hear from someone else that she has been somewhere or had an experience I was not aware of. I am not the center of her universe. Allegra is the center of her universe. She has moved out of my orbit into her own life, and though I am still very much involved, I am no longer the ultimate authority. My ideas about right and wrong are no longer the only ideas that matter. Now her ideas matter too. My concepts of success and happiness remain my own. Hers are still developing, and for her, what constitutes success may have nothing in common with what I feel about the subject.

Success comes in many forms. Few of us arrive in the world assured of a position as the head of a large company or as a prima ballerina or sports star. We often look at those people and think they have reached heights unattainable by us and that they have somehow discovered a version of happiness we'll never understand. For those of us who have children with learning disabilities, it may be a little different. We don't think in terms of CEOs or sports stars. We watch our children grow to be adults, content in the knowledge that we have passed on the best of ourselves to the best of our ability, and we understand that success for them—real, tangible success—may be something as simple as getting behind the wheel of a car and driving somewhere for coffee and a bagel.

Their success is often a matter of the standards they set for themselves. Allegra was challenged by skating and continued to work to improve her abilities. Her determination to do well in the eyes of those who were watching molded her own expectations for herself.

When I look at her today, and I picture her years from now when I am no longer here, I do not have the same frightened questions I had before. I have no fear of the future. I understand and accept her definition of success, and I have seen how much she has achieved, and I have no reason to think anything other than this: "She'll be just fine."

PART IV

Resource Guide
for Parents

Resources

When Allegra first began to show signs of having a learning disability, there were very few resources available. Parents now have many avenues to follow in their attempts to get help for their child. Adults with LD also have many more opportunities for help through support groups, vocational training, and colleges with programs for students with LD.

Resources for Children with Learning Disabilities
- National Learning Disabilities Organizations—serving all ages
- Attention Deficit Disorder
- Government Departments and Agencies
- Legal Issues
- Local Advocacy Support
- School Testing Issues
- Homeschooling
- Summer Camps
- Gifted Children and LD
- Books on Tape
- Technology

Resources for Adults with Learning Disabilities
- National Learning Disabilities Organizations
- Continuing Education Resources
- Employment and Related Issues
- Financial Support
- Independent Living
- Literacy

RESOURCES FOR CHILDREN
WITH LEARNING DISABILITIES

National Learning Disabilities Organizations—Serving All Ages

NATIONAL CENTER FOR LEARNING DISABILITIES (NCLD)
381 Park Avenue South, Suite 1401
New York, NY 10016
Telephone: (212) 545-7510
Toll-free: 1-888-575-7373
Fax: (212) 545-9665
Website: www.LD.org

NCLD seeks to raise public awareness and understanding of LD throughout the life span, furnish national information and resources through their Website, and engage in educational programs and legislative advocacy. NCLD provides educational tools to heighten understanding of learning disabilities, including the quarterly publication called *Our World*, informative articles and newsletters, specific state-by-state resource listings, and informative training programs regarding learning disabilities. In addition, NCLD offers an Anne Ford Scholarship.

ALL KINDS OF MINDS
Website: www.allkindsofminds.org

All Kinds of Minds is a nonprofit institute for the understanding of differences in learning. Each month, the All Kinds of Minds Website explores different areas of learning and learning differences. The site has a library full of articles, book excerpts, audio and video clips, a searchable LearningBase of strategies, and many more resources, including up-to-date information about the institute's programs and products.

COUNCIL FOR EXCEPTIONAL CHILDREN (CEC)
THE DIVISION FOR LEARNING DISABILITIES (DLD)
1110 North Globe Road, Suite 300
Arlington, VA 22201
Telephone: (703) 620-3660
Website: CEC—www.cec.sped.org
DLD—www.dldcec.org

CEC is a nonprofit membership organization with seventeen specialized divisions. This organization is also responsible for administering the Stanley E. Jackson Awards, four scholarships of $500 to students with a "handicapping disability." DLD is the division dedicated to learning disabilities. Both CEC and DLD provide free information and hold conferences.

COUNCIL FOR LEARNING DISABILITIES (CLD)
P.O. Box 40303
Overland Park, KS 66204
Telephone: (913) 492-8755
Fax: (913) 492-2546
Website: www.cldinternational.org
National membership organization dedicated to assisting professionals who work with individuals with learning disabilities by offering daily updated information concerning current issues and recent developments that shape the learning disability community. *The Learning Disabilities Quarterly*, a professional publication is available through CLD.

EDUCATIONAL RESOURCES INFORMATION CENTER (ERIC)
2277 Research Blvd.
MS 4M
Rockville, MD 20850
Toll-free: 1-800-LET-ERIC
Toll-free: 1-800-538-3742
Website: www.eric.ed.gov
Information Clearinghouse funded by the U.S. Department of Education and hosted by the Council for Exceptional Children.

INTERNATIONAL DYSLEXIA ASSOCIATION
(Formerly The Orton Dyslexia Society)
Chester Building, Suite 382
8600 LaSalle Road
Baltimore, MD 21286-2044
Telephone: (410) 296-0232
Toll-free: 1-800-222-3123
Fax: (410) 321-5069
Website: www.interdys.org
International nonprofit membership organization that offers training in language programs and provides publications relating to dyslexia. Chapters are located in most states. The association has forty-two branches across the country, as well as foreign affiliates, offering informational meetings and support groups. Referrals are made for persons seeking resources; in addition, they publish journals and publications regarding dyslexia and hold an annual conference.

LD ONLINE
www.ldonline.com

Comprehensive online resource offering information on learning disabilities for parents, and educators, as well as children and adults with learning disabilities. Features include basic and in-depth information, national events calendar, bulletin boards, audio clips from LD experts, extensive resource listings with hyperlinks, and a special section just for kids. Artwork and writing by young people with learning disabilities are featured weekly.

LEARNING DISABILITIES ASSOCIATION OF AMERICA (LDA)
4156 Library Road
Pittsburgh, PA 15234
Telephone: (412) 341-1515
Fax: (412) 344-0224
Website: www.ldaamerica.org

National nonprofit membership organization, with state and local chapters, which conducts an annual conference and offers information and various publications. The LDA national office has a resource center of over 500 publications for sale; it also operates a film rental service. Call the national headquarters to receive a free information packet.

LEARNING DISABILITIES ASSOCIATION OF CANADA (LDAC)
323 Chapel Street, Suite 200
Ottawa, Ontario, Canada K1N 7Z2
Telephone: (613) 238-5721
Website: www.ldac-taac.ca

Nonprofit membership organization with provincial and territorial offices that conducts programs and provides information for LD children and adults. Resources include books and pamphlets that may be useful to U.S. residents. Offers information in English and French.

NATIONAL ASSOCIATION FOR THE EDUCATION OF AFRICAN AMERICAN CHILDREN WITH LEARNING DISABILITIES (NAEAACLD)
P.O. Box 09521
Columbus, Ohio 43209
Telephone: (614) 237-6021
Fax: (614) 238-0929
Website: www.aacld.org

The NAEAACLD links information and resources provided by an established network of individuals and organizations experienced in minority research and special education with parents, educators, and others responsible for providing an appropriate education for students, specifically African Americans.

NATIONAL ASSOCIATION OF PRIVATE SPECIAL EDUCATION
CENTERS (NAPSEC)
1522 K Street, NW, Suite 1032
Washington, DC 20005
Telephone: (202) 408-3338
Fax: (202) 408-3340
Website: www.napsec.com
Provides referral services for persons interested in private special education placements. Offers publications and sponsors annual conferences.

NATIONAL INFORMATION CENTER FOR YOUTH AND CHILDREN
WITH DISABILITIES (NICHCY)
P.O. Box 1492
Washington, DC 20013-1492
Telephone: (202) 884-8200
Toll-free: 1-800-695-0285
Website: www.nichcy.org
NICHCY is an information clearinghouse that provides free information on disabilities and related issues, focusing on children and youth (birth to age twenty-five). Services include personal responses, referrals, technical assistance, and information searches.

SCHWAB LEARNING
1650 South Amphlett Boulevard, Suite 300
San Mateo, CA 94402
Telephone: (650) 655-2410
Toll-free: 1-800-230-0988
Fax: (650) 655-2411
Websites: www.schwablearning.org
www.sparktop.org
Schwab Learning, a program area of the Charles and Helen Schwab Foundation, is dedicated to helping kids with learning differences be successful in learning and life. The Schwab Learning Website provides practical information and guidance. Developed especially for parents of children who are newly identified as having a learning difference, it is designed to be a parent's guide through the new and unfamiliar landscape of LD.
SparkTop.org is a lively interactive site just for kids to help them understand their learning differences as they engage in activities that focus on their strengths.

Attention Deficit Disorder (ADD/ADHD)

THE ATTENTION DEFICIT INFORMATION NETWORK (AD-IN)
58 Prince Street
Needham, MA 02492
Telephone: (781) 455-9895
Fax: (781) 444-5466
Website: www.addinfonetwork.org
   Nonprofit volunteer organization that provides support and information to families of children with ADD, adults with ADD, and professionals.

CHILDREN AND ADULTS WITH ATTENTION DEFICIT DISORDER
(CHADD)
8181 Professional Place, Suite 201
Landover, MD 20785
Telephone: (301) 306-7070
Toll-free: 1-800-233-4050
Fax: (301) 306-7090
Website: www.chadd.org
   Through family support and advocacy, public and professional education, and encouragement of scientific research, CHADD works to ensure that those with Attention-Deficit/Hyperactivity Disorder (AD/HD) reach their inherent potential. CHADD holds an annual international conference, and local chapters have regular meetings providing support and information.

THE NATIONAL ATTENTION DEFICIT DISORDER ASSOCIATION
(ADDA)
1788 Second Street, Suite 200
Highland Park, IL 60035
Telephone: (847) 432-2332
Fax: (847) 432-5874
Website: www.add.org
   National membership organization that provides referrals to local support groups, holds national conferences and symposiums, and offers materials on ADD and related issues.

Government Departments and Agencies

NATIONAL INSTITUTE FOR CHILD HEALTH AND
HUMAN DEVELOPMENT (NICHD)
National Institutes of Health (NIH)

31 Center Drive
Building 31, Room 2A32
Bethesda, MD 20892-2425
Telephone: (301) 496-5133
Toll-free: 1-800-370-2943
Fax: (301) 496-7101
Website: NICHD—www.nichd.nih.gov
NIH—www.nih.gov
   NICHD provides reviews of literature and information related to
NICHD research.

OFFICE OF SPECIAL EDUCATION AND REHABILITATIVE SERVICES
(OSERS)
U.S. Department of Education
400 Maryland Avenue, SW
MES Building, Room 390
Washington, DC 20202
Telephone: (202) 205-5465
Website: www.ed.gov/offices/OSERS
   Provides grants, technical assistance training, and support to states, as
well as information about special education programs, vocational reha-
bilitation programs, and information about national and international
research regarding disabilities and rehabilitation.

STATE DEPARTMENTS OF EDUCATION
   State Departments of Education can provide information about Individuals with Disabilities Education Act (IDEA) implementation requirements and regulations. Contact directory assistance in your state capital
for further information.

Legal Issues

ADA INFORMATION LINE
Civil Rights Division
Disability Rights Section—NYAVE
950 Pennsylvania Avenue, NW
Washington, DC 20530
Telephone: (202) 514-0301
Toll-free: 1-800-514-0301
Website: www.usdoj.gov/crt/ada/adahom1.htm
   Answers questions about Title II (public services) and Title III (public
accommodations) of the Americans with Disabilities Act. Provides mate-
rials and technical assistance on the provisions of the ADA.

ADA TECHNICAL ASSISTANCE CENTER
Toll-free: 1-800-949-4232
Provides technical assistance and information regarding the Americans with Disabilities Act.

AMERICAN BAR ASSOCIATION CENTER ON CHILDREN
AND THE LAW
750 N. Lake Shore Drive
Chicago, IL 60611
Telephone: 1-800-285-2221
Website: www.abanet.org
Provides information on legal issues and referrals to local bar associations.

NATIONAL ASSOCIATION OF PROTECTION AND
ADVOCACY SYSTEMS
900 Second Street NE, Suite 211
Washington, DC 20002
Telephone: (202) 408-9514
Fax: (202) 408-9520
Website: www.protectionandadvocacy.com
Provides literature on legal issues and referrals to federally mandated programs that advocate for the rights of people with disabilities.

NATIONAL CENTER FOR LAW AND LEARNING DISABILITIES
(NCLLD)
P.O. Box 368
Cabin John, MD 20818
Telephone: (301) 469-8308
Website: www.his.com/~plath3/nclld.html
Nonprofit organization that provides education, advocacy, analysis of legal issues, policy recommendations, and resource materials

OFFICE OF CIVIL RIGHTS (OCR) OF THE U.S. DEPARTMENT
OF EDUCATION
Mary E. Switzer Building
330 C Street, SW
Washington, DC 20202-1100
Toll-free: 1-800-421-3481
Fax: (202) 205-9862
Website: www.ed.gov/offices/OCR
Contact OCR to file a formal civil rights complaint.

WRIGHTSLAW
Website: www.wrightslaw.com
Parents, advocates, educators, and attorneys come to Wrightslaw for accurate, up-to-date information about advocacy for children with disabilities. You will find hundreds of articles, cases, newsletters, and resources about special education law and advocacy in their Advocacy Libraries and Law Libraries.

Local Advocacy Support

PARENT TRAINING AND INFORMATION PROJECT (PTI)
PACER Center
8161 Normandale Blvd.
Minneapolis, MN 55437-1044
Telephone: (952) 838-9000
Toll-free: 1-888-248-0822
Fax: (952) 838-0199
Website: www.taalliance.org
Parent centers in each state provide training and information to parents of infants, toddlers, school-aged children, young adults with disabilities, and the professionals who work with their families.

SIBLING SUPPORT PROJECT
6512 23rd Avenue NW, Suite 213
Seattle, WA 98117
Telephone: (206) 297-6368
Website: www.thearc.org/siblingsupport/
Organization for families that publishes a newsletter and holds support group meetings.

School Testing Issues

Students with documented learning disabilities can apply for test accommodations as appropriate. For more information, contact:

ACT UNIVERSAL TESTING
Information for Life's Transitions
P.O. Box 4028
Iowa City, IA 52243-4028
Telephone: (319) 337-1332
Website: www.act.org

THE COLLEGE BOARD
45 Columbus Avenue
New York, NY 10023-6992
Telephone: (212) 713-8000
Website: www.collegeboard.com
   Students and parents receive information on college admission, guidance, assessment, financial aid, enrollment, and teaching and learning.

EDUCATIONAL RECORDS BUREAU
220 East 42nd Street
New York, NY 10017
Telephone: (212) 705-8888
Toll-free: 1-800-989-3721, ext. 308
Website: www.erbtest.org
   Students with documented LD who take the ERB tests for private schools can obtain accommodations as appropriate.

EDUCATIONAL TESTING SERVICE (ETS)
Rosedale Road
Princeton, NJ 08541
Telephone: (609) 921-9000
Website: www.ets.org
   Tests administered include the SAT, GRE, and GMAT.

THE GENERAL EDUCATIONAL DEVELOPMENT TESTING SERVICE (GEDTS)
One Dupont Circle, Suite 250
Washington, DC 20036
Telephone: (202) 939-9475
Toll-free: 1-800-626-9433
Website: www.acenet.edu/calec/ged/home.html
   Administers the GED exam and publishes information on disability-related accommodations. Operates the GED Hotline, a twenty-four–hour service that provides information on local GED classes and testing services. An accommodations guide for people with learning disabilities is available.

LAW SCHOOL ADMISSIONS COUNCIL
P.O. Box 2000
Newtown, PA 18940-0098
Telephone: (215) 968-1001
Fax: (215) 968-1119
Website: www.lsac.org
   Tests administered include the LSAT and LSDAS.

Homeschooling

HOME SCHOOL LEGAL DEFENSE ASSOCIATION
P.O. Box 3000
Purcellville, VA 20134-9000
Phone: (540) 338-5600
Fax: (540) 338-2733
Website: www.hslda.org
   Membership organization that offers legal assistance on homeschooling issues.

NATIONAL HOMESCHOOL ASSOCIATION (NHA)
P.O. Box 327
Webster, New York 14580-0327
Telephone: (513) 772-9580
Website: www.n-h-a.org/nha.htm
   Nonprofit membership organization that offers lists of support groups, magazines, books, and organizations.

Summer Camps

THE ADVISORY SERVICE ON PRIVATE SCHOOLS AND CAMPS
501 East Boston Post Road
Mamaroneck, NY 10543
Telephone: (914) 381-8096
Website: www.westnet.com/advisoryservice/
   Provides detailed information about private schools and camps.

AMERICAN CAMPING ASSOCIATION
5000 State Road 67 North
Martinsville, IN 46151
Telephone: (765) 342-8456
Toll-free: 1-800-428-2267
Website: www.acacamps.org
   Publishes a guide to accredited camps.

LEARNING DISABILITIES ASSOCIATION OF AMERICA
4156 Library Road
Pittsburgh, PA 15234
Telephone: (412) 341-1515
Website: www.ldanatl.org
   Publishes a summer camp directory.

NATIONAL CAMP ASSOCIATION
610 Fifth Avenue
New York, NY 10185
Toll-free: 1-800-966-CAMP
Telephone (outside U.S.): (212) 645-0653
Website: www.summercamp.org
    Provides personalized guidance and referrals to sleep-away camps.

Gifted Children and LD

THE ASSOCIATION OF THE GIFTED (TAG) OF THE COUNCIL
FOR EXCEPTIONAL CHILDREN
1110 N. Glebe Road, Suite 300
Arlington, VA 22201-5704
Telephone: (703) 620-3660
Toll-free: 1-888-CEC-SPED
Website: www.cec.sped.org
    Membership organization that answers questions and provides information on education for the gifted.

CENTER FOR TALENT DEVELOPMENT
Northwestern University
617 Dartmouth Place
Evanston, IL 60208
Telephone: (847) 491-3782
Website: www.ctd.northwestern.edu
    Dedicated to serving academically gifted children and their families, primarily in the Midwest, but nationally as well.

CENTER FOR TALENTED YOUTH
John Hopkins University
3400 North Charles Court
Baltimore, MD 21218
Telephone: (410) 516-0337
Website: www.jhu.edu/~gifted/
    Comprehensive, university-based initiative that promotes the academic ability of children and youth throughout the world.

DUKE UNIVERSITY TALENT IDENTIFICATION PROGRAM
Box 90747
Durham, NC 27708
Phone: (919) 684-3847
Fax: (919) 681-7921

Website: www.tip.duke.edu
Provides opportunities and resources for gifted students, their parents, and educators.

ERIC CLEARINGHOUSE ON DISABILITIES AND GIFTED EDUCATION
1110 N. Glebe Road
Arlington, VA 22201-5704
Toll-free: 1-800-328-0272
Website: www.ericec.org
Information clearinghouse funded by the federal government and hosted by the Council for Exceptional Children.

HOLLINGWORTH CENTER FOR HIGHLY GIFTED CHILDREN
P.O. Box 434
Portland, ME 04112-0434
Website: www.hollingworth.org
National membership organization that provides information and referrals and publishes a quarterly newsletter and sponsors conferences.

NATIONAL ASSOCIATION FOR GIFTED CHILDREN (NAGC)
1707 L Street NW, Suite 550
Washington, DC 20036
Telephone: (202) 785-4268
Website: www.nagc.org
Membership advocacy organization that provides information to educators, administrators, and parents and publishes a quarterly magazine for parents.

NATIONAL RESEARCH CENTER ON THE GIFTED AND TALENTED
University of Connecticut
2131 Hillside Road, Unit 3007
Storrs, CT 06269-3007
Telephone: (860) 486-4626
Fax: (860) 486-2900
Website: www.gifted.uconn.edu/nrcgt.html/
A broad collaborative research effort with an emphasis on identifying the research needs of economically disadvantaged youth, individuals of limited English proficiency, individuals with handicaps, and other special populations that traditionally have been underserved in programs for gifted and talented students.

ROCKY MOUNTAIN TALENT SEARCH
1981 S. University Blvd.
Denver, CO 80208
Telephone: (303) 871-2983
Website: www.du.edu/education/ces/rmts.html
A program for academically able and highly motivated fifth–ninth grade students in the following states: Colorado, Nevada, Idaho, Montana, New Mexico, Utah, and Wyoming

Books on Tape

NATIONAL LIBRARY SERVICE FOR THE BLIND AND
PHYSICALLY HANDICAPPED (NLSBPH)
Library of Congress
1291 Taylor Street NW
Washington, DC 20542
Telephone: (202) 707-5100
Toll-free: 1-800-424-8567
Website: www.loc.gov/nls
Provides books on tape to children and adults with learning disabilities. Contact your local library for further information.

RECORDING FOR THE BLIND AND DYSLEXIC (RFB&D)
20 Roszel Road
Princeton, NJ 08540
Telephone: (609) 452-0606
Toll-free: 1-800-221-4792
Website: www.rfbd.org
International nonprofit organization that loans recorded and computerized books at all academic levels to people who cannot read standard print.

Technology

ALLIANCE FOR TECHNOLOGY ACCESS
2175 East Francisco Boulevard, Suite L
San Rafael, CA 94901
Telephone: (415) 455-4575
Toll-free: 1-800-455-7970
Fax: (415) 455-0654
Website: www.ataccess.org
Network of forty community-based technology resource centers for people with disabilities. Contact the headquarters for local listings.

CAST
40 Harvard Mills Square, Suite 3
Wakefield, MA 01880-3233
Telephone: (781) 245-2212
Website: www.cast.org
A not-for-profit that seeks to expand educational opportunities for individuals with learning disabilities through the development and innovative uses of technology.

CLOSING THE GAP
Computer Technology in Special Education and Rehabilitation
P.O. Box 68
526 Main Street
Henderson, MN 56044
Telephone: (507) 248-3294
Fax: (507) 248-3810
Website: www.closingthegap.com
Provides newsletter, resource directory, and conducts an annual conference on the use of technology to support students with disabilities

REHABILITATION ENGINEERING AND ASSISTIVE TECHNOLOGY
SOCIETY OF NORTH AMERICA (RESNA)
1700 North Moore Street, Suite 1540
Arlington, VA 22209-1903
Telephone: (703) 524-6686
Fax: (703) 524-6630
Website: www.resna.org
Maintains a listing of state assistive technology programs that are funded under the Technology-related Assistance for Individuals Act of 1988 and its amendments.

RESOURCES FOR ADULTS WITH LEARNING DISABILITIES

National Learning Disabilities Organizations

ERIC CLEARINGHOUSE ON ADULT, CAREER & VOCATIONAL
EDUCATION AT THE CENTER FOR EMPLOYMENT, EDUCATION
& TRAINING AT OHIO STATE UNIVERSITY
College of Education
The Ohio State University
1900 Kenny Road
Columbus, OH 43210-1090

Telephone: (614) 292-7069
Toll-free 1-800-848-4815, ext. 2-7069
FAX: (614) 292-1260
Website: www.ericacve.org

ERIC Clearinghouse representatives are available to provide information, ERIC Digests, annotated bibliographies, and assorted publications, some with information on LD. ERIC does not answer specific questions on disabilities, local programs, or jobs.

HEATH RESOURCE CENTER
(Higher Education and Adult Training for People with Disabilities)
One Dupont Circle, Suite 800
Washington, DC 20036
Telephone: (202) 973-0904
Toll-free: 1-800-544-3284
Fax: (202) 973-0908
Website: www.heath.gwu.edu

National clearinghouse that provides free information on postsecondary education and related issues and publishes a newsletter.

JOB ACCOMMODATION NETWORK (JAN)
West Virginia University
P.O. Box 6080
Morgantown, WV 26506-6080
Toll-free: 1-800-526-7234
Telephone (outside U.S.): (304) 293-7186
Fax: (304) 293-5407
Website: www.jan.wvu.edu

Job Accommodation Network (JAN) has a free consulting service that provides information on equipment, methods, and modifications for disabled persons to improve their work environment. All information is specific to the disability, including LD.

NATIONAL ASSOCIATION FOR ADULTS WITH SPECIAL
LEARNING NEEDS (NAASLN)
c/o CEA
4380 Forbes Boulevard
Lanham, MD 20706
Toll-free: 1-800-496-9222
Website: www.naasln.org

Nonprofit organization comprised of professionals, advocates, and consumers, whose purpose is to educate adults with special learning needs. Publishes a newsletter and holds annual conferences.

NATIONAL INSTITUTE FOR LITERACY
1775 I Street, NW, Suite 730
Washington, DC 20006
Telephone: (202) 233-2025
Fax: (202) 233-2050
Website: www.nifl.gov
A collection of Web-based and other resources on issues affecting adults with learning disabilities and their families, as well as literacy practitioners and other human resource service providers who work with these persons.

Continuing Education Resources

AMERICAN ASSOCIATION FOR VOCATIONAL INSTRUCTIONAL MATERIALS (ASVIM)
220 Smithonia Road
Winterville, GA 30683
Toll-free: 1-800-228-4689
Provides information on educational materials including a Performance Based Teacher Education catalog.

ASSOCIATION ON HIGHER EDUCATION AND DISABILITY (AHEAD)
University of Massachusetts, Boston
100 Morrissey Blvd.
Boston, MA 02125
Telephone: (617) 287-3880
Fax: (617) 287-3881
Website: www.ahead.org
International organization that provides training programs, workshops, conferences, and publications.

THE HIGHER EDUCATION CONSORTIUM FOR
SPECIAL EDUCATION (HECSE)
Department of Special Education
Room 100, Whitehead Hall
Johns Hopkins University
3400 N. Charles Street
Baltimore, MD 21218
Telephone: (410) 516-8273
Nonprofit membership organization for colleges and universities that promotes the improvement of special education training programs.

LEARNING RESOURCES NETWORK (LERN)
P.O. Box 9
River Falls, WI 54022
Toll-free: 1-800-678-5376
Website: www.lern.com

International association in lifelong learning, offering information and consulting resources to providers of lifelong learning programs

OFFICE OF SPECIAL EDUCATION AND REHABILITATIVE SERVICES (OSERS)
U.S. Department of Education
400 Maryland Avenue SW
Washington, DC 20202
Phone: (202) 205-5465
Website: www.ed.gov/offices/OSERS/

These agencies can provide job training, counseling, financial assistance, and employment placement to individuals who meet eligibility criteria.

Employment and Related Issues

EQUAL EMPLOYMENT OPPORTUNITY COMMISSION (EEOC)
1801 L Street NW
Washington, DC 20507
Toll-free: 1-800-663-4900
Website: www.eeoc.gov

Key Federal agency for the implementation of Title I (employment) of the Americans with Disabilities Act (ADA)

JOB ACCOMMODATION NETWORK
West Virginia University
P.O. Box 6080
Morgantown, WV 26506-6080
Toll-free: 1-800-232-9675
Telephone (outside U.S.): (304) 293-7186
Website: www.jan.wvu.edu

International information network and consulting resource that answers questions about workplace accommodations, the Americans with Disabilities Act (ADA), and the Rehabilitation Act of 1973. Offers individualized information packets to employers, rehabilitation professionals, and persons with disabilities.

MAINSTREAM, INC.
6930 Carroll Avenue, Suite 240
Takoma Park, MD 20912
Telephone: (301) 891-8777
Website: www.mainstream-mag.org
    National nonprofit organization dedicated to improving competitive
employment opportunities for people with disabilities. Provides specialized services and acts as a bridge that links people with disabilities, employers, and service providers.

Financial Support

The following sources provide information about financial assistance.
Additional sources may be available at local libraries.

FEDERAL STUDENT AID INFORMATION CENTER
P.O. Box 84
Washington, DC 20044
Toll-free: 1-800-433-3243
Website: www.ed.gov/offices/OSFAP/Students/
    Answers questions and produces several publications about financial
aid.

THE FOUNDATION CENTER
79 Fifth Avenue
New York, NY 10003
Telephone: (212) 620-4230
Toll-free: 1-800-424-9836
Fax: (212) 691-1828
Website: www.fdncenter.org
    Provides referrals to local centers for information regarding scholar-
ships and grants.

HEATH RESOURCE CENTER
One Dupont Circle, Suite 800
Washington, DC 20036
Telephone: (202) 973-0904
Toll-free: 1-800-544-3284
Fax: (202) 973-0908
Website: www.heath.gwu.edu
    National clearinghouse that provides free information on financial
aid available to students with disabilities.

RECORDING FOR THE BLIND & DYSLEXIC (RFB&D)
20 Roszel Road
Princeton, NJ 08540
Toll-free: 1-800-221-4792
Website: www.rbfd.org
   Awards three scholarships of $6,000 each for high school seniors registered with RFB&D for at least a year prior to the deadline.

SOCIAL SECURITY ADMINISTRATION
6401 Security Boulevard
Baltimore, MD 21235
Toll-free: 1-800-772-1213
Website: www.ssa.gov
   Provides financial assistance to those with disabilities who meet eligibility requirements.

Independent Living

LIVING RESEARCH UTILIZATION PROGRAM (ILRU)
2323 South Shepherd, Suite 1000
Houston, TX 77019
Telephone: (713) 520-0232
Fax: (713) 520-5785
Website: www.bcm.tmc.edu/ilru
   National resource center that produces materials, develops and conducts training programs, and publishes a monthly newsletter.

NATIONAL COUNCIL ON INDEPENDENT LIVING (NCIL)
1916 Wilson Blvd., Suite 209
Arlington, VA 22201
Telephone: (703) 525-3406
Fax: (703) 525-3409
Website: www.ncil.org
   Cross-disability grassroots national organization that provides referrals to independent living facilities around the nation.

Literacy

INTERNATIONAL READING ASSOCIATION (IRA)
800 Barksdale Road
P.O. Box 8139
Newark, DE 19714-8139
Telephone: (302) 731-1600

Fax: (302) 731-1057

Website: www.reading.org

Nonprofit membership organization that publishes journals for teachers, researchers, and professionals and holds an annual convention. A catalog of books, videos, and other materials is available.

NATIONAL INSTITUTE FOR LITERACY (NIFL)

1775 I Street, NW, Suite 730

Washington, DC 20006

Telephone: (202) 233-2025

Fax: (202) 233-2050

Website: www.nifl.gov

Federal agency that provides leadership through advocacy, information sharing, and collaboration.

NATIONAL CLEARINGHOUSE ON ESL LITERACY EDUCATION (NCLE)

4646 40th Street NW

Washington, DC 20016-1859

Telephone: (202) 362-0700, ext. 200

Website: www.cal.org/ncle

Provides literacy education for adults and out-of-school youth who are learning English as a second language.

PROLITERACY WORLDWIDE

1320 Jamesville Avenue

Syracuse, NY 13210

Telephone: (315) 442-9121

Toll-free: 1-888-528-2224

Website: www.proliteracy.org

National nonprofit organization that provides literacy opportunities for adults.

Acknowledgments

There are so many people I would like to thank for their encouragement while I was writing this book. Since Allegra was and is so much a part of this project, I asked her to help me express our gratitude for all the friendship and support through the years, not only for the book but for making our lives happier, easier, and more fulfilling.

First, there are the magnificent teachers who helped shape Allegra's formative years and stood by her with unceasing patience and dedication through so many years. Many of them spoke to me as I was writing the book. Dr. Davida Sherwood, Tonya Pulanco, and Virginia Nudell, all from the Gateway School in Manhattan, sat down with me several times to share their memories of Allegra. I was amazed by how much they remembered, starting from her very first evaluation over twenty-five years ago. They have helped countless children who had nowhere else to turn, and I will always be grateful to them. At Riverview, too, there were so many teachers and social workers who helped Allegra in so many ways and guided her with love and friendship. Judy Hafker gave up so much of her personal time to be with Allegra and was always there to listen. I especially want to thank Rick Lavoie. I asked Allegra her thoughts about Rick, and I find I cannot improve upon them: "Rick has always told me to do the right thing and never give up. He told me to be someone's hero and I have tried to be whenever I can. Thank you for all you have done for me." And thanks also to Rick for all his help with this book!

The teachers and counselors at the Threshold Program at Lesley College (now Lesley University) were instrumental in preparing

Allegra for life as an independent young woman. They did this with patience and good humor, and we will never forget them for it. In particular I want to thank Dr. Arlyn Roffman, who was able to look beyond Allegra's academic marks to see her potential. Allegra says, "Whenever I had a bad day, Arlyn knew how to put a smile across my face. Thank you for being so good to me." As for Jane Carroll, "Jane was always like Mom to me away from home." I also want to thank Jane, Carol Novek, and Jim Wilbur for all they did for Allegra, and for their help with the book. I also want to thank Allegra's tutor, Letty Buckley, for her insight and guidance over the years.

School was a major part of Allegra's life, but there were also many family friends who gave us encouragement and support over the years. There are two who are gone now: Judy Braverman and Marianne Ittleson. They were a great part of our lives and we miss them both terribly. Allegra remembers Judy this way: "Mrs. Braverman was a part of my life for a long time. She always loved the cards I sent her and always welcomed me into her home. The very first time I ever stayed over at a friend's house was at Mrs. Braverman's with her daughter Hilary."

Hugh Carey gets an entire chapter in this book and deserves it. Allegra says, "Governor Carey made my life so much fun because he and I almost made it on Broadway. He always told me the sun will come out tomorrow and it did. I love him very much." And Hugh, from me—I love you, too. Thank you for the years of friendship and your extraordinary kindness toward my children.

Diana and Richard Feldman have been friends of our family for many years, and I thank them so much for their kindness to Allegra, as I do Tina McPherson.

Chuck Scarborough was Allegra's stepfather during a very crucial time in her life. Thank you, Chuck, for the countless hours you spent helping Allegra and for your belief in her when it mattered most.

Allegra has had some friends who have stuck by her through thick and thin. Judy Braverman's daughter Hilary was her first skating friend. She says, "It was because of Hilary that I stayed with skating. We always had a great time at the Ice Studio. You will always be a part of my family, and I love you. We have done it!"

Another mother-daughter friendship we have is with Deborah Harris and her daughter Windy. I'll never forget Windy's grace and charm that first night at Riverview when she took Allegra under her wing and made her feel at home. It was Windy's first night away from home, too, but she handled it all with such flair.

Ali Halpern has been Allegra's best friend since the day they first met on the sidewalk when Allegra was six years old. They are close confidants to this day. "Ali has been a part of our family forever," Allegra says. "She is very sweet and loving and is my very best friend." As for me, Ali—I can never thank you enough for being the sister Allegra never had.

We owe a great debt of gratitude to all who made Allegra's life on the ice such a gratifying experience: Archie Walker from the Ice Studio in New York, Bev and Phil Lalande and Michael James in upstate New York, and most especially Allegra's beloved coach, Tammy Lalande. Thank you for giving my daughter such a gratifying sense of accomplishment—it is a priceless gift. For Tammy, Allegra has this message: "You have been a part of my life for fourteen years and I will always love you. Thank you for never giving up on me." Also in upstate New York, Ken Levigne; in Florida, Amy Bigby; and in New York City, Betty McCarthy and Maria Martins—thank you for everything.

In Detroit, Lori Diedrich has been a great counselor to my daughter. Thank you, Lori, for understanding, for advising, for listening, and for loving Allegra.

I was chairman of the National Center for Learning Disabilities from 1988 until 2000. The organization has been and continues to be such an important part of my life. It provided me with a way to use what I had learned with Allegra by reaching out to parents facing similar difficulties. I wish the services of the National Center for Learning Disabilities had been around when I was searching for help. There is not a day that goes by that I don't have to call NCLD and speak to Jim Wendorf or Dr. Sheldon Horowitz about a parent who has called me or written to me or been introduced to me because they have a child with LD and have nowhere else to turn.

Twelve years ago, NCLD was a small organization run out of a borrowed office with five staff members. Since then it has tripled in size, and has become one of the most respected national LD organizations in the United States. Among the most important things they do is advocate on a national level in Washington, D.C., on behalf of those with LD. They have also just created a new screening tool called Get Ready to Read which helps identify preschoolers who may be at risk for future reading difficulties.

I extend a special note of gratitude to the board of directors and the professional advisory board who guided this organization (and me!) over the years with such devotion and skill. I especially want to thank Carrie Rozelle, the first chairman of NCLD; Arlyn Gardner, former executive director of NCLD, a board member, and great friend; and Dr. Mark Griffin who has been there from the beginning. If it wasn't for you three, I don't know if I could have done it. As for the wonderful and dedicated staff members, both past and present, thank you for making my years there so rewarding. I especially want to thank Rose Crawford, Bernadette Colas, Shirley Cramer, the late Bill Ellis, David Fleishman, Marcia Griffith-Pauyo, Dr. Sheldon Horowitz, Norah Mason, Stewart Michael, Janet Weinstein, and Jim Wendorf. You made every day in the office a joy and gave an air of excitement and fun to every challenge we faced. Together we made a real difference. Thank you.

So many people were involved in *Laughing Allegra*, starting with those who were there from the beginning and helped with words of encouragement and sometimes a direct hand in gently guiding us toward a final manuscript. They are Sally Arteseros, Susie Cohen, Anne Colin, Emerson K. Dickman, Esq.; Shirley Gazsi, Dr. Sheldon Horowitz, William Kinsolving, Susan Kornfield, Rick Lavoie, Katie O'Neill, Victor Oristano, Babette Sparr, Alberto Vitale, and Jim Wendorf. My collaborator, John-Richard Thompson, extends additional thanks to Tad Fukunaga, William Lloyd, William McGinn, Bobby Peaco, Carol Rial, Ronaldo Ronquillo, Shelley Mosely Stanzel, and especially his parents, Joan and Edwin Thompson.

We both thank our agent, Phyllis Wender, who was so patient with us and guided us so skillfully through what, for us, was unknown territory. When she called and told us she found a publisher, Newmarket Press, we had no idea we would end up working with such a caring group of professionals. Keith Hollaman, Shannon Berning, Harry Burton, and especially Esther Margolis—thank you for everything.

I owe a special debt of gratitude to Dr. Mel Levine, not only for writing the foreword to this book but also for his many years as one of the leading experts in the field of learning. I have so enjoyed working with him at the National Center for Learning Disabilities, and I am honored to count him among my friends.

Melinda vanden Heuvel is my true soul mate and godmother to Allegra. You have been a very important part of our lives—far too important to put into mere words. In fact, I won't say anything further. Chances are that anything I would say to you and any feeling I wish to express, you already know.

Finally, I want to thank my family.

Sheila Murphy, my cousin and the greatest babysitter the world has ever known, thank you so much for all you did for Allegra and Alessandro. You and your sister Lisa are such a huge part of our lives and we'll always be grateful. The same goes for Maureen Brookman....Get well, Maureen.

To my mother—you are no longer with us, but I know you would be so proud of your "Frida." She has far surpassed both of our expectations. We speak to you daily. And Daddy, I always hope you knew how much you meant to my children and how your "alligator" has become one of Allegra's most cherished memories.

To my brother Edsel, thank you for being such a wonderful godfather and the source of so much great humor.

To my sister Charlotte, your care and devotion, not only to Allegra, but also to Al and me, has been limitless. I love you and Elena very much.

To Alessandro and Kimm, thank you for your understanding and acceptance. Al, I know it was difficult for you at times when you were growing up, but you handled it all with dignity and love, as you continue to do with most things in your life. You are my "perfect son."

And finally, Allegra....I could not have written this book without you. I hope our story will inspire other children and their parents, as you have inspired me.

I love you,
Mom

Index

About the Authors

Anne Ford served as Chairman of the Board of the National Center for Learning Disabilities (NCLD) from 1989 to 2001, and is currently Chairman Emeritus. As with many parents, her interest in the subject was greatly heightened when her daughter was diagnosed with a learning disability. During her term as Chair, Ms. Ford has led the reorganization and broad expansion of NCLD, including establishing a Washington, D.C. office, presenting educational summits on learning disabilities in several regions of the United States, and effectively collaborating with national service organizations outside of the learning disabilities field, representing issues including literacy, school dropout, cultural diversity, and early childhood development (Head Start).

In 1994, Ms. Ford was appointed to the Department of Health and Human Services, Commission on Childhood Disabilities, as the representative for learning disabilities.

Ms. Ford was also a member of the New York State Board of Regents Select Committee on Disabilities. She serves on the Board of Directors of the National Board of Big Brothers, Big Sisters of America; the Board of the Women's Committee of the Central Park Conservancy; and the Board of The Riverview School in East Sandwich, Massachusetts.

In May 1999, the Albert Einstein College of Medicine presented Ms. Ford with the Lizette H. Sarnoff Award for Volunteer Service. In 2001, she was honored by the Lenox Hill Hospital's Center for Attention and Learning Disorders for her many years as a leader in the field of learning disabilities. In 2002 she received a volunteer service award from the Connecticut Association for Children and Adults with Learning Disabilities (CACLD).

Her story has been featured in *Newsweek* and *Newsday* and on ABC, Lifetime, the Oxygen Network, and more. She lives in New York City. Her daughter, Allegra Ford, is now 30 years old and lives in upstate New York.

John-Richard Thompson is an award-winning novelist and playwright. *Indigo Rat*, set in Berlin, Germany, during World War II ran for a year in New York City and received the prestigious MAC Award in 2001. *Indigo Rat* is a follow-up to *Erik and the Snow Maidens*, which is set in Finland during World War I. His other plays include *Rain House, Water Sheerie, Fruit Bat Safari Camp*, and *The Glass Bird*. He currently lives in New York City. For more information, visit his Website at www.j-rt.com.

**For more information on *Laughing Allegra*, visit
www.laughingallegra.com**